for
DIANA and ELIZABETH

Clear and Present Danger

THE FREE SPEECH CONTROVERSY

CLEAR
AND PRESENT
DANGER

THE FREE SPEECH CONTROVERSY

By Nicholas Capaldi

PEGASUS   NEW YORK

Author and Publisher are grateful to:

Mrs. Nell Miller for her letter to the editor of the *New York Times,* May 6, 1969.

Mr. Robert Welch, John Birch Society for pages 157-163 and footnotes, pages xv-xvi, from the fourth printing of the BLUE BOOK OF THE JOHN BIRCH SOCIETY. Quoted by permission of Robert Welch, copyright owner.

Mr. C. B. Baker, *Statecraft,* for "The Revolutionary Imperative" by K. R. Valhal (*Statecraft,* February-March, 1969).

Professor Willard Hutcheon for "Open Letter to the Faculty" (originally submitted to the editor of the *New York Times*).

Mr. Paul Elliott for his letter to the editor of the *New York Times,* May 3, 1969.

Professor Bruce Wallace for his letter to the editor of the *New York Times,* May 1, 1969.

Dr. Charles Steinberg for his letter to the editor of the *New York Times,* May 3, 1969.

Mr. Staughton Lynd for his letter to the editor of the *New York Times,* April 9, 1969 (published April 18, 1969).

The *Columbia Daily Spectator* for excerpts from February 27; March 12; March 17; and March 27, 1969.

The *New York University Alumni News* and Professor Sidney Hook for Professor Hook's "Student Revolts Could Destroy Academic Freedom."

Professor Sidney Hook for his review of Herbert Marcuse, "An Essay on Liberation," *New York Times* Book Review, April 20, 1969.

Harper and Row, Inc. for Chapter 12,

"Concerning Individual Freedom," from THE ORDEAL OF CHANGE by Eric Hoffer. Copyright 1963 by Eric Hoffer. The Viking Press, Inc. for "The College, The Community, and the Bertrand Russell Case," by Yervant Krikorian, from THE BERTRAND RUSSELL CASE edited by John Dewey and Horace M. Kallen. Copyright 1941, copyright renewed 1969 by The Viking Press Inc. Reprinted by permission of The Viking Press, Inc.

The *New York Times:* Excerpts © 1936/68/69 by New York Times Company. Reprinted by permission.

The Beacon Press: © 1965 by Herbert Marcuse (*Repressive Tolerance*); © 1969 by Herbert Marcuse (*Postscript 1968*).

The Macmillan Company: Andrei Y. Vishinsky, THE LAW OF THE SOVIET STATE © 1948 by the American Council of Learned Societies. Doubleday and Company: from CATHOLIC VIEWPOINT ON CENSORSHIP by Harold C. Gardiner. Copyright © 1958, 1961 by Doubleday and Company, Inc. Reprinted by permission of the publisher.

The *New York Review of Books:* for a letter by Dwight MacDonald, July 11, 1968. Reprinted by permission from the *New York Review of Books.* Copyright © 1968 by the *New York Review of Books.*

Columbia University Press for Maximilien Robespierre, "Revolution, the People, and the Press" from INTRODUCTION TO CONTEMPORARY CIVILIZATION IN THE WEST, Volume II.

ACKNOWLEDGMENTS

I HAVE received so many useful suggestions, some of which I could not incorporate, that I hardly know where to begin to thank friends, colleagues, and students. The book grew out of a discussion with Donald Brown, President of Pegasus. It was aided at various stages by Willard Hutcheon, M. Todorovich of University Centers for Rational Alternatives, Joseph Kosiner, Richard Corbin, Walter Volkommer, Yervant H. Krikorian, Mrs. Bea Previti, and Ingrid Bruck. Needless to say, I accept full responsibility for the contents of this book.

CONTENTS

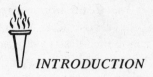

INTRODUCTION

This anthology is meant to be a defense of free speech. By its very nature it must be so. In presenting arguments representative of every point of view, both for and against limitations on the freedom of speech, I have implicitly adopted the axiom that to be completely rational is to be completely fair to every side of every story. One cannot be fair without permitting the freedom necessary for the exploration, articulation, and dissemination of every opinion. In short, without free speech there can be no rational discussion of free speech or anything else.

Three questions naturally suggest themselves: What is free speech? Why is it so important? and Why is it necessary at this time to defend it?

Free speech is here understood to include freedom of speech, the press, and peaceful assembly. It is perhaps most clearly defined, as in John Stuart Mill, as freedom of thought and discussion. Thus, when we speak of *free speech*, we mean the freedom to explore, discover, articulate, and disseminate what it is that we know, think, or feel. What is excluded from the realm of free speech quite clearly is freedom of behavior. Moreover, the notion of "symbolic speech" is also excluded, on the grounds that there is no way of consistently distinguishing symbolic speech from complete freedom of behavior; if the latter is excluded, then so is the former.

The distinction between freedom of speech and freedom of behavior is crucial. No community can exist without some rules and guidelines that place restrictions on behavior. Those restrictions may run the entire gamut from insuring the simple survival of the group to fostering in a positive manner the development of individuals. There is no form of government or political or social philosophy that does not concern itself with specifying restrictions on behavior.

The explanation for the necessity of restricting behavior is also, in general, an explanation for those occasions on which even speech is restricted. To begin with the most extreme and obvious case, during wartime members of the community are not free to divulge important military secrets. Clearly, freedom of speech in this case threatens the existence of the community and is therefore restricted for the same reason that all behavior can be restricted. An important qualification must be added to this point. The existence of a war does not necessarily justify the complete restriction of free speech. On the contrary, one can argue that there must be opportunities for criticizing (positively and negatively) and evaluating the conduct of the war. The justification of this freedom is quite consistent with what we said above, for a badly conducted war is also a threat to the existence of the community.

Somewhere in the middle we find cases such as the celebrated one of the man who hollers fire in a crowded theater when there is no fire and when he knows there is no fire. Again it can be argued that such behavior could threaten the existence of at least some members of the community. A little less obvious are cases of libel and slander. These cases are less obvious because *(a)* they involve the determination of fact and *(b)* they frequently involve political considerations. Thus, in a democracy there may be greater freedom to malign and attack a political leader than to malign and attack an ordinary citizen.

So far we have been concerned with identifying and distinguishing what we mean by free speech. Our discussion, for the most part, would apply to almost any type of community. It is now time to answer the question, Why is free speech so important? It is at this point that the connection between free speech and democracy becomes apparent.

There is no logical reason why free speech cannot be a value in any type of community. But in point of fact, only in democratic societies is a positive value put on free speech, and in many non-democratic societies it is positively forbidden. Why should this be so? A democracy is here defined as a form of government wherein the rules and guidelines for behavior are ultimately decided upon by some form of majority rule. Since the citizens are themselves ultimately responsible for making or participating in such decisions, they must have the information relevant to such decisions, including the opinions of other citizens. Hence free speech on political matters is absolutely essential to a democratic community. There can be no community without a sense of common interest, and one of the justifications for the democratic method of community decision-making is that a man will have a greater sense of identification with the common interest when he helps to shape it. It is also assumed that the common interest is not something over and above the interests of the individual members of the community, so that the members must be consulted. In short, the determination of the common interest (what Rousseau would call the general will) is a matter for rational debate—hence the necessity for free speech.

Nondemocratic forms of government, of course, do not rely upon decisions made by the majority of the citizens. Decisions are made by one man or a relatively small group of men. While free speech may be a right for the ruler or rulers, it is certainly not a right for the rest of the community. Even where it is tolerated, it is not protected by law; so that a citizen who engages in it does so at great risk. In the more extreme cases found in totalitarian societies, free speech is positively forbidden. Frequently the justification for such a policy of restriction on free speech is that the common interest is something over and above the interests of individual members. In such cases the common interest must be determined in a different way, perhaps in the vision or conscience of an all-powerful leader, in the dialectic of history, in the collective wisdom of a small group of wise men, or in the pages of a sacred book. Moreover, and most important, the sense of a common interest is instilled within the community by not permitting the decisions of the leaders to be questioned. It is felt that debate of any kind would undermine the community. In short, free speech is viewed as a threat to the existence of such communities.

As I have already indicated, one purpose of this anthology is to defend free speech. Therefore, I would like to say more in defense of its value. Free speech is not only a positive value within democratic communities, but it is essential to such communities as well. Such communities rely a great deal upon consensus and, ideally, tend to shun the use of coercion, even legal coercion, except in very serious situations. The consensus is the result of give and take. Where communication breaks down, so does the consensus.

Perhaps the strongest argument for free speech is derived from the strongest argument in favor of democracy. That argument was first presented during the Enlightenment and articulated in its modern form in the nineteenth century by John Stuart Mill. No community will be entirely successful in achieving the common interest, much less surviving indefinitely, unless it can truly know what the common interest is. To date there is no general agreement on what the common interest is because there is no scientifically confirmable theory of what man really is. In short, we do not fully comprehend human nature. Moreover, in order to protect pre-existing communities and to achieve limited goals that are conducive to human nature and the common interest as presently conceived, it has often been necessary to adopt policies that restrict the search after man's nature. The strongest arguments for a democratic community are that it (a) does the least to frustrate such a search, (b) does the most to encourage such a search, and (c) will be in the best position to adopt and utilize the factual information that can result from such a search.

Let me elaborate. Since democracies are not committed to any pre-established goals or the ultimate defense of fixed interest-groups, there is no built-in bias to protect. No oligarchy, theocracy, or any form of totalitarian state can exist without rigid commitments to some theory of man. Marxists, for example, must believe that Marx's view of man and the community is ultimately correct. Even where they allow for revision or "clarification," they still operate within a highly restricted framework. Moreover, since democracies can only exist in an atmosphere of competing viewpoints or "experiments" in living, the atmosphere encourages searches in new directions. Free speech is one of the lubricants of the massive machinery for discovering and constructing the consensus. Academic freedom is one of the important instances of free speech, providing a forum not only for discussing pre-existing political viewpoints but also for research into and discovery of man's nature. Finally, since the consensus is continually constructed, more like the growing of an unplanned city than a building with a fixed blueprint, a democratic community is more readily able to incorporate what is new. Only from the point of view of a philosophy of man that is believed to be infallibly correct might democracies seem inefficient.

This is the basis of John Stuart Mill's message in defense of free speech. To forbid it is to assume one's infallibility. To defend limitations on the grounds of the necessity for action is to confuse two things:

> There is the greatest difference between presuming an opinion to be true, because, with every opportunity for contesting it, it has not been refuted, and assuming its truth for the purpose of not permitting its refutation. Complete liberty of contradicting and disproving our opinion is the very condition which justifies us in assuming its truth for purposes of action; and on no other terms can a being with human faculties have any rational assurance of being right.

The foregoing distinction is also a clear answer to those who claim that Mill's ideal turns the community into an ineffective debating society.

If we accept these arguments in favor of free speech, then it would appear that our tasks involve: *(a)* specifying whether an instance of behavior is an instance of the right of free speech or whether it is a form of behavior that goes beyond free speech and falls into the category of overt behavior limited under the law (assuming that we can debate the value of the law); *(b)* calling attention to the various threats to free speech and to the institutions —for instance the university—that rely upon it; *(c)* exposing certain philosophies or points of view that are inimical to free speech. A large part of this book is an attempt to do just that.

There is, however, one threat to free speech that is unique to our time. It is this particular threat that served as the major impetus for creating this book. The threat is so subtle and originates in such unlikely places that it constitutes the gravest danger to the existence of free speech. Specifically, *there is a threat to academic freedom, and it is a threat that originates within the academic community itself.*

Before elaborating upon the danger to academic freedom, it is necessary to engage in the ritualistic cleansing. I clearly recognize that there are many individuals, interest groups, and institutions, including governments, that have in the past, do in the present, and will in the future seek to restrict or destroy academic freedom. There are several places in the book where I have documented that danger.

Ideally, and many times in fact, the university has been and is the haven for free speech. It provides the special atmosphere in which free speech may thrive. It is a place where it is possible to explore, discover, articulate, and disseminate all that we can. It is still a place in many cases where rational dissent is not only tolerated but encouraged. In fact, dissenters are frequently paid a premium. It is even possible to dissent about permitting dissent. Despite its many shortcomings in other respects, the university by and large has managed to preserve academic freedom while performing other social tasks. Its versatility is a tribute to its members and to the vigilance of those who cherish it.

Of late, there has been another task assumed by some members of the academic community, students and faculty alike, and imposed upon others. It is the task of social reform. It is not just the case that the academic community explores and advises. It is now the case that the academic community must advise and consent. Very shortly, it will be the case that the academic community will even seek to effect the contemplated social changes.

We must note an important distinction. The members of the academic community are also members of the community at large and as such are entitled to join or create any institution or group for effecting social change. What members of the academic community do not have a right to do is to use the university as a tool or as a means to bring about that reform. To do so is to engage in a form of behavior that is not protected by the right of free speech. No student or teacher has a right to holler fire in a crowded theater, even if the theater is on campus.

To use the university as a means of social change is to subvert its function and to undermine free speech in general and academic freedom in particular. To begin with, the attitude and atmosphere of a social reform movement is not conducive to research, learning, and the pursuit of knowledge. Conviction rather than the open mind becomes the prime value. After a while, we no longer seek to explore certain theories; rather we seek evidence to reinforce our own ideology. Finally, no social reform movement can succeed if the members are always debating each other; so it becomes necessary to repress dissenters. That repression of academic freedom has already started. It is a fact for which this book adduces evidence.

It is sometimes argued that certain causes, such as the current dissent from the Vietnam war, are so noble that they transcend the ordinary functioning of the university. Even if it were true that the cause is noble, it would still be wrong to disrupt the university. Once the precedent has been set, every extremist and fanatic may claim the nobility of his cause; and there could be no rational debate anywhere since the university would have already abrogated that function. On March 12, 1968, one hundred faculty members and thirty-five hundred students at Columbia University held a moratorium to protest the draft and the war in Vietnam.[1] Six weeks

[1] *The New York Times*, March 14, 1968, p. 45.

later the University was paralyzed by some of the worst disorders ever seen in an American university. More important, who is to decide when a cause is so noble that it transcends every other consideration? Mistakes have been made in the past, and surely we could all make them again. A case in point is that the last time Columbia University held such a protest was on April 12, 1935, when five thousand members of the academic community demonstrated against United States participation in a European war—all this in complete obliviousness to the threat of Nazism.

It is further argued that the administration of the university has in the past and/or is in the present functioning with some policies that are inimical to academic freedom. Therefore, anyone seeking to change these injustices is himself justified in violating some aspects of academic freedom. This argument is a version of "Two wrongs make a right." Unfortunately, it is a double-edged weapon cutting both ways. Anyone could then justifiably repress the reformers on the grounds that the reformers are hypocrites.

One final argument is worth noting. It is claimed in behalf of some who would "politicize" either the university or any other institution that they do not claim to be infallible in what they advocate or that they do not advocate any specific substitute; they are merely opposed to certain policies or opinions that they feel certain are wrong. However, when we claim with absolute certainty that some opinion is wrong or dangerous, we are still invoking our own infallibility, however limited the issue may be.

No community or culture can be destroyed from within unless it has been undermined by its own policies and actions or it loses the confidence of the public. The dissenting intellectual is frequently responsible for the loss of confidence by gnawing away at the sense of common interest. All too often the tragedy of the intellectual is that his dissent does not create a free and noble community but a totalitarian one where the very values and vehicles of the intellectual are swept away.

This anthology is divided into six parts. Part I consists of John Stuart Mill's now classic arguments for free speech. There never has been a clearer, more articulate, and more cogent defense of free speech. To my mind, Mill's position is to date invincible, and the careful reader will be able to find within it all the points necessary to refute any past or present argument opposed to free speech, including the other arguments in this anthology.

Part II consists of Justice Oliver Wendell Holmes's famous ruling popularly known as the doctrine of clear and present danger. Holmes's ruling is consistent with Mill's position and clearly distinguishes the domain of free speech from the domain of what is censorable. What is most remarkable is that other writers have misinterpreted the strictness of Holmes's ruling and so loosened the doctrine that they are ready to declare a clear and present danger on the slightest pretext. This misinterpretation of Holmes is not confined to any political persuasion but is invoked by both the extreme right and the extreme left. William F. Buckley, Jr., in defense of Joseph McCarthy, sees "international Communism" as the clear and present danger, whereas Herbert Marcuse sees the same danger in the "Establishment."

In Part III, entitled "The General Will Versus the Majority," I have brought together a group of articles written by people who (a) claim to be in favor of some form of democracy and freedom, (b) admit the present existence in fact of majority rule, but (c) also claim that the majority has been perverted in its thinking by a premeditated or *de facto* conspiracy. As a result, they all argue for some kind of reverse or reciprocal censorship. They also press the importance of some sort of elite. In no case is there any evidence offered for this conspiracy or any criteria for distinguishing a conspiracy from the consensus; neither is there an explanation for how these writers have escaped being "brainwashed." Once more we find that the extreme right and the extreme left are both capable of and willing to invoke the same argument.

In Part IV, "Beyond Democracy," we clearly move our discussion from the democratic context to a context where there is no commitment to democracy. What is peculiar to these arguments for censorship is that they rest upon the assumption of some inviolable or sacred doctrine. Even where criticism and discussion are permitted, they are circumscribed by the sacred and unchallengeable point of view. It is important to note that this kind of argument is to be found in a totalitarian political state, a conservative religious organization, and in the moral absolutism of some radical student groups. All of these organizations feel justified in disregarding majority rule and rely upon some elite in making decisions.

Part V, "Academic Freedom," contains on the one hand a series of articulate proposals for limiting, restricting, and violating academic freedom, proposals written by members of the academic community who wish to use the university as an instrument of political reform. On the other hand, there are articles written by academics in rebuttal to these proposals.

In Part VI, I have presented a brief journalistic survey of events from the Berkeley affair of 1965 through the spring rites of 1969 in order to show that the problem of free speech has moved from the stage of academic discussion to the critical stage of the implementation of restrictions. The ominous parallel between the present crisis and the Nazi crisis in Germany in the 1930's is also apparent. There are those who will argue that the parallels are misleading, but in the light of actual behavior and articulated policy this is a moot point.

I conclude by noting that there is no argument for limiting free speech in general or academic freedom in particular that cannot be turned against the very people who offer that argument. Moreover there is no noble exception that is not an implicit claim to infallibility. Free speech must be defended lest we become the very thing we fight against.

PART I

The Defense of Free Speech

1. JOHN STUART MILL
    Freedom of Thought and
    Discussion

John Stuart Mill (1806–1873) was the most eminent British philoso-
pher of the nineteenth century. The following selection is Chapter
Two of the famous essay On Liberty (1859), with a few supplemen-
tary passages from the same and other works.

Mill offers four arguments for freedom of thought and discussion,
and he summarizes his case at the end. But the full impact of his
defense of free speech can only be appreciated by following the rich
illustrative material for each argument as well as his replies to
counter-arguments.

It is instructive to compare Mill's distinction between free speech
and freedom of behavior with Justice Holmes's, and to contrast
Mill's analysis of the function of free speech with Marcuse's.

The time, it is to be hoped, is gone by when any defence would
be necessary of the "liberty of the press" as one of the securities
against corrupt or tyrannical government. No argument, we may
suppose, can now be needed, against permitting a legislature or an
executive, not identified in interest with the people, to prescribe
opinions to them, and determine what doctrines or what arguments
they shall be allowed to hear. This aspect of the question, besides,
has been so often and so triumphantly enforced by preceding writers, that it needs not be specially insisted on in this place. Though
the law of England, on the subject of the press, is as servile to this
day as it was in the time of the Tudors, there is little danger of its
being actually put in force against political discussion, except during some temporary panic, when fear of insurrection drives minis-

ters and judges from their propriety; and, speaking generally, it is not, in constitutional countries, to be apprehended, that the government, whether completely responsible to the people or not, will often attempt to control the expression of opinion, except when in doing so it makes itself the organ of the general intolerance of the public. Let us suppose, therefore, that the government is entirely at one with the people, and never thinks of exerting any power of coercion unless in agreement with what it conceives to be their voice. But I deny the right of the people to exercise such coercion, either by themselves or by their government. The power itself is illegitimate. The best government has no more title to it than the worst. It is as noxious, or more noxious, when exerted in accordance with public opinion, than when in opposition to it. If all mankind minus one, were of one opinion, and only one person were of the contrary opinion, mankind would be no more justified in silencing that one person, than he, if he had the power, would be justified in silencing mankind. Were an opinion a personal possession of no value except to the owner; if to be obstructed in the enjoyment of it were simply a private injury, it would make some difference whether the injury was inflicted only on a few persons or on many. But the peculiar evil of silencing the expression of an opinion is, that it is robbing the human race; posterity as well as the existing generation; those who dissent from the opinion, still more than those who hold it. If the opinion is right, they are deprived of the opportunity of exchanging error for truth: if wrong, they lose, what is almost as great a benefit, the clearer perception and livelier impression of truth, produced by its collision with error.

It is necessary to consider separately these two hypotheses, each of which has a distinct branch of the argument corresponding to it. We can never be sure that the opinion we are endeavoring to stifle is a false opinion; and if we were sure, stifling it would be an evil still.

First: the opinion which it is attempted to suppress by authority may possibly be true. Those who desire to suppress it, of course deny its truth; but they are not infallible. They have no authority to decide the question for all mankind, and exclude every other person from the means of judging. To refuse a hearing to an opinion, because they are sure that it is false, is to assume that *their* certainty is the same thing as *absolute* certainty. All silencing of discussion is an assumption of infallibility. Its condemnation may be allowed to rest on this common argument, not the worse for being common.

Unfortunately for the good sense of mankind, the fact of their fallibility is far from carrying the weight in their practical judgment, which is always allowed to it in theory; for while every one well knows himself to be fallible, few think it necessary to take any precautions against their own fallibility, or admit the supposition that any opinion, of which they feel very certain, may be one of the examples of the error to which they acknowledge themselves to be liable. Absolute princes, or others who are accustomed to unlimited deference, usually feel this complete confidence in their own opinions on nearly all subjects. People more happily situated, who sometimes hear their opinions disputed, and are not wholly unused to be set right when they are wrong, place the same unbounded reliance only on such of their opinions as are shared by all who surround them, or to whom they habitually defer: for in proportion to a man's want of confidence in his own solitary judgment, does he usually repose, with implicit trust, on the infallibility of "the world" in general. And the world, to each individual, means the part of it with which he comes in contact; his party, his sect, his church, his class of society: the man may be called, by comparison, almost liberal and large-minded to whom it means anything so comprehensive as his own country or his own age. Nor is his faith in this collective authority at all shaken by his being aware that other ages, countries, sects, churches, classes, and parties have thought, and even now think, the exact reverse. He devolves upon his own world the responsibility of being in the right against the dissentient worlds of other people; and it never troubles him that mere accident has decided which of these numerous worlds is the object of his reliance, and that the same causes which make him a Churchman in London, would have made him a Buddhist or a Confucian in Peking. Yet it is as evident in itself, as any amount of argument can make it, that ages are no more infallible than individuals; every age having held many opinions which subsequent ages have deemed not only false but absurd; and it is as certain that many opinions, now general, will be rejected by future ages, as it is that many, once general, are rejected by the present.

The objection likely to be made to this argument, would probably take some such form as the following. There is no greater assumption of infallibility in forbidding the propagation of error, than in any other thing which is done by public authority on its own judgment and responsibility. Judgment is given to men that they may use it. Because it may be used erroneously, are men to be told that they ought not to use it at all? To prohibit what they think pernicious, is not claiming exemption from error, but fulfilling the duty incumbent on them, although fallible, of acting on their conscientious conviction. If we were never to act on our opinions, because those opinions may be wrong, we should leave all our interests uncared for, and all our duties unperformed. An objection which applies to all conduct, can be no valid objection to any conduct in particular. It is the duty of governments, and of individuals, to form the truest opinions they can; to form them carefully, and never impose them upon others unless they are quite sure of being right. But when they are sure (such reasoners may say), it is not conscientiousness but cowardice to shrink from acting on their opinions, and allow doctrines which they honestly think dangerous to the welfare of mankind, either in this life or in another, to be scattered abroad without restraint, because other people, in less enlightened times, have persecuted opinions now believed to be true. Let us take care, it may be said, not to make the same mistake: but governments and nations have made mistakes in other things, which are not denied to be fit subjects for the exercise of authority: they have laid on bad taxes, made unjust wars. Ought we therefore to lay on no taxes, and, under whatever provocation, make no wars? Men, and governments, must act to the best of their ability. There is no such thing as absolute certainty, but there is assurance sufficient for the purposes of human life. We may, and must, assume our opinion to be true for the guidance of our own conduct: and it is assuming no more when we forbid bad men to pervert society by the propagation of opinions which we regard as false and pernicious.

I answer, that it is assuming very much more. There is the greatest difference between presuming an opinion to be true, because, with every opportunity for contesting it, it has not been refuted, and assuming its truth for the purpose of not permitting its refutation. Complete liberty of contradicting and disproving our opinion, is the very condition which justifies us in assuming its truth for purposes of action; and on no other terms can a being with human faculties have any rational assurance of being right.

When we consider either the history of opinion, or the ordinary conduct of human life, to what is it to be ascribed that the one and the other are no worse than they are? Not certainly to the inherent force of the human understanding; for, on any matter not self-evident, there are ninety-nine persons totally incapable of judging of it, for one who is capable; and the capacity of the hundredth person is only comparative; for the majority of the eminent men of every past generation held many opinions now known to be erroneous, and did or approved numerous things which no one will now justify. Why is it, then, that there is on the whole a preponderance among mankind of rational opinions and rational conduct? If there really is this preponderance—which there must be, unless human affairs are, and have always been, in an almost desperate state—it is owing to a quality of the human mind, the source of everything respectable in man either as an intellectual or as a moral being, namely, that his errors are corrigible. He is capable of rectifying his mistakes, by discussion and experience. Not by experience alone. There must be discussion, to show how experience is to be interpreted. Wrong opinions and practices gradually yield to fact and argument: but facts and arguments, to produce any effect on the mind, must be brought before it. Very few facts are able to tell their own story, without comments to bring out their meaning. The whole strength and value, then, of human judgment, depending on the one property, that it can be set right when it is wrong, reliance can be placed on it only when the means of setting it right are kept constantly at hand. In the case of any person whose judgment is really deserving of confidence, how has it become so? Because he has kept his mind open to criticism of his opinions and conduct. Because it has been his practice to listen to all that could be said against him; to profit by as much of it as was just, and expound to himself, and upon occasion to others, the fallacy of what was fallacious. Because he has felt, that the only way in which a human being can make some approach to knowing the whole of a subject, is by hearing what can be said about it by persons of every variety of opinion, and studying all modes in which it can be looked at by every character of mind. No wise man ever acquired his wisdom in any mode but this; nor is it in the nature of human intellect to become wise in any other manner. The steady habit of correcting and completing his own opinion by collating it with those of others, so far from causing doubt and hesitation in carrying it into practice, is the only stable foundation for a just reliance on it: for, being cognizant of all that can, at least obviously, be said against him, and having taken up his position against all gainsayers knowing that he has sought for objections and difficulties, instead of avoiding them, and has shut out no light which can be thrown upon the subject from any quarter—he has a right to think his judgment better than that of any person, or any multitude, who have not gone through a similar process.

It is not too much to require that what the wisest of mankind, those who are best entitled to trust their own judgment, find necessary to warrant their relying on it, should be submitted to by that miscellaneous collection of a few wise and many foolish individuals, called the public. The most intolerant of churches, the Roman Catholic Church, even at the canonization of a saint, admits, and listens patiently to, a "devil's advocate." The holiest of men, it appears, cannot be admitted to posthumous honors, until all that the devil could say against him is known and weighed. If even the Newtonian philosophy were not permitted to be questioned, mankind could not feel as complete assurance of its truth as they now do. The beliefs which we have most warrant for, have no safeguard to rest on, but a standing invitation to the whole world to prove them unfounded. If the challenge is not accepted, or is accepted and the attempt fails, we are far enough from certainty still; but we have done the best that the existing state of human reason admits of; we have neglected nothing that could give the truth a chance of reaching us: if the lists are kept open, we may hope that if there be a better truth, it will be found when the human mind is capable of receiving it; and in the mean time we may rely on having attained such approach to truth, as is possible in our own day. This is the amount of certainty attainable by a fallible being, and this the sole way of attaining it.

Strange it is, that men should admit the validity of the arguments for free discussion, but object to their being "pushed to an extreme;" not seeing that unless the reasons are good for an extreme case, they are not good for any case. Strange that they should imagine that they are not assuming infallibility, when they acknowledge that there should be free discussion on all subjects which can possibly be *doubtful*, but think that some particular principle or doctrine should be forbidden to be questioned because it is *so certain*, that is, because *they are certain* that it is certain. To call any proposition certain, while there is any one who would deny its certainty if permitted, but who is not permitted, is to assume that we ourselves, and those who agree with us, are the judges of certainty, and judges without hearing the other side.

In the present age—which has been described as "desitute of faith, but terrified at scepticism,"—in which people feel sure, not so much that their opinions are true, as that they should not know what to do without them—the claims of an opinion to be protected from public attack are rested not so much on its truth, as on its importance to society. There are, it is alleged, certain beliefs, so useful, not to say indispensable to well-being, that it is as much the duty of governments to uphold those beliefs, as to protect any other of the interests of society. In a case of such necessity, and so directly in the line of their duty, something less than infallibility may, it is maintained, warrant, and even bind, governments, to act on their own opinion, confirmed by the general opinion of mankind. It is also often argued, and still oftener thought, that none but bad men would desire to weaken these salutary beliefs; and there can be nothing wrong, it is thought, in restraining bad men, and prohibiting what only such men would wish to practise. This mode of thinking makes the justification of restraints on discussion not a question of the truth of doctrines, but of their usefulness; and flatters itself by that means to escape the responsibility of claiming to be an infallible judge of opinions. But those who thus satisfy themselves, do not perceive that the assumption of infallibility is merely shifted from one point to another. The usefulness of an opinion is itself matter of opinion: as disputable, as open to discussion and requiring discussion as much, as the opinion itself. There is the same need of an infallible judge of opinions to decide an opinion to be noxious, as to decide it to be false, unless the opinion condemned has full opportunity of defending itself. And it will not do to say that the heretic may be allowed to maintain the utility or harmlessness of his opinion, though forbidden to maintain its truth. The truth of an opinion is part of its utility. If we would know whether or not it is desirable that a proposition should be believed, is it possible to exclude the consideration of whether or not it is true? In the opinion, not of bad men, but of the best men, no belief which is contrary to truth can be really useful: and can you prevent such men from urging that plea, when they are charged with culpability for denying some doctrine which they are told is useful, but which they believe to be false? Those who are on the side of received opinions, never fail to take all possible advantage of this plea; you do not find *them* handling the question of utility as if it could be completely abstracted from that of truth: on the contrary, it is, above all, because their doctrine is "the truth," that the knowledge or the belief of it is held to be so indispensable. There can be no fair discussion of the question of usefulness, when an argument so vital may be employed on one side, but not on the other. And in point of fact, when law or public feeling do not permit the truth of an opinion to be disputed, they are just as little tolerant of a denial of its usefulness. The utmost they allow is an extenuation of its absolute necessity, or of the positive guilt of rejecting it.

In order more fully to illustrate the mischief of denying a hearing to opinions because we, in our own judgment, have condemned them, it will be desirable to fix down the discussion to a concrete case; and I choose, by preference, the cases which are least favorable to me—in which the argument against freedom of opinion, both on the score of truth and on that of utility, is considered the strongest. Let the opinions impugned be the belief in a God and in a future state, or any of the commonly received doctrines of morality. To fight the battle on such ground, gives a great advantage to an unfair antagonist; since he will be sure to say (and many who have no desire to be unfair will say it internally), Are these the doctrines which you do not deem sufficiently certain to be taken under the protection of law? Is the belief in a God one of the opinions, to feel sure of which, you hold to be assuming infallibility? But I must be permitted to observe, that it is not the feeling sure of a doctrine (be it what it may) which I call an assumption of infallibility. It is the undertaking to decide the question *for others*, without allowing them to hear what can be said on the contrary side. And I denounce and reprobate this pretension not the less, if put forth on the side of my most solemn convictions. However positive any one's persuasion may be, not only of the falsity, but of the pernicious consequences—not only of the pernicious consequences, but (to adopt expressions which I altogether condemn) the immorality and impiety of an opinion; yet if, in pursuance of that private judgment, though backed by the public judgment of his country or his contemporaries, he prevents the opinion from being heard in its defence, he assumes infallibility. And so far from the assumption being less objectionable or less dangerous because the opinion is called immoral or impious, this is the case of all others in which it is most fatal. These are exactly the occasions on which the men of one generation commit those dreadful mistakes, which excite the astonishment and horror of posterity. It is among such that we find the instances memorable in history, when the arm of the law has been employed to root out the best men and the noblest doctrines; with deplorable success as to the men, though some of the doctrines have survived to be (as if in mockery) invoked, in defence of similar conduct towards those who dissent from *them*, or from their received interpretation.

Mankind can hardly be too often reminded, that there was once a man named Socrates, between whom and the legal authorities and public opinion of his time, there took place a memorable collision. Born in an age and country abounding in individual greatness, this man has been handed down to us by those who best knew both him and the age, as the most virtuous man in it; while *we* know him as the head and prototype of all subsequent teachers of virtue, the source equally of the lofty inspiration of Plato and the judicious utilitarianism of Aristotle, *"i maëstri di color che sanno,"* the two headsprings of ethical as of all other philosophy. This acknowledged master of all the eminent thinkers who have since lived— whose fame, still growing after more than two thousand years, all but outweighs the whole remainder of the names which make his native city illustrious—was put to death by his countrymen, after a judicial conviction, for impiety and immorality. Impiety, in denying the gods recognized by the State; indeed his accuser asserted (see the "Apologia") that he believed in no gods at all. Immorality, in being, by his doctrines and instructions, a "corruptor of youth." Of these charges the tribunal, there is every ground for believing, honestly found him guilty, and condemned the man who probably of all then born had deserved best of mankind, to be put to death as a criminal.

To pass from this to the only other instance of judicial iniquity, the mention of which, after the condemnation of Socrates, would not be an anti-climax: the event which took place on Calvary rather more than eighteen hundred years ago. The man who left on the memory of those who witnessed his life and conversation, such an impression of his moral grandeur, that eighteen subsequent centuries have done homage to him as the Almighty in person, was ignominiously put to death, as what? As a blasphemer. Men did not merely mistake their benefactor; they mistook him for the exact contrary of what he was, and treated him as that prodigy of impiety, which they themselves are now held to be, for their treatment of him. The feelings with which mankind now regard these lamentable transactions, especially the later of the two, render them extremely unjust in their judgment of the unhappy actors. These were, to all

appearance, not bad men—not worse than men commonly are, but rather the contrary; men who possessed in a full, or somewhat more than a full measure, the religious, moral, and patriotic feelings of their time and people: the very kind of men who, in all times, our own included, have every chance of passing through life blameless and respected. The high-priest who rent his garments when the words were pronounced, which, according to all the ideas of his country, constituted the blackest guilt, was in all probability quite as sincere in his horror and indignation, as the generality of respectable and pious men now are in the religious and moral sentiments they profess; and most of those who now shudder at his conduct, if they had lived in his time, and been born Jews, would have acted precisely as he did. Orthodox Christians who are tempted to think that those who stoned to death the first martyrs must have been worse men than they themselves are, ought to remember that one of those persecutors was Saint Paul.

Let us add one more example, the most striking of all, if the impressiveness of an error is measured by the wisdom and virtue of him who falls into it. If ever any one, possessed of power, had grounds for thinking himself the best and most enlightened among his contemporaries, it was the Emperor Marcus Aurelius. Absolute monarch of the whole civilized world, he preserved through life not only the most unblemished justice, but what was less to be expected from his Stoical breeding, the tenderest heart. The few failings which are attributed to him, were all on the side of indulgence: while his writings, the highest ethical product of the ancient mind, differ scarcely perceptibly, if they differ at all, from the most characteristic teachings of Christ. This man, a better Christian in all but the dogmatic sense of the word, than almost any of the ostensibly Christian sovereigns who have since reigned, persecuted Christianity. Placed at the summit of all the previous attainments of humanity, with an open, unfettered intellect, and a character which led him of himself to embody in his moral writings the Christian ideal, he yet failed to see that Christianity was to be a good and not an evil to the world, with his duties to which he was so deeply penetrated. Existing society he knew to be in a deplorable state. But

such as it as, he saw or thought he saw, that it was held together and prevented from being worse, by belief and reverence of the received divinities. As a ruler of mankind, he deemed it his duty not to suffer society to fall in pieces; and saw not how, if its existing ties were removed, any others could be formed which could again knit it together. The new religion openly aimed at dissolving these ties: unless, therefore, it was his duty to adopt that religion, it seemed to be his duty to put it down. Inasmuch then as the theology of Christianity did not appear to him true or of divine origin, inasmuch as this strange history of a crucified God was not credible to him, and a system which purported to rest entirely upon a foundation to him so wholly unbelievable, could not be foreseen by him to be that renovating agency which, after all abatements, it has in fact proved to be; the gentlest and most amiable of philosophers and rulers, under a solemn sense of duty, authorized the persecution of Christianity. To my mind this is one of the most tragical facts in all history. It is a bitter thought, how different a thing the Christianity of the world might have been, if the Christian faith had been adopted as the religion of the empire under the auspices of Marcus Aurelius instead of those of Constantine. But it would be equally unjust to him and false to truth, to deny, that no one plea which can be urged for punishing anti-Christian teaching, was wanting to Marcus Aurelius for punishing, as he did, the propagation of Christianity. No Christian more firmly believes that Atheism is false, and tends to the dissolution of society, than Marcus Aurelius believed the same things of Christianity; he who, of all men then living, might have been thought the most capable of appreciating it. Unless any one who approves of punishment for the promulgation of opinions, flatters himself that he is a wiser and better man than Marcus Aurelius—more deeply versed in the wisdom of his time, more elevated in his intellect above it—more earnest in his search for truth, or more single-minded in his devotion to it when found;—let him abstain from that assumption of the joint infallibility of himself and the multitude, which the Great Antoninus made with so unfortunate a result.

Aware of the impossibility of defending the use of punishment for

restraining irreligious opinions, by any argument which will not justify Marcus Antoninus, the enemies of religious freedom, when hard pressed, occasionally accept this consequence, and say, with Dr. Johnson, that the persecutors of Christianity were in the right; that persecution is an ordeal through which truth ought to pass, and always passes successfully, legal penalties being, in the end, powerless against truth, though sometimes beneficially effective against mischievous errors. This is a form of the argument for religious intolerance, sufficiently remarkable not to be passed without notice.

A theory which maintains that truth may justifiably be persecuted because persecution cannot possibly do it any harm, cannot be charged with being intentionally hostile to the reception of new truths; but we cannot commend the generosity of its dealing with the persons to whom mankind are indebted for them. To discover to the world something which deeply concerns it, and of which it was previously ignorant; to prove to it that it had been mistaken on some vital point of temporal or spiritual interest, is as important a service as a human being can render to his fellow-creatures, and in certain cases, as in those of the early Christians and of the Reformers, those who think with Dr. Johnson believe it to have been the most precious gift which could be bestowed on mankind. That the authors of such splendid benefits should be requited by martyrdom; that their reward should be to be dealt with as the vilest of criminals, is not, upon this theory, a deplorable error and misfortune, for which humanity should mourn in sackcloth and ashes, but the normal and justifiable state of things. The propounder of a new truth, according to this doctrine, should stand, as stood, in the legislation of the Locrains, the proposper of a new law, with a halter round his neck, to be instantly tightened if the public assembly did not, on hearing his reasons, then and there adopt his proposition. People who defend this mode of treating benefactors, cannot be supposed to set much value on the benefit; and I believe this view of the subject is mostly confined to the sort of persons who think that new truths may have been desirable once, but that we have had enough of them now.

But, indeed, the dictum that truth always triumphs over persecution, is one of those pleasant falsehoods which men repeat after one another till they pass into commonplaces, but which all experience refutes. History teems with instances of truth put down by persecution. If not suppressed forever, it may be thrown back for centuries. To speak only of religious opinions: the Reformation broke out at least twenty times before Luther, and was put down. Arnold of Brescia was put down. Fra Dolcino was put down. Savonarola was put down. The Albigeois were put down. The Vaudois were put down. The Lollards were put down. The Hussites were put down. Even after the era of Luther, wherever persecution was persisted in, it was successful. In Spain, Italy, Flanders, the Austrian empire, Protestantism was rooted out; and, most likely, would have been so in England, had Queen Mary lived, or Queen Elizabeth died. Persecution has always succeeded, save where the heretics were too strong a party to be effectually persecuted. No reasonable person can doubt that Christianity might have been extirpated in the Roman empire. It spread, and became predominant, because the persecutions were only occasional, lasting but a short time, and separated by long intervals of almost undisturbed propagandism. It is a piece of idle sentimentality that truth, merely as truth, has any inherent power denied to error, of prevailing against the dungeon and the stake. Men are not more zealous for truth than they often are for error, and a sufficient application of legal or even of social penalties will generally succeed in stopping the propagation of either. The real advantage which truth has, consists in this, that when an opinion is true, it may be extinguished once, twice, or many times, but in the course of ages there will generally be found persons to rediscover it, until some one of its reappearances falls on a time when from favorable circumstances it escapes persecution until it has made such head as to withstand all subsequent attempts to suppress it.

It will be said, that we do not now put to death the introducers of new opinions: we are not like our fathers who slew the prophets, we even build sepulchres to them. It is true we no longer put heretics to death; and the amount of penal infliction which modern feeling would probably tolerate, even against the most obnoxious opinions, is not sufficient to extirpate them. But let us not flatter ourselves that we are yet free from the stain even of legal persecution. Penalties for opinion, or at least for its expression, still exist by law; and their enforcement is not, even in these times, so unexampled as to make it at all incredible that they may some day be revived in full force. In the year 1857, at the summer assizes of the county of Cornwall, an unfortunate man, said to be of unexceptionable conduct in all relations of life, was sentenced to twenty-one months imprisonment, for uttering, and writing on a gate, some offensive words concerning Christianity. Within a month of the same time, at the Old Bailey, two persons, on two separate occasions, were rejected as jurymen, and one of them grossly insulted by the judge and by one of the counsel, because they honestly declared that they had no theological belief; and a third, a foreigner, for the same reason, was denied justice against a thief. This refusal of redress took place in virtue of the legal doctrine, that no person can be allowed to give evidence in a court of justice, who does not profess belief in a God (any god is sufficient) and in a future state; which is equivalent to declaring such persons to be outlaws, excluded from the protection of the tribunals; who may not only be robbed or assaulted with impunity, if no one but themselves, or persons of similar opinions, be present; but any one else may be robbed or assaulted with impunity, if the proof of the facts depends on their evidence. The assumption on which this is grounded, is that the oath is worthless, of a person who does not believe in a future state; a proposition which betokens much ignorance of history in those who assent to it (since it is historically true that a large proportion of infidels in all ages have been persons of distinguished integrity and honor); and would be maintained by no one who had the smallest conception how many of the persons in greatest repute with the world, both for virtues and for attainments, are well known, at least to their intimates, to be unbelievers. The rule, besides, is suicidal, and cuts away its own foundation. Under pretence that atheists must be liars, it admits the testimony of all atheists who are willing to lie, and rejects only those who brave the obloquy of publicly confessing a detested creed rather than affirm a falsehood. A rule thus self-convicted of absurdity so far as regards its professed purpose, can be kept in force only as a badge of hatred, a relic of persecution; a persecution, too, having the peculiarity, that the qualification for undergoing it, is the being clearly proved not to deserve it. The rule, and the theory it implies, are hardly less insulting to believers than to infidels. For if he who does not believe in a future state, necessarily lies, it follows that they who do believe are only prevented from lying, if prevented they are, by the fear of hell. We will not do the authors and abettors of the rule the injury of supposing, that the conception which they have formed of Christian virtue is drawn from their own consciousness.

These, indeed, are but rags and remnants of persecution, and may be thought to be not so much an indication of the wish to persecute as an example of that very frequent infirmity of English minds, which makes them take a preposterous pleasure in the assertion of a bad principle, when they are no longer bad enough to desire to carry it really into practice. But unhappily there is no security in the state of the public mind, that the suspension of worse forms of legal persecution, which has lasted for about the space of a generation, will continue. In this age the quiet surface of routine is as often ruffled by attempts to resuscitate past evils, as to introduce new benefits. What is boasted of at the present time as the revival of religion, is always, in narrow and uncultivated minds, at least as much the revival of bigotry; and where there is the strong permanent leaven of intolerance in the feelings of a people, which at all times abides in the middle classes of this country, it needs but little to provoke them into actively persecuting those whom they have never ceased to think proper objects of persecution. For it is this —it is the opinions men entertain, and the feelings they cherish, respecting those who disown the beliefs they deem important, which makes this country not a place of mental freedom. For a long time past, the chief mischief of the legal penalties is that they strengthen the social stigma. It is that stigma which is really effective, and so effective is it, that the profession of opinions which are under the ban of society is much less common in England, than is, in many other countries, the avowal of those which incur risk of judicial punishment. In respect to all persons but those whose pecuniary circumstances make them independent of the good will of other people, opinion, on this subject, is as efficacious as law; men might as well be imprisoned, as excluded from the means of earning their bread. Those whose bread is already secured, and who desire no favors from men in power, or from bodies of men, or from the public, have nothing to fear from the open avowal of any opinions, but to be ill-thought of and ill-spoken of, and this it ought not to require a very heroic mould to enable them to bear. There is no room for any appeal *ad misericordiam* in behalf of such persons. But though we do not now inflict so much evil on those who think differently from us, as it was formerly our custom to do, it may be that we do ourselves as much evil as ever by our treatment of them. Socrates was put to death, but the Socratic philosophy rose like the sun in heaven, and spread its illumination over the whole intellectual firmament. Christians were cast to the lions, but the Christian Church grew up a stately and spreading tree, overtopping the older and less vigorous growths, and stifling them by its shade. Our merely social intolerance, kills no one, roots out no opinions, but induces men to disguise them, or to abstain from any active effort for their diffusion. With us, heretical opinions do not perceptibly gain, or even lose, ground in each decade or generation; they never blaze out far and wide, but continue to smoulder in the narrow circles of thinking and studious persons among whom they originate, without ever lighting up the general affairs of mankind with either a true or a deceptive light. And thus is kept up a state of things very satisfactory to some minds, because, without the unpleasant process of fining or imprisoning anybody, it maintains all prevailing opinions outwardly undisturbed, while it does not absolutely interdict the exercise of reason by dissentients afflicted with the malady of thought. A convenient plan for having peace in the intellectual world, and keeping all things going on therein very much as they do already. But the price paid for this sort of intellectual pacification, is the sacrifice of the entire moral courage of the human mind. A state of things in which a large portion of the most active and inquiring intellects find it advisable to keep the genuine principles and grounds of their convictions within their own breasts, and attempt, in what they address to the public, to fit as much as they can of their own conclusions to premises which they have internally renounced, cannot send forth the open, fearless characters, and logical, consistent intellects who once adorned the thinking world. The sort of men who can be looked for under it, are either mere conformers to commonplace, or time-servers for truth, whose arguments on all great subjects are meant for their hearers, and are not those which have convinced themselves. Those who avoid this alternative, do so by narrowing their thoughts and inter-est to things which can be spoken of without venturing within the region of principles, that is, to small practical matters, which would come right of themselves, if but the minds of mankind were strengthened and enlarged, and which will never be made effectu-ally right until then, while that which would strengthen and enlarge men's minds, free and daring speculation on the highest subjects, is abandoned.

Those in whose eyes this reticence on the part of heretics is no evil, should consider in the first place, that in consequence of it there is never any fair and thorough discussion of heretical opin-ions; and that such of them as could not stand such discussion, though they may be prevented from spreading, do not disappear. But it is not the minds of heretics that are deteriorated most, by the ban placed on all inquiry which does not end in the orthodox conclusions. The greatest harm done is to those who are not heret-ics, and whose whole mental development is cramped, and their reason cowed, by the fear of heresy. Who can compute what the world loses in the multitude of promising intellects combined with timid characters, who dare not follow out any bold, vigorous, in-dependent train of thought, lest it should land them in something which would admit of being considered irreligious or immoral? Among them we may occasionally see some man of deep conscien-tiousness, and subtile and refined understanding, who spends a life in sophisticating with an intellect which he cannot silence, and exhausts the resources of ingenuity in attempting to reconcile the promptings of his conscience and reason with orthodoxy, which yet he does not, perhaps, to the end succeed in doing. No one can be a great thinker who does not recognize, that as a thinker it is his first duty to follow his intellect to whatever conclusions it may lead. Truth gains more even by the errors of one who, with due study and preparation, thinks for himself, than by the true opinions of those who only hold them because they do not suffer themselves to think. Not that it is solely, or chiefly, to form great thinkers, that freedom of thinking is required. On the contrary, it is as much, and even more indispensable, to enable average human beings to attain the mental stature which they are capable of. There have been, and may again be, great individual thinkers, in a general atmosphere of mental slavery. but there never has been, nor ever will be, in that atmosphere, an intellectually active people. Where any people has made a temporary approach to such a character, it has been because the dread of heterodox speculation was for a time suspended. Where there is a tacit convention that principles are not to be disputed; where the discussion of the greatest questions which can occupy humanity is considered to be closed, we cannot hope to find that generally high scale of mental activity which has made some periods of history so remarkable. Never when controversy avoided the subjects which are large and important enough to kindle enthusiasm, was the mind of a people stirred up from its foundations, and the impulse given which raised even persons of the most ordinary intellect to something of the dignity of thinking beings. Of such we have had an example in the condition of Europe during the times immediately following the Reformation; another, though limited to the Continent and to a more cultivated class, in the speculative movement of the latter half of the eighteenth century; and a third, of still briefer duration, in the intellectual fermentation of Germany during the Goethian and Fichtean period. These periods differed widely in the particular opinions which they developed; but were alike in this, that during all three the yoke of authority was broken. In each, an old mental despotism had been thrown off, and no new one had yet taken its place. The impulse given at these three periods has made Europe what it now is. Every single improvement which has taken place either in the human mind or in institutions, may be traced distinctly to one or other of them. Appearances have for some time indicated that all three impulses are well-nigh spent; and we can expect no fresh start, until we again assert our mental freedom.

Let us now pass to the second division of the argument, and dismissing the supposition that any of the received opinions may be false, let us assume them to be true, and examine into the worth of the manner in which they are likely to be held, when their truth is not freely and openly canvassed. However unwillingly a person who has a strong opinion may admit the possibility that his opinion may be false, he ought to be moved by the consideration that however true it may be, if it is not fully, frequently, and fearlessly discussed, it will be held as a dead dogma, not a living truth.

There is a class of persons (happily not quite so numerous as formerly) who think it enough if a person assents undoubtingly to what they think true, though he has no knowledge whatever of the grounds of the opinion, and could not make a tenable defence of it against the most superficial objections. Such persons, if they can once get their creed taught from authority, naturally think that no good, and some harm, comes of its being allowed to be questioned. Where their influence prevails, they make it nearly impossible for the received opinion to be rejected wisely and considerately, though it may still be rejected rashly and ignorantly; for to shut out discussion entirely is seldom possible, and when it once gets in, beliefs not grounded on conviction are apt to give way before the slightest semblance of an argument. Waiving, however, this possibility—assuming that the true opinion abides in the mind, but abides as a prejudice, a belief independent of, and proof against, argument—this is not the way in which truth ought to be held by a rational being. This is not knowing the truth. Truth, thus held, is but one superstition the more, accidentally clinging to the words which enunciate a truth.

If the intellect and judgment of mankind ought to be cultivated, a thing which Protestants at least do not deny, on what can these faculties be more appropriately exercised by any one, than on the things which concern him so much that it is considered necessary for him to hold opinions on them? If the cultivation of the understanding consists in one thing more than in another, it is surely in learning the grounds of one's own opinions. Whatever people believe, on subjects on which it is of the first importance to believe rightly, they ought to be able to defend against at least the common objections. But, some one may say, "Let them be *taught* the grounds of their opinions. It does not follow that opinions must be merely parroted because they are never heard controverted. Persons who learn geometry do not simply commit the theorems to memory, but understand and learn likewise the demonstrations; and it would be absurd to say that they remain ignorant of the grounds of geometrical truths, because they never hear any one deny, and attempt to disprove them." Undoubtedly: and such teaching suffices on a subject like mathematics, where there is nothing at all to be said on the wrong side of the question. The peculiarity of the evidence of mathematical truths is, that all the argument is on one side. There are no objections, and no answers to objections. But on every subject on which difference of opinion is possible, the truth depends on a balance to be struck between two sets of conflicting reasons. Even in natural philosophy, there is always some other explanation possible of the same facts; some geocentric theory instead of heliocentric, some phlogiston instead of oxygen; and it has to be shown why that other theory cannot be the true one: and until this is shown, and until we know how it is shown, we do not understand the grounds of our opinion. But when we turn to subjects infinitely more complicated, to morals, religion, politics, social relations, and the business of life, three-fourths of the arguments for every disputed opinion consist in dispelling the appearances which favor some opinion different from it. The greatest orator, save one, of antiquity, has left it on record that he always studied his adversary's case with as great, if not with still greater, intensity than even his own. What Cicero practised as the means of forensic success, requires to be imitated by all who study any subject in order to arrive at the truth. He who knows only his own side of the case, knows little of that. His reasons may be good, and no one may have been able to refute them. But if he is equally unable to refute the reasons on the opposite side; if he does not so much as know what they are, he has no ground for preferring either opinion. The rational position for him would be suspension of judgment, and unless he contents himself with that, he is either led by authority, or adopts, like the generality of the world, the side to which he feels most inclination. Nor is it enough that he should hear the arguments of adversaries from his own teachers, presented as they state them, and accompanied by what they offer as refutations. That is not the way to do justice to the arguments, or bring them into real contact with his own mind. He must be able to hear them from persons who actually believe them; who defend them in earnest, and do their very utmost for them. He must know them in their most plausible and persuasive form; he must feel the whole force of the difficulty which the true view of the subject has to encounter and dispose of; else he will never really possess himself of the portion of truth which meets and removes that difficulty. Ninety-nine in a hundred of what are called educated men are in this condition, even of those who can argue fluently for their opinions. Their conclusion may be true, but it might be false for anything they know: they have never thrown themselves into the mental position of those who think differently from them, and considered what such persons may have to say; and consequently they do not, in any proper sense of the word, know the doctrine which they themselves profess. They do not know those parts of it which explain and justify the remainder; the considerations which show that a fact which seemingly conflicts with another is reconcilable with it, or that, of two apparently strong reasons, one and not the other ought to be preferred. All that part of the truth which turns the scale, and decides the judgment of a completely informed mind, they are strangers to; nor is it ever really known, but to those who have attended equally and impartially to both sides, and endeavored to see the reasons of both in the strongest light. So essential is this discipline to a real understanding of moral and human subjects, that if opponents of all important truths do not exist, it is indispensable to imagine them, and supply them with the strongest arguments which the most skilful devil's advocate can conjure up.

To abate the force of these considerations, an enemy of free discussion may be supposed to say, that there is no necessity for mankind in general to know and understand all that can be said against or for their opinions by philosophers and theologians. That it is not needful for common men to be able to expose all the misstatements or fallacies of an ingenious opponent. That it is enough if there is always somebody capable of answering them, so that nothing likely to mislead uninstructed persons remains unrefuted. That simple minds, having been taught the obvious grounds of the truths inculcated on them, may trust to authority for the rest, and being aware that they have neither knowledge nor talent to resolve every difficulty which can be raised, may repose in the assurance that all those which have been raised have been or can be answered, by those who are specially trained to the task.

Conceding to this view of the subject the utmost that can be claimed for it by those most easily satisfied with the mount of understanding of truth which ought to accompany the belief of it; even so, the argument for free discussion is no way weakened. For even this doctrine acknowledges that mankind ought to have a rational assurance that all objections have been satisfactorily answered; and how are they to be answered if that which requires to be answered is not spoken? or how can the answer be known to be satisfactory, if the objectors have no opportunity of showing that it is unsatisfactory? If not the public, at least the philosophers and theologians who are to resolve the difficulties, must make themselves familiar with those difficulties in their most puzzling form; and this cannot be accomplished unless they are freely stated, and placed in the most advantageous light which they admit of. The Catholic Church has its own way of dealing with this embarrassing problem. It makes a broad separation between those who can be permitted to receive its doctrines on conviction, and those who must accept them on trust. Neither, indeed, are allowed any choice as to what they will accept; but the clergy, such at least as can be fully confided in, may admissibly and meritoriously make themselves acquainted with the arguments of opponents, in order to answer them, and may, therefore, read heretical books; the laity, not unless by special permission, hard to be obtained. This discipline recognizes a knowledge of the enemy's case as beneficial to the teachers, but finds means, consistent with this, of denying it to the rest of the world: thus giving to the *élite* more mental culture, though not more mental freedom, than it allows to the mass. By this device it succeeds in obtaining the kind of mental superiority which its purposes require; for though culture without freedom never made a large and liberal mind, it can make a clever *nisi prius* advocate of a cause. But in countries professing Protestantism, this resource is denied; since Protestants hold, at least in theory, that the responsibility for the choice of a religion must be borne by each for himself, and cannot be thrown off upon teachers. Besides, in the present state of the world, it is practically impossible that writings which are read by the instructed can be kept from the uninstructed. If the teachers of mankind are to be cognizant of all that they ought to know, everything must be free to be written and published without restraint.

If, however, the mischievous operation of the absence of free discussion, when the received opinions are true, were confined to leaving men ignorant of the grounds of those opinions, it might be thought that this, if an intellectual, is no moral evil, and does not affect the worth of the opinions, regarded in their influence on the character. The fact, however, is, that not only the grounds of the opinion are forgotten in the absence of discussion, but too often the meaning of the opinion itself. The words which convey it, cease to suggest ideas, or suggest only a small portion of those they were originally employed to communicate. Instead of a vivid conception and a living belief, there remain only a few phrases retained by rote; or, if any part, the shell and husk only of the meaning is retained, the finer essence being lost. The great chapter in human history which this fact occupies and fills, cannot be too earnestly studied and meditated on.

It is illustrated in the experience of almost all ethical doctrines and religious creeds. They are all full of meaning and vitality to those who originate them, and to the direct disciples of the originators. Their meaning continues to be felt in undiminished strength, and is perhaps brought out into even fuller consciousness, so long as the struggle lasts to give the doctrine or creed an ascendency over other creeds. At last it either prevails, and becomes the general opinion, or its progress stops; it keeps possession of the ground it has gained, but ceases to spread further. When either of these results has become apparent, controversy on the subject flags, and gradually dies away. The doctrine has taken its place, if not as a received opinion, as one of the admitted sects or divisions of opinion: those who hold it have generally inherited, not adopted it; and conversion from one of these doctrines to another, being now an exceptional fact, occupies little place in the thoughts of their professors. Instead of being, as at first, constantly on the alert either to defend themselves against the world, or to bring the world over to them, they have subsided into acquiescence, and neither listen, when they can help it, to arguments against their creed, nor trouble dissentients (if there be such) with arguments in its favor. From this time may usually be dated the decline in the living power of the doctrine. We often hear the teachers of all creeds lamenting the difficulty of keeping up in the minds of believers a lively apprehension of the truth which they nominally recognize, so that it may penetrate the feelings, and acquire a real mastery over the conduct. No such difficulty is complained of while the creed is still fighting for its existence: even the weaker combatants then know and feel what they are fighting for, and the difference between it and other doctrines; and in that period of every creed's existence, not a few persons may be found, who have realized its fundamental principles in all the forms of thought, have weighed and considered them in all their important bearings, and have experienced the full effect on the character, which belief in that creed ought to produce in a mind thoroughly imbued with it. But when it has come to be an hereditary creed, and to be received passively, not actively—when the mind is no longer compelled, in the same degree as at first, to exercise its vital powers on the questions which its belief presents to it, there is a progressive tendency to forget all of the belief except the formularies, or to give it a dull and torpid assent, as if accepting it on trust dispensed with the necessity of realizing it in consciousness, or tesing it by personal experience; until it almost ceases to connect itself at all with the inner life of the human being. Then are seen the cases, so frequent in this age of the world as almost to form the majority, in which the creed remains as it were outside the mind, encrusting and petrifying it against all other influences addressed to the higher parts of our nature; manifesting its power by not suffering any fresh and living conviction to get in, but itself doing nothing for the mind or heart, except standing sentinel over them to keep them vacant.

To what an extent doctrines intrinsically fitted to make the deepest impression upon the mind may remain in it as dead beliefs, without being ever realized in the imagination, the feelings, or the understanding, is exemplified by the manner in which the majority of believers hold the doctrines of Christianity. By Christianity I here mean what is accounted such by all churches and sects—the maxims and precepts contained in the New Testament. These are considered sacred, and accepted as laws, by all professing Christians. Yet it is scarcely too much to say that not one Christian in a thousand guides or tests his individual conduct by reference to those laws. The standard to which he does refer it, is the custom of his nation, his class, or his religious profession. He has thus, on the one hand, a collection of ethical maxims, which he believes to have been vouchsafed to him by infallible wisdom as rules for his government; and on the other, a set of every-day judgments and practices, which go a certain length with some of those maxims, not so great a length with others, stand in direct opposition to some, and are, on the whole, a compromise between the Christian creed and the interests and suggestions of worldly life. To the first of these standards he gives his homage; to the other his real allegiance. All Christians believe that the blessed are the poor and humble, and those who are ill-used by the world; that it is easier for a camel to pass through the eye of a needle than for a rich man to enter the kingdom of heaven; that they should judge not, lest they be judged; that they should swear not at all; that they should love their neighbor as themselves; that if one take their cloak, they should give him their coat also; that they should take no thought for the morrow;

that if they would be perfect, they should sell all that they have and give it to the poor. They are not insincere when they say that they believe these things. They do believe them, as people believe what they have always heard lauded and never discussed. But in the sense of that living belief which regulates conduct, they believe these doctrines just up to the point to which it is usual to act upon them. The doctrines in their integrity are serviceable to pelt adversaries with; and it is understood that they are to be put forward (when possible) as the reasons for whatever people do that they think laudable. But any one who reminded them that the maxims require an infinity of things which they never even think of doing, would gain nothing but to be classed among those very unpopular characters who affect to be better than other people. The doctrines have no hold on ordinary believers—are not a power in their minds. They have an habitual respect for the sound of them, but no feeling which spreads from the words to the things signified, and forces the mind to take *them* in, and make them conform to the formula. Whenever conduct is concerned, they look around for Mr. A and B to direct them how far to go in obeying Christ.

Now we may be well assured that the case was not thus, but far otherwise, with the early Christians. Had it been thus, Christianity never would have expanded from an obscure sect of the despised Hebrews into the religion of the Roman empire. When their enemies said, "See how these Christians love one another" (a remark not likely to be made by anybody now), they assuredly had a much livelier feeling of the meaning of their creed than they have ever had since. And to this cause, probably, it is chiefly owing that Christianity now makes so little progress in extending its domain, and after eighteen centuries, is still nearly confined to Europeans and the descendants of Europeans. Even with the strictly religious, who are much in earnest about their doctrines, and attach a greater amount of meaning to many of them than people in general, it commonly happens that the part which is thus comparatively active in their minds is that which was made by Calvin, or Knox, or some such person much nearer in character to themselves. The sayings of Christ coexist passively in their minds, producing hardly any effect beyond what is caused by mere listening to words so amiable and bland. There are many reasons, doubtless, why doctrines which are the badge of a sect retain more of their vitality than those common to all recognized sects, and why more pains are taken by teachers to keep their meaning alive; but one reason certainly is, that the peculiar doctrines are more questioned, and have to be oftener defended against open gainsayers. Both teachers and learners go to sleep at their post, as soon as there is no enemy in the field.

The same thing holds true, generally speaking, of all traditional doctrines—those of prudence and knowledge of life, as well as of morals or religion. All languages and literatures are full of general observations on life, both as to what it is, and how to conduct oneself in it; observations which everybody knows, which everybody repeats, or hears with acquiescence, which are received as truisms, yet of which most people first truly learn the meaning, when experience, generally of a painful kind, has made it a reality to them. How often, when smarting under some unforeseen misfortune or disappointment, does a person call to mind some proverb or common saying, familiar to him all his life, the meaning of which, if he had ever before felt it as he does now, would have saved him from the calamity. There are indeed reasons for this, other than the absence of discussion: there are many truths of which the full meaning *cannot* be realized, until personal experience has brought it home. But much more of the meaning even of these would have been understood and what was understood would have been far more deeply impressed on the mind, if the man had been accustomed to hear it argued *pro* and *con* by people who did understand it. The fatal tendency of mankind to leave off thinking about a thing when it is no longer doubtful, is the cause of half their errors. A contemporary author has well spoken of "the deep slumber of a decided opinion."

But what! (it may be asked) Is the absence of unanimity an indispensable condition of true knowledge? Is it necessary that some part of mankind should persist in error, to enable any to realize the truth? Does a belief cease to be real and vital as soon as it is generally received—and is a proposition never thoroughly understood and felt unless some doubt of it remains? As soon as mankind have unanimously accepted a truth, does the truth perish within them? The highest aim and best result of improved intelligence, it has hitherto been thought, is to unite mankind more and more in the acknowledgment of all important truths: and does the intelligence only last as long as it has not achieved its object? Do the fruits of conquest perish by the very completeness of the victory?

I affirm no such thing. As mankind improve, the number of doctrines which are no longer disputed or doubted will be constantly on the increase: and the well-being of mankind may almost be measured by the number and gravity of the truths which have reached the point of being uncontested. The cessation, on one question after another, of serious controversy, is one of the necessary incidents of the consolidation of opinion; a consolidation as salutary in the case of true opinions, as it is dangerous and noxious when the opinions are erroneous. But though this gradual narrowing of the bounds of diversity of opinion is necessary in both senses of the term, being at once inevitable and indispensable, we are not therefore obliged to conclude that all its consequences must be beneficial. The loss of so important an aid to the intelligent and living apprehension of a truth, as is afforded by the necessity of explaining it to, or defending it against, opponents, though not sufficient to outweigh, is no trifling drawback from, the benefit of its universal recognition. Where this advantage can no longer be had, I confess I should like to see the teachers of mankind endeavoring to provide a substitute for it; some contrivance for making the difficulties of the question as present to the learner's consciousness, as if they were pressed upon him by a dissentient champion, eager for his conversion.

But instead of seeking contrivances for this purpose, they have lost those they formerly had. The Socratic dialectics, so magnificently exemplified in the dialogues of Plato, were a contrivance of this description. They were essentially a negative discussion of the great questions of philosophy and life, directed with consummate skill to the purpose of convincing any one who had merely adopted the commonplaces of received opinion, that he did not understand the subject—that he as yet attached no definite meaning to the doctrines he professed; in order that, becoming aware of his ignorance, he might be put in the way to attain a stable belief, resting on a clear apprehension both of the meaning of doctrines and of their evidence. The school disputations of the Middle Ages had a somewhat similar object. They were intended to make sure that the pupil understood his own opinion, and (by necessary correlation) the opinion opposed to it, and could enforce the grounds of the one and confute those of the other. These last-mentioned contests had indeed the incurable defect, that the premises appealed to were taken from authority, not from reason; and, as a discipline to the mind, they were in every respect inferior to the powerful dialectics which formed the intellects of the "Socratici viri": but the modern mind owes far more to both than it is generally willing to admit, and the present modes of education contain nothing which in the smallest degree supplies the place either of the one or of the other. A person who derives all his instruction from teachers or books, even if he escape the besetting temptation of contenting himself with cram, is under no compulsion to hear both sides; accordingly it is far from a frequent accomplishment, even among thinkers, to know both sides; and the weakest part of what everybody says in defence of his opinion, is what he intends as a reply to antagonists. It is the fashion of the present time to disparage negative logic—that which points out weaknesses in theory or errors in practice, without establishing positive truths. Such negative criticism would indeed be poor enough as an ultimate result; but as a means to attaining any positive knowledge or conviction worthy the name, it cannot be valued too highly; and until people are again systematically trained to it, there will be few great thinkers, and a low general average of intellect, in any but the mathematical and physical departments of speculation. On any other subject no one's opinions deserve the name of knowledge, except so far as he has either had forced upon him by others, or gone through of himself, the same mental process which would have been required of him in carrying on an active controversy with opponents. That, therefore, which when absent, it is so indispensable, but so difficult, to create, how worse than absurd is it to forego, when spontaneously offering itself! If there are any persons who contest a received opinion, or who will do so if law or opinion will let them, let us thank them for it, open our minds to listen to them, and rejoice that there is some one to do for us what we otherwise ought, if we have any regard for either the certainty or the vitality of our convictions, to do with much greater labor for ourselves.

It still remains to speak of one of the principal causes which make diversity of opinion advantageous, and will continue to do so until mankind shall have entered a stage of intellectual advancement which at present seems at an incalculable distance. We have hitherto considered only two possibilities: that the received opinion may be false, and some other opinion, consequently, true; or that, the received opinion being true, a conflict with the opposite error is essential to a clear apprehension and deep feeling of its truth. But there is a commoner case than either of these; when the conflicting doctrines, instead of being one true and the other false, share the truth between them; and the nonconforming opinion is needed to supply the remainder of the truth, of which the received doctrine embodies only a part. Popular opinions, on subjects not palpable to sense, are often true, but seldom or never the whole truth. They are a part of the truth; sometimes a greater, sometimes a smaller part, but exaggerated, distorted, and disjoined from the truths by which they ought to be accompanied and limited. Heretical opinions, on the other hand, are generally some of these suppressed and neglected truths, bursting the bonds which kept them down, and either seeking reconciliation with the truth contained in the common opinion, or fronting it as enemies, and setting themselves up, with similar exclusiveness, as the whole truth. The latter case is hitherto the most frequent, as, in the human mind, one-sidedness has always been the rule, and many-sidedness the exception. Hence, even in revolutions of opinion, one part of the truth usually sets while another rises. Even progress, which ought to superadd, for the most part only substitutes one partial and incomplete truth for another; improvement consisting chiefly in this, that the new fragment of truth is more wanted, more adapted to the needs of the time, than that which it displaces. Such being the partial character of prevailing opinions, even when resting on a true foundation; every opinion which embodies somewhat of the portion of truth which the common opinion omits, ought to be considered precious, with whatever amount of error and confusion that truth may be blended. No sober judge of human affairs will feel bound to be indignant because those who force on our notice truths which we should otherwise have overlooked, overlook some of those which we see. Rather, he will think that so long as popular truth is one-sided, it is more desirable than otherwise that unpopular truth should have one-sided asserters too; such being usually the most energetic, and the most likely to compel reluctant attention to the fragment of wisdom which they proclaim as if it were the whole.

Thus, in the eighteenth century, when nearly all the instructed, and all those of the uninstructed who were led by them, were lost in admiration of what is called civilization, and of the marvels of modern science, literature, and philosophy, and while greatly overrating the amount of unlikeness between the men of modern and those of ancient times, indulged the belief that the whole of the difference was in their own favor; with what a salutary shock did the paradoxes of Rousseau explode like bombshells in the midst, dislocating the compact mass of one-sided opinion, and forcing its elements to recombine in a better form and with additional ingredients. Not that the current opinions were on the whole farther from the truth than Rousseau's were; on the contrary, they were nearer to it; they contained more of positive truth, and very much less of error. Nevertheless there lay in Rousseau's doctrine, and has floated down the stream of opinion along with it, a considerable amount of exactly those truths which the popular opinion wanted; and these are the deposit which was left behind when the flood subsided. The superior worth of simplicity of life, the enervating and demoralizing effect of the trammels and hypocrisies of artificial society, are ideas which have never been entirely absent from cultivated minds since Rousseau wrote; and they will in time produce their due effect, though at present needing to be asserted as much as ever, and to be asserted by deeds, for words, on this subject, have nearly exhausted their power.

In politics, again, it is almost a commonplace, that a party of order or stability, and a party of progress or reform, are both necessary elements of a healthy state of political life; until the one or the other shall have so enlarged its mental grasp as to be a party equally of order and of progress, knowing and distinguishing what is fit to be preserved from what ought to be swept away. Each of these modes of thinking derives its utility from the deficiencies of the other; but it is in a great measure the opposition of the other that keeps each within the limits of reason and sanity. Unless opinions favorable to democracy and to aristocracy, to property and to equality, to coöperation and to competition, to luxury and to abstinence, to sociality and individuality, to liberty and discipline, and all the other standing antagonisms of practical life, are expressed with equal freedom, and enforced and defended with equal talent and energy, there is no chance of both elements obtaining their due; one scale is sure to go up, and the other down. Truth, in the great practical concerns of life, is so much a question of the reconciling and combining of opposites, that very few have minds sufficiently capacious and impartial to make the adjustment with an approach to correctness, and it has to be made by the rough process of a struggle between combatants fighting under hostile banners. On any of the great open questions just enumerated, if either of the two opinions has a better claim than the other, not merely to be tolerated, but to be encouraged and countenanced, it is the one which happens at the particular time and place to be in a minority. That is the opinion which, for the time being, represents the neglected interests, the side of human well-being which is in danger of obtaining less than its share. I am aware that there is not, in this country, any intolerance of differences of opinion on most of these topics. They are adduced to show, by admitted and multiplied examples, the universality of the fact, that only through diversity of opinion is there, in the existing state of human intellect, a chance of fair play to all sides of the truth. When there are persons to be found, who form an exception to the apparent unanimity of the world on any subject, even if the world is in the right, it is always probable that dissentients have something worth hearing to say for themselves, and that truth would lose something by their silence.

It may be objected, "But *some* received principles, especially on the highest and most vital subjects, are more than half-truths. The Christian morality, for instance, is the whole truth on that subject, and if any one teaches a morality which varies from it, he is wholly in error." As this is of all cases the most important in practice, none can be fitter to test the general maxim. But before pronouncing what Christian morality is or is not, it would be desirable to decide what is meant by Christian morality. If it means the morality of the New Testament, I wonder that any one who derives his knowledge of this from the book itself, can suppose that it was announced, or intended, as a complete doctrine of morals. The Gospel always refers to a preëxisting morality, and confines its precepts to the particulars in which that morality was to be corrected, or superseded by a wider and higher; expressing itself, moreover, in terms most general, often impossible to be interpreted literally, and possessing rather the impressiveness of poetry or eloquence than the precision of legislation. To extract from it a body of ethical doctrine, has never been possible without eking it out from the Old Testament, that is, from a system elaborate indeed, but in many respects barbarous, and intended only for a barbarous people. St. Paul, a declared enemy to this Judaical mode of interpreting the doctrine and filling up the scheme of his Master, equally assumes a preëxisting morality, namely, that of the Greeks and Romans; and his advice to Christians is in a great measure a system of accommodation to that; even to the extent of giving an apparent sanction to slavery. What is called Christian, but should rather be termed theological, morality, was not the work of Christ or the Apostles, but is of much later origin, having been gradually built up by the Catholic Church of the first five centuries, and though not implicitly adopted by moderns and Protestants, has been much less modified by them than might have been expected. For the most part,indeed, they have contented themselves with cutting off the additions which had been made to it in the Middle Ages, each sect supplying the place by fresh additions, adopted to its own character and tendencies. That mankind owe a great debt to this morality, and to its early teachers, I should be the last person to deny; but I do not scruple to say of it, that it is, in many important points, incomplete and one-sided, and that unless ideas and feelings, not sanctioned by it, had contributed to the formation of European life and character, human affairs would have been in a worse condition than they now are. Christian morality (so called) has all the characters of a re-action; it is, in great part, a protest against Paganism. Its ideal is negative rather than positive; passive rather than active; Innocence rather than Nobleness; Abstinence from Evil, rather than energetic Pursuit of Good: in its precepts (as has been well said) "thou shalt not" predominates unduly over "thou shalt." In its horror of sensu-ality, it made an idol of asceticism, which has been gradually com-promised away into one of legality. It holds out the hope of heaven and the threat of hell, as the appointed and appropriate motives to a virtuous life: in this falling far below the best of the ancients, and doing what lies in it to give to human morality an essentially selfish character, by disconnecting each man's feelings of duty from the interests of his fellow-creatures, except so far as a self-interested inducement is offered to him for consulting them. It is essentially a doctrine of passive obedience; it inculcates submission to all authorities found established; who indeed are not to be actively obeyed when they command what religion forbids, but who are not to be resisted, far less rebelled against, for any amount of wrong to ourselves. And while, in the morality of the best Pagan nations, duty to the State holds even a disproportionate place, infringing on the just liberty of the individual; in purely Christian ethics, that grand department of duty is scarcely noticed or acknowledged. It is in the Koran, not the New Testament, that we read the maxim —"A ruler who appoints any man to an office, when there is in his dominions another man better qualified for it, sins against God and against the State." What little recognition the idea of obligation to the public obtains in modern morality, is derived from Greek and Roman sources, not from Christian; as, even in the morality of private life, whatever exists of magnanimity, high-mindedness, personal dignity, even the sense of honor, is derived from the purely human, not the religious part of our education, and never could have grown out of a standard of ethics in which the only worth, professedly recognized, is that of obedience.

I am as far as any one from pretending that these defects are necessarily inherent in the Christian ethics, in every manner in which it can be conceived, or that the many requisites of a complete moral doctrine which it does not contain, do not admit of being reconciled with it. Far less would I insinuate this of the doctrines and precepts of Christ himself. I believe that the sayings of Christ are all, that I can see any evidence of their having been intended to be; that they are irreconcilable with nothing which a comprehensive morality requires; that everything which is excellent in ethics may be brought within them, with no greater violence to their language than has been done to it by all who have attempted to deduce from them any practical system of conduct whatever. But it is quite consistent with this, to believe that they contain, and were meant to contain, only a part of the truth; that many essential elements of the highest morality are among the things which are not provided for, nor intended to be provided for in the recorded deliverances of the Founder of Christianity, and which have been entirely thrown aside in the system of ethics erected on the basis of those deliverances by the Christian Church. And this being so, I think it a great error to persist in attempting to find in the Christian doctrine that complete rule for our guidance, which its author intended it to sanction and enforce, but only partially to provide. I believe, too, that this narrow theory is becoming a grave practical evil, detracting greatly from the value of the moral training and instruction, which so many well-meaning persons are now at length exerting themselves to promote. I much fear that by attempting to form the mind and feelings on an exclusively religious type, and discarding those secular standards (as for want of a better name they may be called) which heretofore coexisted with and supplemented the Christian ethics, receiving some of its spirit, and infusing into it some of theirs, there will result, and is even now resulting, a low, abject, servile type of character, which, submit itself as it may to what it deems the Supreme Will, is incapable of rising to or sympathizing in the conception of Supreme Goodness. I believe that other ethics than any which can be evolved from exclusively Christian sources, must exist side by side with Christian ethics to produce the moral regeneration of mankind; and that the Christian system is no exception to the rule, that in an imperfect state of the human mind, the interests of truth require a diversity of opinions. It is not necessary that in ceasing to ignore the moral truths not contained in Christianity, men should ignore any of those which it does contain. Such prejudice, or oversight, when it occurs, is altogether an evil; but it is one from which we cannot hope to be always exempt, and must be regarded as the price paid for an inestimable good. The exclusive pretension made by a part of the truth to be the whole, must and ought to be protested against, and if a reactionary impulse should make the protestors unjust in their turn, this one-sidedness, like the other, may be lamented, but must be tolerated. If Christians would teach infidels to be just to Christianity, they should themselves be just to infidelity. It can do truth no service to blink the fact, known to all who have the most ordinary acquaintance with literary history, that a large portion of the noblest and most valuable moral teaching has been the work, not only of men who did not know, but of men who knew and rejected, the Christian faith.

I do not pretend that the most unlimited use of the freedom of enunciating all possible opinions would put an end to the evils of religious or philosophical sectarianism. Every truth which men of narrow capacity are in earnest about, is sure to be asserted, inculcated, and in many ways even acted on, as if no other truth existed in the world, or at all events none that could limit or qualify the first. I acknowledge that the tendency of all opinions to become sectarian is not cured by the freest discussion, but is often heightened and exacerbated thereby; the truth which ought to have been, but was not, seen, being rejected all the more violently because proclaimed by persons regarded as opponents. But it is not on the impassioned partisan, it is on the calmer and more disinterested by-stander, that this collision of opinions works its salutary effect.

Not the violent conflict between parts of the truth, but the quiet suppression of half of it, is the formidable evil: there is always hope when people are forced to listen to both sides; it is when they attend only to one that errors harden into prejudices, and truth itself ceases to have the effect of truth, by being exaggerated into falsehood. And since there are few mental attributes more rare than that judicial faculty which can sit in intelligent judgment between two sides of a question, of which only one is represented by an advocate before it, truth has no chance but in proportion as every side of it, every opinion which embodies any fraction of the truth, not only finds advocates, but is so advocated as to be listened to.

We have now recognized the necessity to the mental well-being of mankind (on which all their other well-being depends) of freedom of opinion, and freedom of the expression of opinion, on four distinct grounds; which we will now briefly recapitulate.

First, if any opinion is compelled to silence, that opinion may, for aught we can certainly know, be true. To deny this is to assume our own infallibility.

Secondly, though the silenced opinion be an error, it may, and very commonly does, contain a portion of truth; and since the general or prevailing opinion on any subject is rarely or never the whole truth, it is only by the collision of adverse opinions that the remainder of the truth has any chance of being supplied.

Thirdly, even if the received opinion be not only true, but the whole truth; unless it is suffered to be, and actually is, vigorously and earnestly contested, it will, by most of those who receive it, be held in the manner of a prejudice, with little comprehension or feeling of its rational grounds. And not only this, but, fourthly, the meaning of the doctrine itself will be in danger of being lost, or enfeebled, and deprived of its vital effect on the character and conduct: the dogma becoming a mere formal profession, inefficacious for good, but cumbering the ground, and preventing the growth of any real and heartfelt conviction, from reason or personal experience.

Before quitting the subject of freedom of opinion, it is fit to take some notice of those who say, that the free expression of all opinions should be permitted, on condition that the manner be temperate, and do not pass the bounds of fair discussion. Much might be said on the impossibility of fixing where these supposed bounds are to be placed; for if the test be offence to those whose opinion is attacked, I think experience testifies that this offence is given whenever the attack is telling and powerful, and that every opponent who pushes them hard, and whom they find it difficult to answer, appears to them, if he shows any strong feeling on the subject, an intemperate opponent. But this, though an important consideration in a practical point of view, merges in a more fundamental objection. Undoubtedly the manner of asserting an opinion, even though it be a true one, may be very objectionable, and may justly incur severe censure. But the principal offences of the kind are such as it is mostly impossible, unless by accidental self-betrayal, to bring home to conviction. The gravest of them is, to argue sophistically, to suppress facts or arguments, to misstate the elements of the case, or misrepresent the opposite opinion. But all this, even to the most aggravated degree, is so continually done in perfect good faith, by persons who are not considered, and in many other respects may not deserve to be considered, ignorant or incompetent, that it is rarely possible on adequate grounds conscientiously to stamp the misrepresentation as morally culpable; and still less could law presume to interfere with this kind of controversial misconduct. With regard to what is commonly meant by intemperate discussion, namely, invective, sarcasm, personality, and the like, the denunciation of these weapons would deserve more sympathy if it were ever proposed to interdict them equally to both sides; but it is only desired to restrain the employment of them against the prevailing opinion: against the unprevailing they may not only be used without general disapproval, but will be likely to obtain for him who uses them the praise of honest zeal and righteous indignation. Yet whatever mischief arises from their use, is greatest when they are employed against the comparatively defenceless; and whatever unfair advantage can be derived by any opinion from this mode of asserting it, accrues almost exclusively to received opinions. The worst offence of this kind which can be committed by a polemic, is to stigmatize those who hold the contrary opinion as bad and immoral men. To calumny of this sort, those who hold any unpopular opinion are peculiarly exposed, because they are in general few and uninfluential, and nobody but themselves feels much interest in seeing justice done them; but this weapon is, from the nature of the case, denied to those who attack a prevailing opinion: they can neither use it with safety to themselves, nor, if they could, would it do anything but recoil on their own cause. In general, opinions contrary to those commonly received can only obtain a hearing by studied moderation of language, and the most cautious avoidance of unnecessary offence, from which they hardly ever deviate even in a slight degree without losing ground: while unmeasured vituperation employed on the side of the prevailing opinion, really does deter people from professing contrary opinions, and from listening to those who profess them. For the interest, therefore, of truth and justice, it is far more important to restrain this employment of vituperative language than the other; and, for example, if it were necessary to choose, there would be much more need to discourage offensive attacks on infidelity, than on religion. It is, however, obvious that law and authority have no business with restraining either, while opinion ought, in every instance, to determine its verdict by the circumstances of the individual case; condemning every one, on whichever side of the argument he places himself, in whose mode of advocacy either want of candor, or malignity, bigotry, or intolerance of feeling manifest themselves; but not inferring these vices from the side which a person takes, though it be the contrary side of the question to our own: and giving merited honor to every one, whatever opinion he may hold, who has calmness to see and honesty to state what his opponents and their opinions really are, exaggerating nothing to their discredit, keeping nothing back which tells, or can be supposed to tell, in their favor. This is the real morality of public discussion; and if often violated, I am happy to think that there are many controversialists who to a great extent observe it, and a still greater number who conscientiously strive towards it.

Such being the reasons which make it imperative that human

beings should be free to form opinions, and to express their opinions without reserve; and such the baneful consequences to the intellectual, and through that to the moral nature of man, unless this liberty is either conceded, or asserted in spite of prohibition; let us next examine whether the same reasons do not require that men should be free to act upon their opinions—to carry these out in their lives, without hindrance, either physical or moral, from their fellow-men, so long as it is at their own risk and peril. This last proviso is of course indispensable. No one pretends that actions should be as free as opinions. On the contrary, even opinions lose their immunity, when the circumstances in which they are expressed are such as to constitute their expression a positive instigation to some mischievous act. An opinion that corn-dealers are starvers of the poor, or that private property is robbery, ought to be unmolested when simply circulated through the press, but may justly incur punishment when delivered orally to an excited mob assembled before the house of a corn-dealer, or when handed about among the same mob in the form of a placard. Acts, of whatever kind, which, without justifiable cause, do harm to others, may be, and in the more important cases absolutely require to be, controlled by the unfavorable sentiments, and, when needful, by the active interference of mankind. The liberty of the individual must be thus far limited; he must not make himself a nuisance to other people. But if he refrains from molesting others in what concerns them, and merely acts according to his own inclination and judgment in things which concern himself, the same reasons which show that opinion should be free, prove also that he should be allowed, without molestation, to carry his opinions into practice at his own cost. That mankind are not infallible; that their truths, for the most part, are only half-truths; that unity of opinion, unless resulting from the fullest and freest comparison of opposite opinions, is not desirable, and diversity not an evil, but a good, until mankind are much more capable than at present of recognizing all sides of the truth, are principles applicable to men's modes of action, not less than to their opinions. As it is useful that while mankind are imperfect there should be different opinions, so is it that there should be different experiments of living; that free scope should be given to varieties of character, short of injury to others; and that the worth of different modes of life should be proved practically, when any one thinks fit to try them. It is desirable, in short, that in things which do not primarily concern others, individuality should assert itself. Where, not the person's own character, but the traditions or customs of other people are the rule of conduct, there is wanting one of the principal ingredients of human happiness, and quite the chief ingredient of individual and social progress.

Looking at democracy in the way in which it is commonly conceived, as the rule of the numerical majority; it is surely possible that the ruling power may be under the dominion of sectional or class interests, pointing to conduct different from that which would be dictated by impartial regard for the interest of all. Suppose the majority to be whites, the minority negroes, or *vice versa:* is it likely that the majority would allow equal justice to the minority?*7

[The elite proposed by Mill would have an advisory function, not a power function:]
  . . . In the false democracy which, instead of giving representation to all gives it only to the local majorities, the voice of the instructed minority may have no organs at all in the representative body. . . . Against this evil the system of personal representation, proposed by Mr. Hare†is almost a specific. The minority of instructed minds scattered through the local constituencies would unite to return a number proportioned to their own numbers, of the very ablest men the country contains. They would be under the strongest inducement to choose such men, since in no other mode could they make their small numerical strength tell for anything

* *Representative Government,* "Of the Infirmities and Dangers to Which Representative Government Is Liable."
† Thomas Hare, *Treatise on the Election of Representatives* (1859) [Ed.]

considerable. The representatives of the majority, besides that they would themselves be improved in quality by the operation of the system, would no longer have the whole field to themselves. They would indeed outnumber the others, as much as the one class of electors outnumbers the other in the country: they could always outvote them, but they would speak and vote in their presence, and subject to their criticism. When any difference arose, they would have to meet the arguments of the instructed few by reasons, at least apparently, as cogent; and since they could not, as those do who are speaking to persons already unanimous, simply assume that they are in the right, it would occasionally happen to them to become convinced that they were in the wrong. As they would in general be well-meaning (for thus much may reasonably be expected from a fairly-chosen national representation), their own minds would be insensibly raised by the influence of the minds with which they were in contact, or even in conflict. The champions of unpopular doctrines would not put forth their arguments merely in books and periodicals, read only by their own side; the opposing ranks would meet face to face and hand to hand, and there would be a fair comparison of their intellectual strength in the presence of the country. It would then be found out whether the opinion which prevailed by counting votes would also prevail if the votes were weighed as well as counted. The multitude have often a true instinct for distinguishing an able man, when he has the means of displaying his ability in a fair field before them. If such a man fails to obtain at least some portion of his just weight, it is through institutions or usages which keep him out of sight. In the old democracies there were no means of keeping out of sight any able man: the bema was open to him; he needed nobody's consent to become a public adviser. It is not so in a representative government; and the best friends of representative democracy can hardly be without misgivings that the Themistocles or Demosthenes, whose counsels would have saved the nation, might be unable during his whole life ever to obtain a seat. But if the presence in the representative assembly can be insured of even a few of the first minds in the country, though the remainder consist only of average minds, the influence of these leading spirits is sure to make itself sensibly felt in the general deliberations, even though they be known to be, in many respects, opposed to the tone of popular opinion and feeling. I am unable to conceive any mode by which the presence of such minds can be so positively insured as by that proposed by Mr. Hare.*

[For the following reasons, Mill believed his essay *On Liberty* to be unusually timely]

... The fears we expressed, lest the inevitable growth of social equality and of the government of public opinion, should impose on mankind an oppressive yoke of uniformity in opinion and practice, might easily have appeared chimerical to those who looked more at present facts than at tendencies; for the gradual revolution that is taking place in society and institutions has, thus far, been decidedly favourable to the development of new opinions, and has procured for them a much more unprejudiced hearing than they previously met with. But this is a feature belonging to periods of transition, when old notions and feelings have been unsettled, and no new doctrines have yet succeeded to their ascendancy. At such times people of any mental activity, having given up their old beliefs, and not feeling quite sure that those they still retain can stand unmodified, listen eagerly to new opinions. But this state of things is necessarily transitory: some particular body of doctrine in time rallies the majority round it, organizes social institutions and modes of action conformably to itself, education impresses this new creed upon the new generations without the mental processes that have led to it, and by degrees it acquires the very same power of compression, so long exercised by the creeds of which it had taken the place. Whether this noxious power will be exercised, depends on whether mankind have by that time become aware that it cannot be exercised without stunting and dwarfing human nature. It is then that the teachings of the 'Liberty' will have their greatest value.

Representative Government, Chapter VII, "Of True and False Democracy."

And it is to be feared that they will retain that value a long time.*

... the importance, in the present imperfect state of mental and social science, of antagonistic modes of thought; which it will one day be felt, are as necessary to one another in speculation, as mutually checking powers are in a political constitution.†

*_Autobiography_, Chapter VII, "General View of the Remainder of My Life."
†_Essay on Coleridge_.

PART II

The Clear and Present Danger

Oliver Wendell Holmes (1841–1935) was Associate Justice of the United States Supreme Court (1902–1932) and was known as the "great dissenter." His decisions and opinions are now legendary.

The doctrine of "clear and present danger" was the result of the Schenck v. United States case (1919) and grew out of the attempt by Schenck to obstruct the draft during World War I. In 1917 Congress had passed an espionage and sedition act. Interestingly enough, in this case Holmes wrote the unanimous opinion of the Court. Holmes's ruling is very clear and strict. Speech is not protected by the First Amendment if it (a) is "of such a nature as to create a clear and present danger"; *(b) is* used in special "circumstances"; and *(c)* "will bring about the substantive evils that Congress has a right to prevent."

This is an indictment in three counts. The first charges a conspiracy to violate the Espionage Act of June 15, 1917, c. 30, § 3, 40 Stat. 217, 219, by causing and attempting to cause insubordination, &c., in the military and naval forces of the United States, and to obstruct the recruiting and enlistment service of the United States, when the United States was at war with the German Empire, to-wit, that the defendants, wilfully conspired to have printed and circulated to men who had been called and accepted for military service under the Act of May 18, 1917, a document set forth and alleged to be calculated to cause such insubordination and obstruction. The count alleges overt acts in pursuance of the conspiracy, ending in the distribution of the document set forth. The second count alleges a conspiracy to commit an offense against the United States, to-wit, to use the mails for transmission of matter declared to be non-mailable by Title XII, §2, of the Act of June 15, 1917, to-wit, the above-mentioned document, with an averment of the same overt acts. The third count charges an unlawful use of the mails for the transmission of the same matter and otherwise as above. The defendants were found guilty on all the counts. They set up the First Amendment to the Constitution forbidding Congress to make any law abridging the freedom of speech, or of the press, and bringing the case here on that ground have argued some other points also of which we must dispose.

It is argued that the evidence, if admissible, was not sufficient to prove that the defendant Schenck was concerned in sending the documents. According to the testimony Schenck said he was general secretary of the Socialist Party and had charge of the Socialist headquarters from which the documents were sent. He identified a book found there as the minutes of the Executive Committee of the party. The book showed a resolution of August 13, 1917, that fifteen thousand leaflets should be printed on the other side of one of them in use, to be mailed to men who had passed exemption boards, and for distribution. Schenck personally attended to the printing. On August 20 the general secretary's report said, "Obtained new leaflets from printer and started work addressing envelopes," &c.; and there was a resolve that Comrade Schenck be allowed $125 for sending leaflets through the mail. He said that he had about fifteen or sixteen thousand printed. There were files of the circular in question in the inner office which he said were printed on the other side of the one-sided circular and were there for distribution. Other copies were proved to have been sent through the mails to drafted men. Without going into confirmatory details that were proved, no reasonable man could doubt that the defendant Schenck was largely instrumental in sending the circulars about. As to the defendant Baer, there was evidence that she was a member of the Executive Board and that the minutes of its transactions were hers. The argument as to the sufficiency of the evidence that the defendants conspired to send the documents only impairs the seriousness of the real defence.

It is objected that the documentary evidence was not admissible because obtained upon a search warrant, valid so far as appears. The contrary is established. *Adams* v. *New York*, 192 U. S. 585; *Weeks* v. *United States*, 232 U. S. 383, 395, 396. The search warrant did not issue against the defendant but against the Socialist headquarters at 1326 Arch Street and it would seem that the documents technically were not even in the defendant's possession. See *Johnson* v. *United States*, 288 U. S. 457. Notwithstanding some protest in argument the notion that evidence even directly proceeding from the defendant in a criminal proceeding is excluded in all cases by the Fifth Amendment is plainly unsound. *Holt* v. *United States*, 218 U. S. 245, 252, 253.

The document in question upon its first printed side recited the first section of the Thirteenth Amendment, said that the idea embodied in it was violated by the Conscription Act and that a conscript is little better than a convict. In impassioned language it intimated that conscription was despotism in its worst form and a monstrous wrong against humanity in the interest of Wall Street's chosen few. It said, "Do not submit to intimidation," but in form at least confined itself to peaceful measures such as a petition or the repeal of the Act. The other and later printed side of the sheet was headed, "Assert Your Rights." It stated reasons for alleging that anyone violated the Constitution when he refused to recognize "your right to assert your opposition to the draft," and went on, "If you do not assert and support your rights, you are helping to deny or disparage rights which it is the solemn duty of all citizens and residents of the United States to retain." It described the arguments on the other side as coming from cunning politicians and a mercenary capitalist press, and even silent assent to the conscription law as helping to support an infamous conspiracy. It denied the power to send our citizens away to foreign shores to shoot up the people of other lands, and added that words could not express the condemnation such cold-blooded ruthlessness deserves; &c., &c., winding up, "You must do your share to maintain, support and uphold the rights of the people of this country." Of course the document would not have been sent unless it had been intended to have some effect, and we do not see what effect it could be expected to have upon persons subject to the draft except to influence them to obstruct the carrying of it out. The defendants do not deny that the jury might find against them on this point.

But it is said, suppose that that was the tendency of this circular, it is protected by the First Amendment to the Constitution. Two of the strongest expressions are said to be quoted respectively from well-known public men. It well may be that the prohibition of laws abridging the freedom of speech is not confined to previous restraints, although to prevent them may have been the main purpose, as intimated in *Patterson* v. *Colorado*, 205 U. S. 454, 462. We admit that in many places and in ordinary times the defendants in saying all that was said in the circular would have been within their constitutional rights. But the character of every act depends upon the circumstances in which it is done. *Aikens* v. *Wisconsin*, 195 U. S. 194, 205, 206. The most stringent protection of free speech would not protect a man in falsely shouting fire in a theater and causing a panic. It does not even protect a man from an injunction against uttering words that may have all the effect of force. *Gompers* v. *Bucks Stove & Range Co.*, 221 U. S. 418, 439. The question in every case is whether the words used are used in such circumstances and are of such a nature as to create a clear and present danger that they will bring about the substantive evils that Congress has a right to prevent. It is a question of proximity and degree. When a nation is at war many things that might be said in time of peace are such a hindrance to its effort that their utterance will not be endured so long as men fight and that no court could regard them as protected by any constitutional right. It seems to be admitted that if an actual obstruction of the recruiting service were proved, liability for words that produced that effect might be enforced. The statute of 1917 in §4 punishes conspiracies to obstruct as well as actual obstruction. If the act (speaking, or circulating a paper), its tendency and the intent with which it is done are the same, we perceive no ground for saying that success alone warrants making the act a crime. *Goldman* v. *United States*, 245 U. S. 474, 477. Indeed that case might be said to dispose of the present contention if the precedent covers all *media concludendi*. But as the right to free speech was not referred to specially, we have thought fit to add a few words.

It was not argued that a conspiracy to obstruct the draft was not within the words of the Act of 1917. The words are "obstruct the recruiting or enlistment service," and it might be suggested that they refer only to making it hard to get volunteers. Recruiting heretofore usually having been accomplished by getting volunteers, the word is apt to call up that method only in our minds. But recruiting is gaining fresh supplies for the forces, as well by draft as otherwise. It is put as an alternative to enlistment or voluntary enrollment in this Act. The fact that the Act of 1917 was enlarged by the amending Act of May 16, 1918, c. 75, 40 Stat. 553, of course, does not affect the present indictment and would not, even if the former Act had been repealed. Rev. St. ¶ 13.

William F. Buckley, Jr., is the well-known editor of the National Review. **L. Brent Bozell** is a frequent contributor to the *National Review.*

Of special importance in this article is an extended argument for the unavoidable existence of "thought control." Moreover, Buckley and Bozell argue that there is a clear and present danger posed by international Communism, and that the late Senator Joseph McCarthy attempted to combat it. The reader should contrast Buckley and Bozell's use of the term "society" with Marcuse's use of the term "Establishment."

McCarthyism, we are saying, has narrowed the limits within which political proselytizing can safely go forward in the American community. The assertion that there is a "reign of terror" directed at all who disagree with Senator McCarthy, we are saying further, is irresponsible nonsense. But something is abroad in the land, and we have no objection to its being called a "reign of terror" provided it is clear that a metaphor is being used, and that the victims are the Communists and their sympathizers. We may concede that America has come to insist on "conformity," if you will, *on the Communist issue.*

One of the problems that arises is that of stating precisely what the conformity, encouraged by McCarthyism, actually involves:

From William F. Buckley, Jr., and L. Brent Bozell, *McCarthy and His Enemies* (Chicago, 1954), pp. 316-335. Reprinted by permission of Henry Regnery Company.

what sanctions are being imposed upon *what people* to discour *what sort* of activity. Defining the conformity is difficult, if for no other reason than that its shape and coloring vary sharply from one part of the country to another, and from one field of activity to another. Another question entirely is whether we approve of the sanctions and of their being visited on the particular people they are being visited on. But there is a third question: What about the argument underlying the liberals' determined assault on McCarthyism—the argument that "conformity," *in any area whatever*, is undesirable? A number of serious writers on the subject profess to be disturbed not so much with the peculiar orientation of a "conformist" society, as with the fact that a conformity—*any* orthodoxy whatever—should exist at all. McCarthyism is bad, we are told, and must be bad, just to the extent that it obstructs the free flow of commerce in the "marketplace of ideas."

The objection requires thorough consideration—not because it is profound, but because it elicits reflexive and emotion-charged support from so many people who, for excellent reasons, are concerned with protecting "freedom of the mind."

Opposition to conformity of *any* sort arises from a failure to understand the ways of society, a failure to recognize that *some* conformity, in varying degrees and in diverse fields, has characterized every society known to man; and for the reason that some conformity is just as indispensable as some heresy.

The word "conformity" is too often used to connote collective adherence by an insensate and irrational society to an unimaginative and erroneous doctrine. Thus the frequent references to the "threat of conformity," to "arid conformity," to "stultifying conformity," and so on. The word "conformity" is not necessarily misused when it is given that meaning. But it is also a useful word to describe the prevailing value preferences of *highly civilized societies;* and in that sense conformity may be a blessing rather than something to be avoided. In short, we rightly deplore the "conformity" obtained in Germany during the thirties—the orthodoxy which evokes so vividly the image of an authoritarian, secular, ethnocentric society, savage in its elimination of dissidents. But we may also

onformity" of English sentiment on, say, the subject
ry government—and with some enthusiasm. In the
tion was wedded to an evil social doctrine which it
imposing brutal punitive sanctions upon dissidents.
England, however, is wedded to what we deem a highly commend-
able political process—and wedded to it by the voluntary acquiescence of all, or nearly all, of its citizens.

Our indictment of Nazi conformity is therefore based on two
counts: *(a)* we don't like the values the Nazis encouraged, and *(b)*
we don't like the fact that they violated persons who disagreed with
them. Our approval of England's conformity with parliamentary
rule is based on our approval of the institution of popular government, and also on our approval of the fact that Englishmen are not
embarked on an active campaign against dissidents.

The conformity we are concerned with in this book—the one
McCarthyism is promoting—resembles the English conformity on
the first count: the vast majority of Americans are certainly in
sympathy with those values Communism threatens. It is equally
clear—as regards the second count—that McCarthyism (understood as including all the legal, economic and social measures that
are being used to discourage adherence to Communism) has little
in common with pogroms and concentration camps. But on this
score the conformity encouraged by McCarthyism is not like contemporary English conformity either: for it *is* a calculated, purpose-
ful national campaign levelled against Communist dissidents. Do
we conclude, then—from this difference—that conformity, Eng-
lish-style, is desirable, while conformity, McCarthy style, is reprehensible?

It is easier to understand the conformity McCarthyism is urging,
and the sanctions being used to promote that conformity, if we
recognize that some coercive measures—i.e., restrictive sanctions
of some sort—against dissidents are indispensable to the achievement of *any* conformity. *Coercion takes different forms.* It may be
exercised through education, through social pressure, or through
laws. But it must be exercised in one form or another if naturally
diverse minds are to form a common tendency.

What liberals fail to understand is that even the orthodoxies they approve of have not come about through spontaneous consent. To act as though the Paraclete had, one bright morning, breathed into the hearts of Englishmen their allegiance to parliamentary rule is, among other things, to do a severe injustice to the thousands of men who devoted their lives to dislodging British absolutism. England had to fight for her form of government; and it was several hundred tumultuous years before popular rule emerged as the imperious and unchallenged orthodoxy that reigns today.

In short, we are apt to forget that conformity, in order to "be," must first "become." We cannot have our cake without first baking it. England's conformity with parliamentarianism does not, today, depend on coercive measures to preserve its supremacy, because it is *mature*, because it is institutionalized to the point that it goes virtually unchallenged. McCarthyism, however, involves an orthodoxy still-in-the-making; and therefore, as with all imperfect conformities, some coercive sanctions are being exercised in its behalf.

The sanctions imposed on behalf of favored values have often been violent, as when the guillotine was used as an instrument for winning converts to French republicanism, or when civil war and the Thirteenth Amendment were adopted as deterrents to slavery in this country, or when the Income Tax was written into our laws to encourage financial support of the government. Or, the sanctions may be relatively gentle: for example, the ubiquitous pressures which, for two decades now, have emanated from the classroom and from the bureaucrat's desk, from political podiums and from a preponderance of our literature, in behalf of the leviathan State.

The sanctions imposed by McCarthyism are of both kinds. The legal sanctions, the anti-Communist *laws*, are, in a sense, "harsh" measures. The Smith Act, for example, punishes with imprisonment anyone who conspires to advocate the overthrow of the government by force. The McCarran Act harasses members of fellow-travelling organizations. The Feinberg Law denies employment to teachers who are members of subversive organizations. Miscellaneous laws and executive orders deny government employment to persons regarded as loyalty or security risks.

The social sanctions of McCarthyism are of the other, relatively mild variety—as when individual schools refuse to hire Communist professors, or radio stations close their doors to Communist artists, or labor unions deny membership to Communist workers. They are ordinarily milder because, in the absence of a law on the subject, there may be other schools, radio stations, and unions that will give the Communists shelter.

To sum up, then, a drive for some conformity, and the turbulence often attendant on such drive, are not unusual phenomena in our society or any other. And judging by past experience, if Americans, by the year 1999, learn to despise fellow-travelling with the same intensity and unanimity with which today they regard, say, slave-owning, it is predictable that the liberals of that day will not bewail America's anti-Communist orthodoxy.

But we must probe deeper into the alleged threat to freedom of the mind posed by McCarthyism. Although the measures by which McCarthyism encourages conformity are clearly the same measures by which societies *have* traditionally protected favored values, liberals are not obliged to *approve* of what societies have done in the past. They can repudiate *all* sanctions designed to influence opinion, past, present and future; and they seem to be doing this when they universalize about the evils of "thought control" each time the subject of McCarthyism is brought up.

It is perfectly true that the sanctions of McCarthyism (like those that have been used in the past on behalf of democracy, freedom for trade unions, and so on) *do* constitute "thought control" in the sense that they hack away, and are intended to hack away, at opposition to certain values. But to condemn these sanctions is to condemn the natural processes of society.

Freedom of the mind, we are told by the liberals, is an absolute value; and thought control, "since it impairs this freedom," an absolute evil. Few liberals are aware that the first of these statements does not necessarily justify the second. The only freedom that an individual may never sacrifice is, providentially, one that he will never be without: the freedom to act as a moral agent *at the choice level*—to select, as between whatever alternatives are left open to him, the one which most closely coincides with the "good." In religious terms, man's only absolute freedom is his freedom to earn salvation; and this freedom is irrevocable because man has a free will. The Russian serf, even within the area in which he is allowed by the State to act, can triumph over evil every bit as decisively as can the American freeman.

There remains, however, the alluring *political* argument that if democracy is to prosper, sanctions must not be used to delimit the number of ideas our minds consider, or to make one idea appear more attractive than another. Democracy, so the argument goes, thrives on the "free market in ideas," and to tamper with the market is, ultimately, to sabotage the machinery that makes possible enlightened self-government. In a democracy, therefore, every idea must be allowed to display its inherent attractiveness, so that it can be judged on its merits. All ideas must, so to speak, start out even in the race; and if an idea is to be rejected, this must be done by each individual for himself—free from coercion by his fellow men. McCarthyism embodies such coercion. Thus, *ipso facto* it is anti-democratic.

Unquestionably, the claims of the free market in ideas are very strong. Hard experience through centuries has taught us to exercise self-restraint in insisting upon our own notions of what decisions society should make. Societies, we have learned, fare better when they have a wide selection of ideas from which to choose, if only because their citizens are then better able to articulate, and therefore to realize, their wants. But when the liberals go on from here to formulate an inflexible doctrine which, in the name of freedom of the mind, would prohibit a society from exercising sanctions of *any* sort, and when they talk as if even the freest society could manage this feat, they are talking very dangerous nonsense.

Part of the liberals' difficulty is that when they think of sanctions against ideas, they think in drastic terms. They think in terms of denying employment to, or imprisoning the carriers of, "objectionable ideas." They ignore altogether the areas in which the process of "controlling" thought takes a less dramatic form. They do not consider, and hence do not weigh, the more subtle, but infinitely more important sanctions through which societies defend favored ideas.

Our schools, for example, have thoroughly indoctrinated the average American with the virtues of democracy. A sanction of the subtle variety has been exercised; and one that will unquestionably affect his political judgment in a thousand ways favorable to one favored concept—the perpetuation of democracy. Where, again for example, social disfavor attends Jew-baiting, a sanction (not the less effective because it is subtle) is being imposed against racial intolerance. Once again, does anyone contend that polygamy is getting a fair break in the market of ideas?

In short, every idea presented to our minds, as we grow up, is accompanied by sanctions of approval or disapproval which add to, or subtract from, that idea's naked appeal. And these sanctions are "thought control"—whether they urge political conformity with democracy by jailing Communist conspirators, or aesthetic conformity with classicism by disparaging, in the classroom, musical romanticism.

The practice of thought control is so ubiquitous and so commonplace as to make us wonder at the success of the liberals in frightening people with only one, the crudest, of its many manifestations. They turn the trick, it seems, by dramatizing the sanctions that are deliberately and purposefully imposed, while keeping silent about the haphazard process by which society subsidizes approved prejudices and preferences. And they disarm us by an impressive array of swear words which they apply only to the overt, dramatic type of sanction.

Not long ago, in the course of upholding (on the grounds of precedent) the constitutionality of Atlanta's banning of the movie *Lost Boundaries* (which dramatizes, among other things, the evils of Jim Crow), a U. S. District Court launched into a ringing liberal lament, excoriating all such laws. The fate they deserve, the Court insisted, is "interment in the attic which contains the ghosts of those who, arrayed in the robe of Bigotry, armed with the spear of Intolerance, and mounted on the steed of Hatred, have through all the ages sought to patrol the highway of the mind."

The judge apparently disapproved the action taken by Atlantans to forbid the propagation of certain ideas on their screens. This, he suggested, was "thought control." Yet the question cannot be avoided: does the *withholding* of the ideas embodied in *Lost Boundaries* from audiences in Atlanta constitute "thought control" in some sense in which the *presentation* of those ideas to New York audiences does not? Was the Atlanta Board of Censors tampering with freedom of thought in some sense in which a dozen movie producers do not regularly do, month in month out, as they decide what pictures advocating what ideas shall be produced? Clearly, the *encouragement* of certain ideas on race relations can affect thought, just as the *discouragement* of these ideas can—as, for example, when they are suppressed. We may feel that it is a mistake to suppress such ideas; that Atlantans would profit from a sympathetic presentation of a Negro family's assimilation by white society. Yet this is merely a euphemistic way of saying that we would like to influence contrarily disposed minds in the direction of our own point of view—which is to plead guilty to the charge of thought control. We are certainly not less guilty than our fellow countrymen in Atlanta, who seek to incline minds the other way.

In short, it is characteristic of society that it uses sanctions in support of its own folkways and mores, and that in doing so it urges conformity. What we call the "institutions" of a society are nothing but the values that society has settled on over the years and now defends by sanctions. Most of us take fierce pride in our society's institutions—quite reasonably, since it is our institutions that make us what we are. But it is well to remember that in exhibiting this pride, we are applauding just so many manifestations of conformity which were brought about by the practice of "thought control" through many generations.

Not only is it *characteristic* of society to create institutions and to defend them with sanctions. Societies *must* do so—or else they cease to exist. The members of a society must share certain values if that society is to cohere; and cohere it must if it is to survive. In order to assert and perpetuate these values, it must do constant battle against competing values. A democratic society, for example, dare not take for granted that the premises of democracy will, unaided (i.e., solely in virtue of their ideological superiority), drive Communism out of the market. If the contest were to be adjudicated by a divine tribunal, society could sit back with folded hands and watch the show. But it is not; and hence a concomitant of man's selecting freedom as against Communism is his acting rationally in *behalf* of freedom and *against* Communism. If the contest were to be adjudicated by a divine tribunal, a society could afford to be capricious and patronizing towards the enemy's ideas. It could even afford to act on liberal premises relating to "freedom of the mind"—by seeing to it, for example, that the New York *Daily Worker* circulated as many copies as the New York *Journal American.*

A hard and indelible fact of freedom is that a conformity of sorts is always dominant, as evidenced by such minutiae as that the *Journal American* and the New York *Post* are more heavily subscribed than the *Daily Worker.* And since a conformity of sorts will always be with us, the freeman's principal concern is that it shall be a conformity that honors the values he esteems rather than those he rejects.

This is not to say, of course, that society never makes mistakes in this area, and that the conformities selected by societies are, invariably, conformities with the eternal verities. Even free and enlightened men may use the power of sanctions in behalf of false and inferior values. But democracy is meaningless unless, having brought to bear on today's problems their intelligence, their insights, and their experience, freemen take vigorous action on behalf of the truth as they see it.

Thus liberal spokesmen, who are forever warning us against attempting to get an inside run for our favored values, show a fundamental misunderstanding of the free society.

The liberals are forever warning us about the dangers of coming down hard on those who oppose the basic values of our society. The Communist problem, for example, according to one of the liberals' favorite lines of argument, is not inherently different from that which, prior to the Revolutionary War, our forefathers posed to the English; and we have no more business assuming our own infallibility *vis à vis* the Communists than the English had in assuming theirs *vis à vis* the American Revolutionaries. "In 1940," writes Alan Barth, "the Alien Registration Act forbade all Americans to teach or advocate the duty or necessity of overthrowing by force or violence a government created by just such advocacy."

Two implications are clearly present in such a statement, namely, *(a)* that the revolution America is seeking to frustrate through the Smith Act and, one supposes, through McCarthyism in general, cannot be written off as morally reprehensible unless we are prepared to write off, in like manner, the Revolution to which we owe our existence as a nation; and *(b)* that the English ought not to have resisted our insurrectionary forefathers.

Both of these notions, we contend, are false, and the freeman must reject them as a matter of course: the one as contrary to his considered estimate of Communism, the other as politically egocentric to the point of sheer naivete.

We believe on the strength of the evidence, that the American Revolution against George III was a revolution in the interests of freedom and of civilization. But it does not follow that the English should have recognized it as such, and should, accordingly, have given it their blessing. Still less does it follow that the Communist revolution is in the interests of freedom and of civilization, and that we should give it *our* blessing. For each free society must decide these questions by its own lights as they arise, and there is no place to which it can turn for the kind of guidance that will exclude the possibility of error. Certainly not to such doctrines as "the divine right of revolution."

The individual freeman may, of course, find himself in disagreement with his society's decision. If so, it is his duty to resist the majority, even if it be very large, to just the extent called for by the intensity of his disagreement. But let him not deny society's right to consolidate around the institutions it favors. Or at least let him not deny this right in the name of a free society.

The preaching of the liberals on the subject of conformity, as we have already suggested, does not conform with their practice. In the light of their own habits, their sense of outrage in the presence of McCarthyism becomes difficult to explain. For where movements are concerned that conform with liberalism, the liberals talk out of the other side of their mouths.

The drum-beating for a "bi-partisan" foreign policy, for example, insistent and deafening as it was during the post-war years (and is even today), is a call for "conformity" in one aspect of public affairs. And who has beat that drum more assiduously than the liberals? Every time a diehard crosses the aisle and joins the bipartisan ranks there is jubilation in the Liberal Camp. That no such acclamation greets the regeneration of a Louis Budenz, a Whittaker Chambers, or an Elizabeth Bentley, is something for which the liberals have yet to offer a convincing explanation.

Where were the liberals when the weapons they now forbid us to use against the Communists were being used, fifteen years ago, against American fascists and against a number of Americans who were *not* fascists? And how do the liberals account for their past and present ruthlessness in assaulting all persons, groups, or even ideas, that are out of harmony with the liberal orthodoxy? That liberal weapons have been effectively wielded, many a business-man, many a so-called isolationist, and many a hard anti-Commu-nist can prove by pointing to his scars.

What is more, the liberals have been signally successful in many of their drives for conformity. Not many years ago, for example, most Americans believed employers were entitled to recognize or not recognize labor unions as bargaining agents for workers as they themselves saw fit. But more and more Americans became con-vinced that the ends of social justice would be better served if workers enjoyed a stronger bargaining position. The liberals, how-ever, were not content with a slow evolution of public sentiment. They were in a hurry. And no sooner did they win a Congress and a president of their persuasion, than they passed a law making collective bargaining *mandatory*. The nonconforming employer could thenceforward *(a)* close up shop or *(b)* go to jail for contempt. It was, to be sure, the employer's actions rather than his thought that the Wagner Act was intended to control. But it has also proved an extremely effective instrument of creeping thought control, since it has produced a gradual consolidation of public opinion around the ideas of its authors. If the collective bargaining clause of the Act were repealed tomorrow, a few employers might conceivably turn the unions out. But an overwhelming majority would not. Sixteen years of collective bargaining, sanctioned by law and by society, have so deeply implanted this practice in our public morality that it has become, quite simply, an American "institution."

The liberals, in short, do want conformity—with liberalism. The overriding sin, in their attitude toward McCarthyism as a drive toward conformity, is their duplicity. The fulminations of those liberals who know what they are about are prompted not by a dread of conformity as such, but by the approaching conformity with values to which they do not subscribe.

To say that all societies encourage conformity leaves open the question of *how* they ought to encourage it. And there is a consensus that a society concerned with preserving individual freedom will not take away from dissidents one iota of freedom that does not *have* to be taken away in order to protect its institutions.

The traditional view among libertarians has always been that freedom tends to be maximized for both majorities and minorities, and thus for society in general, if social sanctions are preferred to legal ones. This view has normally been supported by two arguments: *(a)* that the *genus State* (which goes into action when legal sanctions are imposed) has natural aggressive tendencies that tend to feed upon each successive new grant of power; and *(b)* that social sanctions more accurately reflect the real "lay" of community sentiment.

The first of these arguments is grounded in long centuries of experience which have taught us that the State has attributes one of which is a tendency to usurp functions that can be equally well and, in most cases, better performed by the citizens acting individually or through voluntary and spontaneous associations. The end result of such usurpations is, of course, fatal to freedom. Thus, wisdom instructs freemen not to whet the State's always enormous appetite for power by passing laws that add *unnecessarily* to the paraphernalia of the State.

The second argument rests upon what we have learned in the long pull of history about the plight of dissenting minorities, even in the freest societies. A legal sanction is, in theory, one hundred per cent effective: all the citizens are made to conform, even if only fifty-one per cent of them entertain the views that prompted the legislation. Thus, half the citizens of the State of New York, plus one, can through control of the legislature, pass a law that will prevent Communists from teaching in any State school—even though half of the community, minus one, believes such a law to be bad or at least inadvisable. Social sanctions, by contrast, are effective roughly in proportion to the number of persons who wish to exercise them: if only fifty-one per cent of New Yorkers want Communist teachers kept out of the schools, and only social sanctions are used, then Communists will be kept out of, roughly fifty-one per cent of the schools; the minority is left free to resist the pressure exerted by the majority.

In other words, minorities remain freer when majorities content themselves with the degree of conformity they can achieve without calling in the police. Freemen, other things being equal, will ardently desire to maximize the minority's freedom; and to the extent that they do they will advocate social evolution rather than legal revolution. The freeman who objects to nudism may inflict social indignities on the sun cultist, but he will not advocate legislation outlawing nudist colonies. The freeman will join in making life uncomfortable for Gerald L. K. Smith, but will not back a law forbidding Smith to publish his scurrilous literature.

It is interesting that the liberals have been far less concerned than libertarians about freedom for the minorities. They have a congenital fondness for passing laws, and a congenital distaste for waiting around while social sanctions engender conformity on this issue or that. The sure and swift machinery of the State fascinates them the way a *real* pistol fascinates youthful admirers of Hopalong Cassidy; their faith in it knows no bounds. Thus, for example, the proposed federal Fair Employment Practice Law is a sturdy rallying point for all liberals; while the libertarian prefers to encourage racial conciliation through education and social pressures.

The balanced libertarian does not, to be sure, hold that the majority members of a free society must *never* be "in a hurry," and that in no circumstances may they take the short cut conveniently provided by the statute-book. He well knows there are times when legal sanctions must be used, and he knows we live in such times today. He will advise the majority not to adopt *unnecessary* legal measures of a restrictive character; but not to hesitate to adopt the *necessary* ones, i.e., those that the exigencies of the situation clearly call for.

Mr. Justice Holmes laid down a famous test by which free societies can distinguish between the unnecessary and the necessary in this area. The "clear and present danger" doctrine is useful, and, probably, the best we have. The doctrine is, of course, incapable of furnishing wholly objective and unvarying standards, as Supreme Court experience with it has proved. But the central meaning of Holmes' test is clear and serviceable as applied to deeds as well as speech. It authorizes the use of legal sanctions against any activity that offers an imminent threat to the survival of existing institutions, or an imminent threat to the safety of persons or property. It forbids their use against all other deeds and utterances, and insists, indirectly, that a free society, when not in jeopardy, protect its values through the use of social pressure.

However we translate Holmes' test, most of us are agreed that activity on behalf of the enemy in time of war poses a clear and present danger.

We cannot avoid the fact that the United States is at war against international communism, and that McCarthyism is a program of action against those in our land who help the enemy. McCarthyism is (and, in our opinion, is likely to remain), nine parts social sanction to one part legal sanction. But that one part legal sanction is entirely legitimate. The resulting restrictions on a minority's freedom are certainly mild when compared with the drastic restrictions the majority imposes upon itself through such measures as military conscription. It is perhaps the crowning anomaly of present-day liberalism that it should, on the one hand, sanction the total tyranny of compulsory military service, and yet balk restricting the least freedom of our enemy's domestic allies.

Finally, the liberals insist, our society cannot, even during wartime, afford to cut itself off from *innovation*. Whatever the emergencies of today, the argument runs, we must think about tomorrow. We must make sure that our conformity shall not be so rigid as to barricade our minds against new ideas. The most terrifying nightmare of our intellectuals is that America may some day pass the hemlock to a Socrates, hang a Thomas More, or force a Galileo to recant. It can happen here, we are warned, if we give McCarthyism its rein.

This argument forgets that societies are, after all, educated as well as educable. It is one thing for society to give a hearing to new ideas, and quite another thing for it to feel impelled to put new ideas —simply because they are new or unorthodox—on a plane of equality with cherished ideas that have met the test of time. It is, for example, one thing to study Jean Paul Sartre and allow the free circulation of his books (which this country is doing) and quite another thing to give existentialist ideas the inside run in the curriculum of our university philosophy departments (which this country is not doing). It should after all be clear that a free market in ideas ceases to be free or a market if the latest huckster to arrive can claim his share of trade without regard to the quality or appeal of the commodity he is selling, and merely because he is a parvenu. The liberals, bewitched as they are with the value of innovation, tend to forget that a free market is one where the customers can, if they so wish, keep on trading with the same old butcher.

Moreover, the argument tends to equate "innovation" with progress. The innovator can regale society with a cornucopia of wealth and happiness; but he can also open a Pandora's box. A measure of healthy skepticism about new ideas is not a sign of obscurantism —nor, necessarily, an indication of stagnancy. Most of what we correctly call progress is a matter of the natural development and growth of old ideas. The statement that the heterodoxy of today is the orthodoxy of tomorrow, which we hear so often in this connection, is a piece of absurd oversimplification. *One* of today's heterodoxies may become tomorrow's orthodoxy; but if so, then, by definition, the remainder will not. And today's heterodoxies are always numerous in a way that the cliché fails to recognize. Witness in our country the brief flowering and unlamented demise of Know-Nothingism and Ku-Kluxism—both of them heterodoxies that did not, on the morrow, become orthodoxies. Nor is it true, as the argument suggests, that there is net social gain, or progress, necessarily and as a matter of course, every time a heterodoxy displaces an orthodoxy. Societies often progress backwards.

Even so, progress *does* occur, and no intelligent society should adhere to a conformity so rigid as to make the airing of alternatives dangerous or impossible. Our major differences with the liberals in this area have to do with whether McCarthyism tends in any such direction. And this brings us, at last, to the question: What is the actual extent of the conformity McCarthyism seeks to impose?

McCARTHYISM's CALL TO CONFORMITY

McCarthyism, on the record, is not in any sense an attempt to prevent the airing of new ideas. It is directed not at *new* ideas but at *Communist* ideas, of which the last thing that can be said is that they are new or untried. The McCarthyites are doing their resourceful best to make our society inhospitable to Communists, fellow-travelers, and security risks in the government. To this end, they are conducting operations on two fronts: (1) they seek to vitalize existing legal sanctions, and (2) they seek to harden existing anti-Communist prejudices and channel them into effective social sanctions.

Valid laws and auxiliary Executive Orders prohibited Communists—or persons about whose loyalty or reliability there was a reasonable doubt—from holding government posts long before Senator McCarthy started talking; but they were frequently evaded, and sloppily administered. McCarthy and his allies have simply insisted that they be vigorously enforced. McCarthyism is primarily the maintenance of a steady flow of criticism (raillery, the liberals call it) calculated to pressure the President, Cabinet members, high officials, and above all the political party in power, to get on with the elimination of security risks in government. In a sense, the major "victims" of McCarthy's drive for conformity have been those responsible for the so-called loyalty program, whom he has tried to inch into performing their clear legal duties.

On the second front, McCarthy has tied into fellow-travellers who have no tangible affiliation with the government. For example, he early aimed his fire at Harlow Shapley, Frederick Schuman, and Owen Lattimore. McCarthy exposed their party-lining and did what he could to build up social pressure against them. He has not, or at least not yet, succeeded in eliminating them from positions of power and influence in national academic life: all three continue to teach at important universities. But there is no doubting the fact that they are less influential than they were before. Their pronouncements on foreign policy are no longer cited as authoritative. Lattimore's future books about solutions in Asia are unlikely to become bestsellers.

The conformity attendant upon McCarthyism, then, adds up to something like this: (1) *persons who conspire to overthrow the government by force* are subject to legal sanctions (the Smith Act, for example), primarily that of imprisonment; (2) *persons in public service about whose loyalty or security there is a "reasonable doubt"* are subject to legal sanctions (the various security regulations), primarily that of exclusion from government employment; (3) *persons other than government employees about whom there exist reasonable grounds for believing they are "proCommunist,"* are to some extent subject to legal sanctions (possibly the McCarran Act or the Attorney General's list of subversive organizations), primarily that of having their activities officially labeled as "Communist" or "subversive" or (as with the Feinberg Law or the statutory loyalty oath requirements) that of being excluded from certain jobs; they are furthermore subject, increasingly, to social sanctions, primarily of the type that have been aimed at Lattimore and Schuman and Shapley.

These sanctions are not the same all over the country. In some localities, in sections of the Midwest for example, the sanctions hit people who might escape them elsewhere. In the rare instance, a single Communist-front affiliation may engender public hostility and bring down severe social sanctions on a man's head. In the academic arena of the East, by contrast, the level of enforced conformity is decidedly lower, and sometimes descends nearly to zero. Southern Baptist College X fires Jones when there are apparently no reasonable grounds for believing him to be a pro-Communist. But Harvard, Williams and Johns Hopkins retain Shapley, Schuman and Lattimore on their faculties when reasonable grounds abound for believing them to be pro-Communist.

The claim is often made that McCarthyism has as its ultimate objective the exclusion of liberals from positions of power, prestige, and influence in the American community; and that the present campaign against Communists and fellow-travellers is merely the thin edge of the wedge. It is therefore curious that the one instance which lent a modicum of factual support to this fear received little or no attention from liberal publicists.

In October of 1952, Senator McCarthy delivered his widely heralded attack on Adlai Stevenson, which people generally expected would turn into an attempt to connect the Democratic candidate with Communism. With millions of listeners glued to radio and TV, McCarthy reached, not for a red paint brush, but for a list of some of Stevenson's top advisors: Archibald MacLeish, Bernard De Voto, Arthur Schlesinger, Jr. Was his point that these men were *Communists?* No, that was not McCarthy's point. His objection to these men was not that they were Communists, or even pro-Communists, but that they were liberals—atheistic, soft-headed, anti-anti-Communist, ADA liberals. And his major point turned out to be that this was sufficient reason for rejecting the candidate for whom they were serving as Edgar Bergens.

Whether the speech was a conscious effort to narrow the limits of tolerable opinion so as to exclude left-wing liberals, only McCarthy can say. The fact that he has not reiterated the point suggests that, if this *was* his intent, he was not very serious about it. It is far more likely that he intended to deliver a traditional political campaign speech highlighting the disqualifications of his party's opponents. But it may well be we have not heard the last of his idea. Some day, the patience of America may at last be exhausted, and we will strike out against liberals. Not because they are treacherous like Communists, but because, with James Burnham, we will conclude "that they are mistaken in their predictions, false in their analyses, wrong in their advice, and through the results of their actions injurious to the interests of the nation. That is reason enough to strive to free the conduct of the country's affairs from the influence of them and their works." But the real point, for our purposes, is that the mainstream of McCarthyism flows past the liberals as gently as the Afton; and that the MacLeishes, De Votos and Schlesingers have no grounds for arguing that any sustained effort is being made to read *them* out of the community.

It is still only *Communist* ideas that are beyond the pale. And the evidence is convincing that the function of Senator McCarthy and his colleagues is not that of defining or creating a new orthodoxy with which individuals are being called upon to conform. The American community affirmed anti-Communism long before McCarthy started in. McCarthy's function has been to harden the *existing* conformity.

We are left with the final question: whether the conformity urged by McCarthyism is doing a service to America and, therefore, whether we should view it with approval. Certainly the vast majority of the American people have already given *their* answer to the question; for, after all, the approaching conformity is of their own making, and they must be presumed to approve what they are doing. Most Americans, the available evidence seems to say, favor anti-Communism, and tight security in the civil service. But we are asking, of course, whether the majority is *right;* and therefore we must take account of the misgivings of the intelligentsia. What should be said of their resolute and impassioned opposition to McCarthyism?

Simply this. They are confused, they have misread history, and they fail to understand social processes. What is more, they do not feel the faith they so often and so ardently express in democracy. There is only one alternative to this explanation: that they are opposed to the decline of Communist influence at home. The determination of the American people to curb Communism cannot be dismissed as a capricious, ignorant, or impetuous decision. There is, we contend, a great deal of difference between a society's harassing the exponents of an idea that has been thoroughly examined and found objectionable, and its harassing the exponents of an idea simply because it hurls a novel challenge at traditional notions. Our Schumans, Shapleys, and Lattimores have become unacceptable not because they are known to hold ideas and values at variance with those of the majority of Americans, but because they expound a *particular* set of ideas and values which Americans have explored and emphatically rejected, and because the propagation of these ideas fortifies an implacable foreign power bent on the destruction of American independence.

The ideas of the Schumans, Shapleys and Lattimores are not, as we say, new ideas; they are exploded ideas. America has had access to the literature of Communism for more than a generation. Everything from *Das Kapital* and *The Problems of Leninism* to monthlies, weeklies and dailies reflecting the least adjustment in the party line, has for years circulated freely in American classrooms, libraries, and living rooms. Communist missionaries have roamed the land to urge their ideas through the spoken word. In short, America could hardly have given Communism a fairer or more exhaustive hearing without inviting over a dozen commissars to conduct an American Five Year Plan.

Having heard the case, America has rejected it. And because the case is championed by a mobilized, aggressive, titanic enemy state, America has gone further: she has turned to the offensive against Communism. We are at war, and there are many strategies, many tactics, many weapons, many courses of action open to us. Our lines could be advanced by innumerable enterprises, some foolish, some proper—by assassinating Malenkov, by atom-bombing Soviet industrial plants, by subsidizing a Russian underground, by providing leadership and funds for prominent European and Asiatic anti-

Communists, by imprisoning violators of the Smith Act, by purging the civil service, and by exposing and persecuting Communist apologists in whatever occupation they are engaged. One thing is certain: Communism will not be defeated—any more than freedom was won—by postulating the virtues of democracy and of Christianity as evident truths and letting it go at that.

McCarthyism, then, is a weapon in the American arsenal. To the extent that McCarthyism, out of ignorance or impetuosity or malice, urges the imposition of sanctions upon persons who are *not* pro-Communist or security risks, we should certainly oppose it. When persons about whose loyalty or security reliability there is *no* reasonable doubt are flushed from government service for security reasons, those responsible should be criticized and held to an accounting both at the polls and before investigating committees. Whenever the anti-Communist conformity excludes well-meaning liberals, we should, in other words, go to their rescue. But as long as McCarthyism fixes its goal with its present precision, it is a movement around which men of good will and stern morality can close ranks.

Herbert Marcuse is Professor of Philosophy at the University of California at San Diego. He emigrated from Germany in 1934 and during World War II served as consultant to the United States government. Idolized by the New Left, he is a Marxist who believes that society is a conflict between haves and have-nots, and that society must be changed by the oppressed and the youthful intellectuals. Like all Marxists, he views history as eschatology. Hence public opinion at any one point seems to be a closed monolithic system. He also believes that truth is more than logic and science.

In order to understand the full meaning and the implications of Professor Marcuse's position, the reader should note his conception of democracy, his view of the role of dissent (which should be sharply contrasted with John Stuart Mill's conception of *discussion),* and his belief that the existence of the Cold War is a case of "clear and present danger."

This essay is dedicated to my students at Brandeis University.

This essay examines the idea of tolerance in our advanced industrial society. The conclusion reached is that the realization of the objective of tolerance would call for intolerance toward prevailing policies, attitudes, opinions, and the extension of tolerance to policies, attitudes, and opinions which are outlawed or suppressed. In other words, today tolerance appears again as what it was in its origins, at the beginning of the modern period—a partisan goal, a subversive liberating notion and practice. Conversely, what is proclaimed and practiced as tolerance today, is in many of its most effective manifestations serving the cause of oppression.

The author is fully aware that, at present, no power, no authority, no government exists which would translate liberating tolerance into practice, but he believes that it is the task and duty of the intellectual to recall and preserve historical possibilities which seem to have become utopian possibilities—that it is his task to break the concreteness of oppression in order to open the mental space in which this society can be recognized as what it is and does.

Tolerance is an end in itself. The elimination of violence, and the reduction of suppression to the extent required for protecting man and animals from cruelty and aggression are preconditions for the creation of a humane society. Such a society does not yet exist; progress toward it is perhaps more than before arrested by violence and suppression on a global scale. As deterrents against nuclear war, as police action against subversion, as technical aid in the fight against imperialism and communism, as methods of pacification in neo-colonial massacres, violence and suppression are promulgated, practiced, and defended by democratic and authoritarian governments alike, and the people subjected to these governments are educated to sustain such practices as necessary for the preservation of the status quo. Tolerance is extended to policies, conditions, and modes of behavior which should not be tolerated because they are impeding, if not destroying, the chances of creating an existence without fear and misery.

This sort of tolerance strengthens the tyranny of the majority against which authentic liberals protested. The political locus of tolerance has changed: while it is more or less quietly and constitutionally withdrawn from the opposition, it is made compulsory behavior with respect to established policies. Tolerance is turned from an active into a passive state, from practice to nonpractice: laissez-faire the constituted authorities. It is the people who tolerate the government, which in turn tolerates opposition within the framework determined by the constituted authorities.

Tolerance toward that which is radically evil now appears as good because it serves the cohesion of the whole on the road to affluence or more affluence. The toleration of the systematic moronization of children and adults alike by publicity and propaganda, the release of destructiveness in aggressive driving, the recruitment for and training of special forces, the impotent and benevolent tolerance toward outright deception in merchandising, waste, and planned obsolescence are not distortions and aberrations, they are the essence of a system which fosters tolerance as a means for perpetuating the struggle for existence and suppressing the alternatives. The authorities in education, morals, and psychology are vociferous against the increase in juvenile delinquency; they are less vociferous against the proud presentation, in word and deed and pictures, of ever more powerful missiles, rockets, bombs—the mature delinquency of a whole civilization.

According to a dialectical proposition it is the whole which determines the truth—not in the sense that the whole is prior or superior to its parts, but in the sense that its structure and function determine every particular condition and relation. Thus, within a repressive society, even progressive movements threaten to turn into their opposite to the degree to which they accept the rules of the game. To take a most controversial case: the exercise of political rights (such as voting, letter-writing to the press, to Senators, etc., protest-demonstrations with a priori renunciation of counterviolence) in a society of total administration serves to strengthen this administration by testifying to the existence of democratic liberties which, in reality, have changed their content and lost their effectiveness. In such a case, freedom (of opinion, of assembly, of speech) becomes an instrument for absolving servitude. And yet (and only here the dialectical proposition shows its full intent) the existence and practice of these liberties remain a precondition for the restoration of their original oppositional function, provided that the effort to transcend their (often self-imposed) limitations is intensified. Generally, the function and value of tolerance depend on the equality prevalent in the society in which tolerance is practiced. Tolerance itself stands subject to overriding criteria: its range and its limits cannot be defined in terms of the respective society. In other words, tolerance is an end in itself only when it is truly universal, practiced by the rulers as well as by the ruled, by the lords as well as by the peasants, by the sheriffs as well as by their victims. And such universal tolerance is possible only when no real or alleged enemy requires in the national interest the education and training of people in military violence and destruction. As long as these conditions do not prevail, the conditions of tolerance are "loaded": they are determined and defined by the institutionalized inequality (which is certainly compatible with constitutional equality), i.e., by the class structure of society. In such a society, tolerance is *de facto* limited on the dual ground of legalized violence or suppression (police, armed forces, guards of all sorts) and of the privileged position held by the predominant interests and their "connections."

These background limitations of tolerance are normally prior to the explicit and judicial limitations as defined by the courts, custom, governments, etc. (for example, "clear and present danger," threat to national security, heresy). Within the framework of such a social structure, tolerance can be safely practiced and proclaimed. It is of two kinds: (1) the passive toleration of entrenched and established attitudes and ideas even if their damaging effect on man and nature is evident; and (2) the active, official tolerance granted to the Right as well as to the Left, to movements of aggression as well as to that of humanity. I call this non-partisan tolerance "abstract" or "pure" inasmuch as it refrains from taking sides—but in doing so it actually protects the already established machinery of discrimination.

The tolerance which enlarged the range and content of freedom was always partisan—intolerant toward the protagonists of the repressive status quo. The issue was only the degree and extent of intolerance. In the firmly established liberal society of England and the United States, freedom of speech and assembly was granted even to the radical enemies of society, provided they did not make the transition from word to deed, from speech to action.

Relying on the effective background limitations imposed by its class structure, the society seemed to practice general tolerance. But liberalist theory had already placed an important condition on tolerance: it was "to apply only to human beings in the maturity of their faculties." John Stuart Mill does not only speak of children and minors; he elaborates: "Liberty, as a principle, has no application to any state of things anterior to the time when mankind have become capable of being improved by free and equal discussion." Anterior to that time, men may still be barbarians, and "despotism is a legitimate mode of government in dealing with barbarians, provided the end be their improvement, and the means justified by actually effecting that end." Mill's often-quoted words have a less familiar implication on which their meaning depends: the internal connection between liberty and truth. There is a sense in which truth is the end of liberty, and liberty must be defined and confined by truth. Now in what sense can liberty be for the sake of truth? Liberty is self-determination, autonomy—this is almost a tautology, but a tautology which results from a whole series of synthetic judgments. It stipulates the ability to determine one's own life: to be able to determine what to do and what not to do, what to suffer and what not. But the subject of this autonomy is never the contingent, private individual as that which he actually is or happens to be; it is rather the individual as a human being who is capable of being free with the others. And the problem of making possible such a harmony between every individual liberty and the other is not that of finding a compromise between competitors, or between freedom and law, between general and individual interest, common and private welfare in an *established* society, but of *creating* the society in which man is no longer enslaved by institutions which vitiate self-determination from the beginning. In other words, freedom is still to be created even for the freest of the existing societies. And the direction in which it must be sought, and the institutional and cultural changes which may help to attain the goal are, at least in developed civilization, *comprehensible*, that is to say, they can be identified and projected, on the basis of experience, by human reason.

In the interplay of theory and practice, true and false solutions become distinguishable—never with the evidence of necessity, never as the positive, only with the certainty of a reasoned and reasonable chance, and with the persuasive force of the negative. For the true positive is the society of the future and therefore beyond definition and determination, while the existing positive is that which must be surmounted. But the experience and understanding of the existent society may well be capable of identifying what is *not* conducive to a free and rational society, what impedes and distorts the possibilities of its creation. Freedom is liberation, a specific historical process in theory and practice, and as such it has its right and wrong, its truth and falsehood.

The uncertainty of chance in this distinction does not cancel the historical objectivity, but it necessitates freedom of thought and expression as preconditions of finding the way to freedom—it necessitates *tolerance.* However, this tolerance cannot be indiscriminate and equal with respect to the contents of expression, neither in word nor in deed; it cannot protect false words and wrong deeds which demonstrate that they contradict and counteract the possibilities of liberation. Such indiscriminate tolerance is justified in harmless debates, in conversation, in academic discussion; it is indispensable in the scientific enterprise, in private religion. But society cannot be indiscriminate where the pacification of existence, where freedom and happiness themselves are at stake: here, certain things cannot be said, certain ideas cannot be expressed, certain policies cannot be proposed, certain behavior cannot be permitted without making tolerance an instrument for the continuation of servitude.

The danger of "destructive tolerance" (Baudelaire), of "benevolent neutrality" toward *art* has been recognized: the market, which absorbs equally well (although with often quite sudden fluctuations) art, anti-art, and non-art, all possible conflicting styles, schools, forms, provides a "complacent receptacle, a friendly abyss"* in which the radical impact of art, the protest of art against the established reality is swallowed up. However, censorship of art and literature is regressive under all circumstances. The authentic oeuvre is not and cannot be a prop of oppression, and pseudo-art (which can be such a prop) is not art. Art stands against history,

*Edgar Wind, *Art and Anarchy* (New York: Alfred A. Knopf, 1964), p. 101.

withstands history which has been the history of oppression, for art subjects reality to laws other than the established ones: to the laws of the Form which creates a different reality—negation of the established one even where art depicts the established reality. But in its struggle with history, art subjects itself to history: history enters the definition of art and enters into the distinction between art and pseudo-art. Thus it happens that what was once art becomes pseudo-art. Previous forms, styles, and qualities, previous modes of protest and refusal cannot be recaptured in or against a different society. There are cases where an authentic oeuvre carries a regressive political message—Dostoevski is a case in point. But then, the message is canceled by the oeuvre itself: the regressive political content is absorbed, *aufgehoben* in the artistic form: in the work as literature.

Tolerance of free speech is the way of improvement, of progress in liberation, *not* because there is no objective truth, and improvement must necessarily be a compromise between a variety of opinions, but because there *is* an objective truth which can be discovered, ascertained only in learning and comprehending that which is and that which can be and ought to be done for the sake of improving the lot of mankind. This common and historical "ought" is not immediately evident, at hand: it has to be uncovered by "cutting through," "splitting," "breaking asunder" *(dis-cutio)* the given material—separating right and wrong, good and bad, correct and incorrect. The subject whose "improvement" depends on a progressive historical practice is each man as man, and this universality is reflected in that of the discussion, which a priori does not exclude any group or individual. But even the all-inclusive character of liberalist tolerance was, at least in theory, based on the proposition that men were (potential) *individuals* who could learn to hear and see and feel by themselves, to develop their own thoughts, to grasp their true interests and rights and capabilities, also against established authority and opinion. This was the rationale of free speech and assembly. Universal toleration becomes questionable when its rationale no longer prevails, when tolerance is administered to manipulated and indoctrinated individuals who parrot, as their own, the opinion of their masters, for whom heteronomy has become autonomy.

The telos of tolerance is truth. It is clear from the historical record that the authentic spokesmen of tolerance had more and other truth in mind than that of propositional logic and academic theory. John Stuart Mill speaks of the truth which is persecuted in history and which does *not* triumph over persecution by virtue of its "inherent power," which in fact has no inherent power "against the dungeon and the stake." And he enumerates the "truths" which were cruelly and successfully liquidated in the dungeons and at the stake: that of Arnold of Brescia, of Fra Dolcino, of Savonarola, of the Albigensians, Waldensians, Lollards, and Hussites. Tolerance is first and foremost for the sake of the heretics—the historical road toward *humanitas* appears as heresy: target of persecution by the powers that be. Heresy by itself, however, is no token of truth.

The criterion of progress in freedom according to which Mill judges these movements is the Reformation. The evaluation is *ex post*, and his list includes opposites (Savonarola too would have burned Fra Dolcino). Even the ex post evaluation is contestable as to its truth: history corrects the judgment—too late. The correction does not help the victims and does not absolve their executioners. However, the lesson is clear: intolerance has delayed progress and has prolonged the slaughter and torture of innocents for hundreds of years. Does this clinch the case for indiscriminate, "pure" tolerance? Are there historical conditions in which such toleration impedes liberation and multiplies the victims who are sacrificed to the status quo? Can the indiscriminate guaranty of political rights and liberties be repressive? Can such tolerance serve to contain qualitative social change?

I shall discuss this question only with reference to political movements, attitudes, schools of thought, philosophies which are "political" in the widest sense—affecting the society as a whole, demonstrably transcending the sphere of privacy. Moreover, I propose a shift in the focus of the discussion: it will be concerned not only, and not primarily, with tolerance toward radical extremes, minorities, subversives, etc., but rather with tolerance toward majorities, toward official and public opinion, toward the established protectors of freedom. In this case, the discussion can have as a frame of reference only a democratic society, in which the people, as individuals and as members of political and other organizations, participate in the making, sustaining, and changing policies. In an authoritarian system, the people do not tolerate—they suffer established policies.

Under a system of constitutionally guaranteed and (generally and without too many and too glaring exceptions) practiced civil rights and liberties, opposition and dissent are tolerated unless they issue in violence and/or in exhortation to and organization of violent subversion. The underlying assumption is that the established society is free, and that any improvement, even a change in the social structure and social values, would come about in the normal course of events, prepared, defined, and tested in free and equal discussion, on the open marketplace of ideas and goods.* Now in recalling John Stuart Mill's passage, I drew attention to the premise hidden in this assumption: free and equal discussion can fulfill the function attributed to it only if it is *rational*—expression and development of independent thinking, free from indoctrination, manipulation, extraneous authority. The notion of pluralism and countervailing powers is no substitute for this requirement. One might in theory construct a state in which a multitude of different pressures, interests, and authorities balance each other out and result in a truly general and rational interest. However, such a construct badly fits a society in which powers are and remain unequal and even increase their unequal weight when they run their own course. It fits even worse when the variety of pressures unifies and coagulates into an overwhelming whole, integrating the particular countervailing powers by virtue of an increasing standard of living and an increasing concentration of power. Then, the laborer,

---

*I wish to reiterate for the following discussion that, *de facto*, tolerance is *not* indiscriminate and "pure" even in the most democratic society. The "background limitations" stated on page 85 restrict tolerance before it begins to operate. The antagonistic structure of society rigs the rules of the game. Those who stand against the established system are a priori at a disadvantage, which is not removed by the toleration of their ideas, speeches, and newspapers.

whose real interest conflicts with that of management, the common consumer whose real interest conflicts with that of the producer, the intellectual whose vocation conflicts with that of his employer find themselves submitting to a system against which they are powerless and appear unreasonable. The ideas of the available alternatives evaporates into an utterly utopian dimension in which it is at home, for a free society is indeed unrealistically and undefinably different from the existing ones. Under these circumstances, whatever improvement may occur "in the normal course of events" and without subversion is likely to be improvement in the direction determined by the particular interests which control the whole.

By the same token, those minorities which strive for a change of the whole itself will, under optimal conditions which rarely prevail, be left free to deliberate and discuss, to speak and to assemble—and will be left harmless and helpless in the face of the overwhelming majority, which militates against qualitative social change. This majority is firmly grounded in the increasing satisfaction of needs, and technological and mental coordination, which testify to the general helplessness of radical groups in a well-functioning social system.

Within the affluent democracy, the affluent discussion prevails, and within the established framework, it is tolerant to a large extent. All points of view can be heard: the Communist and the Fascist, the Left and the Right, the white and the Negro, the crusaders for armament and for disarmament. Moreover, in endlessly dragging debates over the media, the stupid opinion is treated with the same respect as the intelligent one, the misinformed may talk as long as the informed, and propaganda rides along with education, truth with falsehood. This pure toleration of sense and nonsense is justified by the democratic argument that nobody, neither group nor individual, is in possession of the truth and capable of defining what is right and wrong, good and bad. Therefore, all contesting opinions must be submitted to "the people" for its deliberation and choice. But I have already suggested that the democratic argument implies a necessary condition, namely, that the people must be capable of deliberating and choosing on the basis of knowledge, that they must have access to authentic information, and that, on this basis, their evaluation must be the result of autonomous thought.

In the contemporary period, the democratic argument for abstract tolerance tends to be invalidated by the invalidation of the democratic process itself. The liberating force of democracy was the chance it gave to effective dissent, on the individual as well as social scale, its openness to qualitatively different forms of government, of culture, education, work—of the human existence in general. The toleration of free discussion and the equal right of opposites was to define and clarify the different forms of dissent: their direction, content, prospect. But with the concentration of economic and political power and the integration of opposites in a society which uses technology as an instrument of domination, effective dissent is blocked where it could freely emerge: in the formation of opinion, in information and communication, in speech and assembly. Under the rule of monopolistic media—themselves the mere instruments of economic and political power—a mentality is created for which right and wrong, true and false are predefined wherever they affect the vital interest of the society. This is, prior to all expression and communication, a matter of semantics: the blocking of effective dissent, of the recognition of that which is not of the Establishment which begins in the language that is publicized and administered. The meaning of words is rigidly stabilized. Rational persuasion, persuasion to the opposite is all but precluded. The avenues of entrance are closed to the meaning of words and ideas other than the established one—established by the publicity of the powers that be, and verified in their practices. Other words can be spoken and heard, other ideas can be expressed, but, at the massive scale of the conservative majority (outside such enclaves as the intelligentsia), they are immediately "evaluated" (i.e. automatically understood) in terms of the public language—a language which determines a priori the direction in which the thought process moves. Thus the process of reflection ends where it started: in the given conditions and relations. Self-validating, the argument of the discussion repels the contradiction because the antithesis is redefined in terms of the thesis. For example, thesis: we work for peace; antithesis: we prepare for war (or even: we wage war); unification of opposites: preparing for war *is* working for peace. Peace is redefined as necessarily, in the prevailing situation, including preparation for war (or even war) and in this Orwellian form, the meaning of the word "peace" is stabilized. Thus, the basic vocabulary of the Orwellian language operates as a priori categories of understanding: preforming all content. These conditions invallidate the logic of tolerance which involves the rational development of meaning and precludes the closing of meaning. Consequently, persuasion through discussion and the equal presentation of opposites (even where it is really equal) easily lose their liberating force as factors of understanding and learning; they are far more likely to strengthen the established thesis and to repel the alternatives.

Impartiality to the utmost, equal treatment of competing and conflicting issues is indeed a basic requirement for decision-making in the democratic process—it is an equally basic requirement for defining the limits of tolerance. But in a democracy with totalitarian organization, objectivity may fulfill a very different function, namely, to foster a mental attitude which tends to obliterate the difference between true and false, information and indoctrination, right and wrong. In fact, the decision between opposed opinions has been made before the presentation and discussion get under way— made, not by a conspiracy or a sponsor or a publisher, not by any dictatorship, but rather by the "normal course of events," which is the course of administered events, and by the mentality shaped in this course. Here, too, it is the whole which determines the truth. Then the decision asserts itself, without any open violation of objectivity, in such things as the make-up of a newspaper (with the breaking up of vital information into bits interspersed between extraneous material, irrelevant items, relegating of some radically negative news to an obscure place), in the juxtaposition of gorgeous ads with unmitigated horrors, in the introduction and interruption of the broadcasting of facts by overwhelming commercials. The result is a *neutralization* of opposites, a neutralization, however, which takes place on the firm grounds of the structural limitation of tolerance and within a preformed mentality. When a magazine prints side by side a negative and a positive report on the FBI, it fulfills honestly the requirements of objectivity: however, the chances are that the positive wins because the image of the institution is deeply engraved in the mind of the people. Or, if a newscaster reports the torture and murder of civil rights workers in the same unemotional tone he uses to describe the stock-market or the weather, or with the same great emotion with which he says his commercials, then such objectivity is spurious—more, it offends against humanity and truth by being calm where one should be enraged, by refraining from accusation where accusation is in the facts themselves. The tolerance expressed in such impartiality serves to minimize or even absolve prevailing intolerance and suppression. If objectivity has anything to do with truth, and if truth is more than a matter of logic and science, then this kind of objectivity is false, and this kind of tolerance inhuman. And if it is necessary to break the established universe of meaning (and the practice enclosed in this universe) in order to enable man to find out what is true and false, this deceptive impartiality would have to be abandoned. The people exposed to this impartiality are no *tabulae rasae*, they are indoctrinated by the conditions under which they live and think and which they do not transcend. To enable them to become autonomous, to find by themselves what is true and what is false for man in the existing society, they would have to be freed from the prevailing indoctrination (which is no longer recognized as indoctrination). But this means that the trend would have to be reversed: they would have to get information slanted in the opposite direction. For the facts are never given immediately and never accessible immediately; they are established, "mediated" by those who made them; the truth, "the whole truth" surpasses these facts and requires the rupture with their appearance. This rupture —prerequisite and token of all freedom of thought and of speech —cannot be accomplished within the established framework of abstract tolerance and spurious objectivity because these are precisely the factors which precondition the mind *against* the rupture.

The factual barriers which totalitarian democracy erects against the efficacy of qualitative dissent are weak and pleasant enough compared with the practices of a dictatorship which claims to educate the people in the truth. With all its limitations and distortions, democratic tolerance is under all circumstances more humane than an institutionalized intolerance which sacrifices the rights and liberties of the living generations for the sake of future generations. The question is whether this is the only alternative. I shall presently try to suggest the direction in which an answer may be sought. In any case, the contrast is not between democracy in the abstract and dictatorship in the abstract.

Democracy is a form of government which fits very different types of society (this holds true even for a democracy with universal suffrage and equality before the law), and the human costs of a democracy are always and everywhere those exacted by the society whose government it is. Their range extends all the way from normal exploitation, poverty, and insecurity to the victims of wars, police actions, military aid, etc., in which the society is engaged—and not only to the victims within its own frontiers. These considerations can never justify the exacting of different sacrifices and different victims on behalf of a future better society, but they do allow weighing the costs involved in the perpetuation of an existing society against the risk of promoting alternatives which offer a reasonable chance of pacification and liberation. Surely, no government can be expected to foster its own subversion, but in a democracy such right is vested in the people (i.e. in the majority of the people). This means that the ways should not be blocked on which a subversive majority could develop, and if they are blocked by organized repression and indoctrination, their reopening may require apparently undemocratic means. They would include the withdrawal of toleration of speech and assembly from groups and movements which promote aggressive policies, armament, chauvinism, discrimination on the grounds of race and religion, or which oppose the extension of public services, social security, medical care, etc. Moreover, the restoration of freedom of thought may necessitate new and rigid restrictions on teachings and practices in the educational institutions which, by their very methods and concepts, serve to enclose the mind within the established universe of discourse and behavior—thereby precluding a priori a rational evaluation of the alternatives. And to the degree to which freedom of thought involves the struggle against inhumanity, restoration of such freedom would also imply intolerance toward scientific research in the interest of deadly "deterrents," of abnormal human endurance under inhuman conditions, etc. I shall presently discuss the question as to who is to decide on the distinction between liberating and repressive, human and inhuman teachings and practices; I have already suggested that this distinction is not a matter of value-preference but of rational criteria.

While the reversal of the trend in the educational enterprise at least could conceivably be enforced by the students and teachers themselves, and thus be self-imposed, the systematic withdrawal of tolerance toward regressive and repressive opinions and movements could only be envisaged as results of large-scale pressure which would amount to an upheaval. In other words, it would presuppose that which is still to be accomplished: the reversal of the trend. However, resistance at particular occasions, boycott, non-participation at the local and small-group level may perhaps prepare the ground. The subversive character of the restoration of freedom appears most clearly in that dimension of society where false tolerance and free enterprise do perhaps the most serious and lasting damage, namely, in business and publicity. Against the emphatic insistence on the part of spokesmen for labor, I maintain that practices such as planned obsolescence, collusion between union leadership and management, slanted publicity are not simply imposed from above on a powerless rank and file, but are *tolerated* by them—and by the consumer at large. However, it would be ridiculous to speak of a possible withdrawal of tolerance with respect to these practices and to the ideologies promoted by them. For they pertain to the basis on which the repressive affluent society rests and reproduces itself and its vital defenses—their removal would be that total revolution which this society so effectively repels.

To discuss tolerance in such a society means to re-examine the issue of violence and the traditional distinction between violent and non-violent action. The discussion should not, from the beginning, be clouded by ideologies which serve the perpetuation of violence. Even in the advanced centers of civilization, violence actually prevails: it is practiced by the police, in the prisons and mental institutions, in the fight against racial minorities; it is carried, by the defenders of metropolitan freedom, into the backward countries. This violence indeed breeds violence. But to refrain from violence in the face of vastly superior violence is one thing, to renounce a priori violence against violence, on ethical or psychological grounds (because it may antagonize sympathizers) is another. Non-violence is normally not only preached to but exacted from the weak—it is a necessity rather than a virtue, and normally it does not seriously harm the case of the strong. (Is the case of India an exception? There, passive resistance was carried through on a massive scale, which disrupted, or threatened to disrupt, the economic life of the country. Quantity turns into quality: on such a scale, passive resistance is no longer passive—it ceases to be non-violent. The same holds true for the General Strike.) Robespierre's distinction between the terror of liberty and the terror of despotism, and his moral glorification of the former belongs to the most convincingly condemned aberrations, even if the white terror was more bloody than the red terror. The comparative evaluation in terms of the number of victims is the quantifying approach which reveals the man-made horror throughout history that made violence a necessity. In terms of historical function, there is a difference between revolutionary and reactionary violence, between violence practiced by the oppressed and by the oppressors. In terms of ethics, both forms of violence are inhuman and evil—but since when is history made in accordance with ethical standards? To start applying them at the point where the oppressed rebel against the oppressors, the have-nots against the haves is serving the cause of actual violence by weakening the protest against it.

Comprenez enfin ceci: si la violence a commencé ce soir, si l'exploitation ni l'oppression n'ont jamais existé sur terre, peut-être la non-violence affichée peut apaiser la querelle. Mais si le régime tout entier et jusqu'à vos non-violentes pensées sont conditionnées par une oppression millénaire, votre passivité ne sert qu'à vous ranger du côté des oppresseurs.*

The very notion of false tolerance, and the distinction between right and wrong limitations on tolerance, between progressive and regressive indoctrination, revolutionary and reactionary violence demand the statement of criteria for its validity. These standards must be prior to whatever constitutional and legal criteria are set up and applied in an existing society (such as "clear and present danger," and other established definitions of civil rights and liberties), for such definitions themselves presuppose standards of freedom and repression as applicable or not applicable in the respective society: they are specifications of more general concepts. By whom, and according to what standard, can the political distinction between true and false, progressive and regressive (for in this sphere, these pairs are equivalent) be made and its validity be justified? At the outset, I propose that the question cannot be answered in terms of the alternative between democracy and dictatorship, according to which, in the latter, one individual or group, without any effective control from below, arrogate to themselves the decision. Historically, even in the most democratic democracies, the vital and final decisions affecting the society as a whole have been made, constitutionally or in fact, by one or several groups without effective control by the people themselves. The ironical question: who educates the educators (i.e. the political leaders) also applies to democracy. The only authentic alternative and negation of dictatorship (with respect to this question) would be a society in which "the people" have become autonomous individuals, freed from the repressive requirements of a struggle for existence in the interest of domination, and as such human beings choosing their government and determining their life. Such a society does not yet exist anywhere. In the meantime, the question must be treated *in abstracto* —abstraction, not from the historical possibilities, but from the realities of the prevailing societies.

I suggested that the distinction between true and false tolerance,

*Jean-Paul Sartre, Preface to Frantz Fanon, *Les Damnés de la Terre* (Paris: Maspéro, 1961), p. 22.

between progress and regression can be made rationally on empirical grounds. The real possibilities of human freedom are relative to the attained stage of civilization. They depend on the material and intellectual resources available at the respective stage, and they are quantifiable and calculable to a high degree. So are, at the stage of advanced industrial society, the most rational ways of using these resources and distributing the social product with priority on the satisfaction of vital needs and with a minimum of toil and injustice. In other words, it is possible to define the direction in which prevailing institutions, policies, opinions would have to be changed in order to improve the chance of a peace which is not identical with cold war and a little hot war, and a satisfaction of needs which does not feed on poverty, oppression, and exploitation. Consequently, it is also possible to identify policies, opinions, movements which would promote this chance, and those which would do the opposite. Suppression of the regressive ones is a prerequisite for the strengthening of the progressive ones.

The question, who is qualified to make all these distinctions, definitions, identifications for the society as a whole, has now one logical answer, namely, everyone "in the maturity of his faculties" as a human being, everyone who has learned to think rationally and autonomously. The answer to Plato's educational dictatorship is the democratic educational dictatorship of free men. John Stuart Mill's conception of the *res publica* is not the opposite of Plato's: the liberal too demands the authority of Reason not only as an intellectual but also as a political power. In Plato, rationality is confined to the small number of philosopher-kings; in Mill, every rational human being participates in the discussion and decision—but only as a rational being. Where society has entered the phase of total administration and indoctrination, this would be a small number indeed, and not necessarily that of the elected representatives of the people. The problem is not that of an educational dictatorship, but that of breaking the tyranny of public opinion and its makers in the closed society.

However, granted the empirical rationality of the distinction between progress and regression, and granted that it may be applicable to tolerance, and may justify strongly discriminatory tolerance on political grounds (cancellation of the liberal creed of free and equal discussion), another impossible consequence would follow. I said that, by virtue of its inner logic, withdrawal of tolerance from regressive movements, and discriminatory tolerance in favor of progressive tendencies would be tantamount to the "official" promotion of subversion. The historical calculus of progress (which is actually the calculus of the prospective reduction of cruelty, misery, suppression) seems to involve the calculated choice between two forms of political violence: that on the part of the legally constituted powers (by their legitimate action, or by their tacit consent, or by their inability to prevent violence), and that on the part of potentially subversive movements. Moreover, with respect to the latter, a policy of unequal treatment would protect radicalism on the Left against that on the Right. Can the historical calculus be reasonably extended to the justification of one form of violence as against another? Or better (since "justification" carries a moral connotation), is there historical evidence to the effect that the social origin and impetus of violence (from among the ruled or the ruling classes, the haves or the have-nots, the Left or the Right) is in a demonstrable relation to progress (as defined above)?

With all the qualifications of a hypothesis based on an "open" historical record, it seems that the violence emanating from the rebellion of the oppressed classes broke the historical continuum of injustice, cruelty, and silence for a brief moment, brief but explosive enough to achieve an increase in the scope of freedom and justice, and a better and more equitable distribution of misery and oppression in a new social system—in one word: progress in civilization. The English civil wars, the French Revolution, the Chinese and the Cuban Revolutions may illustrate the hypothesis. In contrast, the one historical change from one social system to another, marking the beginning of a new period in civilization, which was *not* sparked and driven by an effective movement "from below," namely, the collapse of the Roman Empire in the West, brought about a long period of regression for long centuries, until a new, higher period of civilization was painfully born in the violence of the heretic revolts of the thirteenth century and in the peasant and laborer revolts of the fourteenth century.*

With respect to historical violence emanating from among ruling classes, no such relation to progress seems to obtain. The long series of dynastic and imperialist wars, the liquidation of Spartacus in Germany in 1919, Fascism and Nazism did not break but rather tightened and streamlined the continuum of suppression. I said emanating "from among ruling classes": to be sure, there is hardly any organized violence from above that does not mobilize and activate mass support from below; the decisive question is, on behalf of and in the interest of which groups and institutions is such violence released? And the answer is not necessarily ex post: in the historical examples just mentioned, it could be and was anticipated whether the movement would serve the revamping of the old order or the emergence of the new.

Liberating tolerance, then, would mean intolerance against movements from the Right, and toleration of movements from the Left. As to the scope of this tolerance and intolerance: . . . it would extend to the stage of action as well as of discussion and propaganda, of deed as well as of word. The traditional criterion of clear and present danger seems no longer adequate to a stage where the whole society is in the situation of the theater audience when somebody cries: "fire." It is a situation in which the total catastrophe could be triggered off any moment, not only by a technical error, but also by a rational miscalculation of risks, or by a rash speech of one of the leaders. In past and different circumstances, the speeches of the Fascist and Nazi leaders were the immediate prologue to the massacre. The distance between the propaganda and the action, between the organization and its release on the people had become too short. But the spreading of the word could have been stopped before it was too late: if democratic tolerance had been withdrawn when the future leaders started their campaign, mankind would have had a chance of avoiding Auschwitz and a World War.

The whole post-fascist period is one of clear and present danger.

---

*In modern times, fascism has been a consequence of the transition to industrial society *without* a revolution. See Barrington Moore's *Social Origins of Dictatorship and Democracy* (Boston: Beacon Press, 1966).

Consequently, true pacification requires the withdrawal of tolerance before the deed, at the stage of communication in word, print, and picture. Such extreme suspension of the right of free speech and free assembly is indeed justified only if the whole of society is in extreme danger. I maintain that our society is in such an emergency situation, and that it has become the normal state of affairs. Different opinions and "philosophies" can no longer compete peacefully for adherence and persuasion on rational grounds: the "marketplace of ideas" is organized and delimited by those who determine the national and the individual interest. In this society, for which the ideologists have proclaimed the "end of ideology," the false consciousness has become the general consciousness—from the government down to its last objects. The small and powerless minorities which struggle against the false consciousness and its beneficiaries must be helped: their continued existence is more important than the preservation of abused rights and liberties which grant constitutional powers to those who oppress these minorities. It should be evident by now that the exercise of civil rights by those who don't have them presupposes the withdrawal of civil rights from those who prevent their exercise, and that liberation of the Damned of the Earth presupposes suppression not only of their old but also of their new masters.

Withdrawal of tolerance from regressive movements *before* they can become active; intolerance even toward thought, opinion, and word, and finally, intolerance in the opposite direction, that is, toward the self-styled conservatives to the political Right—these anti-democratic notions respond to the actual development of the democratic society which has destroyed the basis for universal tolerance. The conditions under which tolerance can again become a liberating and humanizing force have still to be created. When tolerance mainly serves the protection and preservation of a repressive society, when it serves to neutralize opposition and to render men immune against other and better forms of life, then tolerance has been perverted. And when this perversion starts in the mind of the individual, in his consciousness, his needs, when heteronomous interests occupy him before he can experience his servitude, then the efforts to counteract his dehumanization must begin at the place of entrance, there where the false consciousness takes form (or rather: is systematically formed)—it must begin with stopping the words and images which feed this consciousness. To be sure, this is censorship, even precensorship, but openly directed against the more or less hidden censorship that permeates the free media. Where the false consciousness has become prevalent in national and popular behavior, it translates itself almost immediately into practice: the safe distance between ideology and reality, repressive thought and repressive action, between the word of destruction and the deed of destruction is dangerously shortened. Thus, the break through the false consciousness may provide the Archimedean point for a larger emancipation—at an infinitesimally small spot, to be sure, but it is on the enlargement of such small spots that the chance of change depends.

The forces of emancipation cannot be identified with any social class which, by virtue of its material condition, is free from false consciousness. Today, they are hopelessly dispersed throughout the society, and the fighting minorities and isolated groups are often in opposition to their own leadership. In the society at large, the mental space for denial and reflection must first be recreated. Repulsed by the concreteness of the administered society, the effort of emancipation becomes "abstract"; it is reduced to facilitating the recognition of what is going on, to freeing language from the tyranny of the Orwellian syntax and logic, to developing the concepts that comprehend reality. More than ever, the proposition holds true that progress in freedom demands progress in the *consciousness* of freedom. Where the mind has been made into a subject-object of politics and policies, intellectual autonomy, the realm of "pure" thought has become a matter of *political education* (or rather: counter-education).

This means that previously neutral, value-free, formal aspects of learning and teaching now become, on their own grounds and in their own right, political: learning to know the facts, the whole truth, and to comprehend it is radical criticism throughout, intellectual subversion. In a world in which the human faculties and needs are arrested or perverted, autonomous thinking leads into a "perverted world": contradiction and counter-image of the established world of repression. And this contradiction is not simply stipulated, is not simply the product of confused thinking or phantasy, but is the logical development of the given, the existing world. To the degree to which this development is actually impeded by the sheer weight of a repressive society and the necessity of making a living in it, repression invades the academic enterprise itself, even prior to all restrictions on academic freedom. The pre-empting of the mind vitiates impartiality and objectivity: unless the student learns to think in the opposite direction, he will be inclined to place the facts into the predominant framework of values. Scholarship, i.e. the acquisition and communication of knowledge, prohibits the purification and isolation of facts from the context of the whole truth. An essential part of the latter is recognition of the frightening extent to which history was made and recorded by and for the victors, that is, the extent to which history was the development of oppression. And this oppression is in the facts themselves which it establishes; thus they themselves carry a negative value as part and aspect of their facticity. To treat the great crusades *against* humanity (like that against the Albigensians) with the same impartiality as the desperate struggles *for* humanity means neutralizing their opposite historical function, reconciling the executioners with their victims, distorting the record. Such spurious neutrality serves to reproduce acceptance of the dominion of the victors in the consciousness of man. Here, too, in the education of those who are not yet maturely integrated, in the mind of the young, the ground for liberating tolerance is still to be created.

Education offers still another example of spurious, abstract tolerance in the guise of concreteness and truth: it is epitomized in the concept of self-actualization. From the permissiveness of all sorts of license to the child, to the constant psychological concern with the personal problems of the student, a large-scale movement is under way against the evils of repression and the need for being oneself. Frequently brushed aside is the question as to what has to be repressed before one can be a self; oneself. The individual potential is first a negative one, a portion of the potential of his society: of aggression, guilt feeling, ignorance, resentment, cruelty which vitiate his life instincts. If the identity of the self is to be more than the immediate realization of this potential (undesirable for the individual as human being), then it requires repression and sublimation, conscious transformation. This process involves at each stage (to use the ridiculed terms which here reveal their succinct concreteness) the negation of the negation, mediation of the immediate, and identity is no more and no less than this process. "Alienation" is the constant and essential element of identity, the objective side of the subject—and not, as it is made to appear today, a disease, a psychological condition. Freud well knew the difference between progressive and regressive, liberating and destructive repression. The publicity of self-actualization promotes the removal of the one and the other, it promotes existence in that immediacy which, in a repressive society, is (to use another Hegelian term) bad immediacy *(schlechte Unmittelbarkeit)*. It isolates the individual from the one dimension where he could "find himself": from his political existence, which is at the core of his entire existence. Instead, it encourages non-conformity and letting-go in ways which leave the real engines of repression in the society entirely intact, which even strengthen these engines by substituting the satisfactions of private and personal, and therefore more authentic, opposition. The desublimation involved in this sort of self-actualization is itself repressive inasmuch as it weakens the necessity and the power of the intellect, the catalytic force of that unhappy consciousness which does not revel in the archetypal personal release of frustration—hopeless resurgence of the Id which will sooner or later succumb to the omnipresent rationality of the administered world—but which recognizes the horror of the whole in the most private frustration and actualizes itself in this recognition.

I have tried to show how the changes in advanced democratic societies, which have undermined the basis of economic and political liberalism, have also altered the liberal function of tolerance. The tolerance which was the great achievement of the liberal era is still professed and (with strong qualifications) practiced, while the economic and political process is subjected to an ubiquitous and effective administration in accordance with the predominant interests. The result is an objective contradiction between the economic and political structure on the one side, and the theory and practice of toleration on the other. The altered social structure tends to weaken the effectiveness of tolerance toward dissenting and oppositional movements and to strengthen conservative and reactionary forces. Equality of tolerance becomes abstract, spurious. With the actual decline of dissenting forces in the society, the opposition is insulated in small and frequently antagonistic groups who, even where tolerated within the narrow limits set by the hierarchical structure of society, are powerless while they keep within these limits. But the tolerance shown to them is deceptive and promotes coordination. And on the firm foundations of a coordinated society all but closed against qualitative change, tolerance itself serves to contain such change rather than to promote it.

These same conditions render the critique of such tolerance abstract and academic, and the proposition that the balance between tolerance toward the Right and toward the Left would have to be radically redressed in order to restore the liberating function of tolerance becomes only an unrealistic speculation. Indeed, such a redressing seems to be tantamount to the establishment of a "right of resistance" to the point of subversion. There is not, there cannot be any such right for any group or individual against a constitutional government sustained by a majority of the population. But I believe that there is a "natural right" of resistance for oppressed and overpowered minorities to use extralegal means if the legal ones have proved to be inadequate. Law and order are always and everywhere the law and order which protect the established hierarchy; it is nonsensical to invoke the absolute authority of this law and this order against those who suffer from it and struggle against it—not for personal advantages and revenge, but for their share of humanity. There is no other judge over them than the constituted authorities, the police, and their own conscience. If they use violence, they do not start a new chain of violence but try to break an established one. Since they will be punished, they know the risk, and when they are willing to take it, no third person, and least of all the educator and intellectual, has the right to preach them abstention.

PART III

The General Will Versus the Majority

Maximilien Robespierre (1758–1794) was a French lawyer. He believed in a democracy of equals and in universal suffrage; he opposed capital punishment. His idealistic temperament earned him the name "incorruptible."

When he became the leading spokesman of the Jacobins during the French Revolution, he identified Rousseau's "general will" with the will of the Jacobins and finally with himself. He also instituted the reign of terror epitomized by the guillotine.

The Vendée is a department of France, on the western Atlantic coast; its conservative Catholics opposed the French Revolution. The sans-culottes ("without knee breeches") were the Parisian supporters of the Revolution who wore long trousers.

MAY 8, 1793

The armies of the Vendée, the armies of Brittany and of Coblenz are marching against Paris.

Parisians! The feudal masters are arming themselves because you are the vanguard of humanity. All the great powers of Europe are equipping themselves against you and all the base and depraved persons in France support them.

We now know the entire plan of our enemies, and have means for our defense in our hands. I am not stating secrets to you, I am merely repeating the speech I delivered this morning in the Convention. I declared this morning in the Convention that the Parisians will march to La Vendée, and that on all the roads and in all the cities on our journey we shall gather friends and brothers, and that we must extinguish in a single blow all of them, all the rebels. All the friends of the Republic must rise in order to annihilate all the aristocrats in La Vendée.

This morning in the Convention I said that the rascals in La Vendée have allies in the very heart of Paris, and I demanded emphatically that the Parisian fighters who have borne the terrible burden of the Revolution for five years, a portion of whom will now take the field—that these republicans must not lose their wives and children during their absence, at the murderous hands of the counter-revolution. And no one to-day dared in the Convention to dispute the necessity of these measures.

Parisians! Let us hasten to meet the bandits of La Vendée!

Do you know why La Vendée is becoming a danger to us? La Vendée is a danger because great precautions have been taken to disarm a section of the population. But we shall create new republican legions and we shall not hand over our wives and children to the daggers of the counter-revolution.

This morning, in the Convention, I demanded the destruction of the rebels from La Vendée, and I also demanded that all aristocrats and moderates should at once be excluded from the Paris sections, and I also demanded that these suspected persons should be jailed.

We do not regard a person as a suspect merely because he was once a nobleman, a farmer general or a trader. Those persons are suspects who have not proved their quality as citizens, and they shall remain in our prisons until such time as the war may be terminated victoriously.

I asked money this morning in the Convention for the *sans-culottes*, for we must deliberate in the sections, and the workingman cannot deliberate and work at home at the same time. But he must receive pay for his task of guarding the city. I have asked millions for the *sans-culottes* of Paris. . . . I have asked that people cease calumniating in the Convention the people of Paris and that the newspaper writers who desire to contaminate public opinion have their mouths stopped for them.

I demanded this morning in the Convention, and I demand it here again—and neither in the Convention nor here do I hear any contrary voices—that an army be held in readiness in Paris, an army not like that of Dumouriez, but an army consisting of *sans-culottes* and workingmen. And this army must investigate Paris, must keep the moderates in check, must occupy all posts and inspire all enemies with terror.

I asked in the Convention that the forges in all public squares be set to work in order to forge weapons, weapons, and again weapons, and I asked that the Council of Ministers should supervise this production of arms.

The tyrants of this earth have made their plans. The defenders of the Republic are to be their sacrifices. Very well—in this most grave of all moments, we shall save freedom by the severest measures, we shall not consent to be murdered one by one.

Citizens! Certain representatives of the people have attempted to play off the Parisians against the Departments, the Departments against Paris, the Convention against the provinces, and the people in the galleries against the masses of the Parisians. They will not succeed. I have informed these gentlemen to this effect, and if the entire people of France could hear me, the entire people of France would be on my side.

Citizens! Do not be dismayed. We are told of immeasurably large foreign armies, of their connections with La Vendée, of their connections with Paris. Very well! What will all their efforts avail them against millions of *sans-culottes?*

We have an immense people of strong *sans-culottes* at our disposal, who cannot be permitted to drop their work. Let the rich pay! We have a Convention; perhaps not all its members are poor and resolute, but the corrupt section will for all that not be able to prevent us from fighting. Do you believe that the Mountain has not enough forces to defeat the adherents of Dumouriez, Orléans and Coburg combined? Parisians, the fate of all France, of all Europe, and all humanity is in your hands. The Mountain needs the People. The people needs the Mountain. And I brand the reports that the provinces are turning their arms against the Jacobins as fabrications on the part of our enemies.

In conclusion, I demand what I demanded in the Convention this morning, namely, that the Parisians shall be the revolutionary nucleus of the army, strong enough to drag the *sans-culottes* with them, that an army should remain in Paris in order to keep our enemies in check, that all enemies who are caught shall be placed under arrest, and that money must be confiscated from the rich in order to enable the poor to continue the struggle.

What is our aim? Using the constitution for the benefit of the people.

Who are likely to oppose us? The rich and the corrupt.

What means will they employ? Slander and hypocrisy.

Why do they use these means? Because the *sans-culottes* are ignorant. The people must be educated.

What are the obstacles to their education? The paid journalists who mislead them everyday by irresponsible misrepresentations.

What conclusion follows? That we should limit these writers as the most dangerous enemies of the country, and widely circulate the right kind of information. . . .

When will the people be educated? . . . when the rich and the government cease bribing treacherous pens and tongues to deceive the people; when their interests are identified with those of the people.

When will this be? Never!*

---

*Maximilien Robespierre, private memorandum recorded by E. B. Courtois in *Rapport fait au nom de la commission chargée de l'examen des papiers trouvés chez Robespierre et ses complices* (1795), Pièce justificative, No. 44. Translated by N. Capaldi.

Adolf Hitler (1889-1945) was the founder of the Nazi party and became German Führer in 1934.

Hitler's critique of the democratic Weimar Republic of Germany was based upon (a) the claim that it was a sham democracy wherein public opinion was surreptitiously controlled by an international conspiracy of Jews; *(b)* the charge that traditional democracies were ineffective since they placed "final decisions into the hands of a mass assembly of people, of whom only a small portion has the knowledge and experience required by the affairs under consideration"; and *(c)* a distinction between democratic parliamentarianism and "true Germanic democracy"—where the latter is described as the "free choice of a leader with the latter's obligation to take over fully all responsibility for what he does or does not do. There will be no voting by a majority on single questions."

What cause finally had America to enter the war against Germany? With the outbreak of the World War, which Judah had desired so passionately and so long, all the large Jewish firms of the United States began supplying ammunitions. They supplied the European "war-market" to an extent which perhaps even they themselves had never dreamed of—a gigantic harvest! Yet nothing satisfied the insatiable greed of the Jew. And so the venal press which depended upon the Stock Exchange kings began an unparalleled propaganda campaign. *A gigantic organization for newspaper lying was built up. And once more it is a Jewish concern, the Hearst press, which set the tone of the agitation against Germany.* The hatred of these "Americans" was not directed solely against commercial Germany or against military Germany. It was directed specially against social Germany, because this Germany had up to that time kept itself outside of the principles which governed the world trusts. The old Reich had at least made an honorable attempt to be socially-minded. We had to show for ourselves such an initiative in social institutions as no other country in the wide world could boast. . . . This explains why, even in Germany itself, the "comrades" under Jewish leadership fought against their own vital interests. This explains the agitation carried on throughout the world under the same watchword. For this reason the Jewish-democratic press of America had to accomplish its masterpiece—that is to say, it had to drive into the most horrible of all wars a great peace-loving people which was as little concerned in European struggles as it was in the North Pole: America was to intervene "in defense of civilization," and the Americans were persuaded so to do by an atrocity propaganda conducted in the name of civilization which from A to Z was a scandalous invention the like of which has never yet been seen—a farrago of lies and forgeries. Because this last State in the world where social aims were being realized had to be destroyed, therefore twenty-six peoples were incited one against the other by this press which is exclusively in the possession of one and the same world people, of one and the same race, and that race on principle the deadly foe of all national States.

Who could have prevented the World War? Not the *Kultur-solidarität*, the "solidarity of civilization," in whose name the Jews carried on their propaganda: not the so-called World Pacifism—again an exclusively Jewish invention. Could the so-called "Solidarity of the Proletariat?" . . . "All the wheels stand silent, still, If that be your strong arm's will. . . ." The German wheel on November 9, 1918, was indeed brought to a standstill. The Social Democratic party in its principal organ, *Vorwärts*, declared in so many words that it was not in the interest of the workers that Germany should win the war. . . .

Could the Freemasons perhaps stop the war?—this most noble of philanthropic institutions who foretold the good fortune of the people louder than anyone and who at the same time was the principal leader in promoting the war. Who, after all, are the Freemasons? You have to distinguish two grades. To the lower grade in Germany belong the ordinary citizens who through the claptrap which is served up to them can feel themselves to be "somebodies," but the responsible authorities are those many-sided folk who can stand any climate, those 300 Rathenaus who all know each other, who guide the history of the world over the heads of Kings and Presidents, those who will undertake any office without scruples, who know how brutally to enslave all peoples—once more the Jews!

Why have the Jews been against Germany? That is made quite clear today—proved by countless facts. They use the age-old tactics of the hyena—when fighters are tired out, then go for them! Then make your harvest! In war and revolutions the Jew attained the unattainable. Hundreds of thousands of escaped Orientals become modern "Europeans." Times of unrest produce miracles. Before 1914 how long would it have taken, for instance, in Bavaria before a Galician Jew became—Prime Minister?—Or in Russia before an anarchist from the New York Ghetto, Bronstein (Trotsky), became —Dictator? Only a few wars and revolutions—that was enough to put the Jewish people into possession of the red gold and thereby to make them masters of the world.

Before 1914 there were two States above all, Germany and Russia, which prevented the Jew from reaching his goal—the mastery of the world. Here not everything which they already possessed in the Western democracies had fallen to the Jews. Here they were not the sole lords alike in the intellectual and economic life. Here, too, the Parliaments were not yet exclusively instruments of Jewish capital and of the will of the Jew. The German and the genuine Russian had still preserved a certain aloofness from the Jew. In both peoples there still lived the healthy instinct of scorn for the Jew, and there was a real danger that in these monarchies there might one day arise a Frederick the Great, a William I, and that democracy and a parliamentary regime might be sent to the devil. So the Jews became revolutionaries! The Republic should bring them to wealth and to power. This aim they disguised: they cried "Down with the monarchies!" "Enthrone the 'sovereign' people!" I do not know whether today one could venture to call the German or the Russian people "sovereign." At least one cannot see any trace of it! What the German people can trace, however, what every day stands in the most crass form before its eyes, is debauchery, gluttony, speculation ruling unchecked, the open mockery of the Jew. . . .

So Russia and Germany had to be overthrown in order that the ancient prophecy might be fulfilled. So the whole world was lashed into fury. So every lie and propaganda agency was brutally set in action against the State of the last—the German—idealists! *And thus it was that Judah won the World War. Or would you wish to maintain that the French, the English, or the American "people" won the war? They, one and all, victors and vanquished are alike defeated:* one thing raises itself above them all: the World Stock Exchange which has become the master of the people.

What guilt had Germany herself for the outbreak of the war? Her guilt consisted in this: that at the moment when the ring closed about her existence Germany neglected to organize her defense with such vigor that through this demonstration of her power either the others, despite their abominable purposes, would have been robbed of their will to strike or else the victory of the Reich would have been assured. The guilt of the German people lies in this: that when in 1912 a criminal Reichstag in its unfathomable baseness and folly had refused to allow the raising of three army corps the people did not create for itself those army corps in the Reichstag's despite. With these additional 120,000 men the Battle of the Marne would have been won and the issue of the war decided. Two million fewer German heroes would have sunk into their graves. Who was it in 1912 as in 1918 struck its weapons from the hands of the German people? Who was it that in 1912, as in the last year of the war, infatuated the German people with his theory that if Germany throws down her arms the whole world will follow her example— who?—the democratic-Marxist Jew who at the same hour incited and still today incites the others to—arm and to subjugate "barbarous" Germany.

But someone may perhaps yet raise the question whether it is expedient today to talk about the guilt for the war. Most assuredly we have the duty to talk about it! For the murderers of our Fatherland who all the years through have betrayed and sold Germany, they are the same men who, as the November criminals, have plunged us into the depths of misfortune. We have the duty to speak since in the near future, when we have gained power, we shall have the further duty of taking these creators of ruin, these clouts, these traitors to their State and of hanging them on the gallows to which they belong. Only let no one think that in them there has come a change of heart. On the contrary, these November scoundrels who still are free to go as they will in our midst, they are, even today, going against us. From the recognition of the facts comes the will to rise again. Two millions have remained on the field of battle. They, too, have their rights and not we, the survivors, alone. There are millions of orphans, of cripples, of widows in our midst. They, too, have rights. For the Germany of today not one of them died, not one of them became a cripple, an orphan, or a widow. We owe it to these millions that we build a new Germany!

Herbert Marcuse (see page 82) is convinced of the importance of preventing people like Hitler from coming to power. Marcuse believes that Hitler's rise was the result of the failure of present forms of democracy, and he analyzes that failure as due to (a) the fact that public opinion is not free but controlled by the Establishment; *(b)* the fact that decisions are made by "politicians" and not "really qualified" people; and *(c)* the need for a "real" and "true" democracy that "puts qualified people in government" and in which it is recognized that the "majority is not always right."

"Two things I'm repeatedly accused of," Dr. Marcuse commented amiably, "are favoring restriction of free expression, and favoring rule by an autocratic elite. I think these points are misunderstood.

"I'm trying to conceive of real democracy. I would restrict expression only in the case of movements which are definitely aggressive and destructive.

"For instance," he continued, "the Hitler movement. I was there. I saw it. If he had been restricted while there was still time, we would have avoided a horrible war. The fact that he was not restricted was a failure in applying the democratic process in an effective way.

"If you had the people in government who were really qualified, problems like that would not arise. The fact that government is turned over to politicians is a violation of the democratic process.

134

"I've never advocated government by an elite group. What I have said is that to have really democratic rule, you have to have a system that puts qualified people in government. You have to have completely free formation of public opinion.

"There has to be equal freedom to both the right and the left, which you don't have today, in terms of money or of access to the communications media. The majority is not always right. New movements, new ideas, always start with a minority, and they must be protected somehow, it seems to me. I may be terribly naïve about this.

"Chicago [the Democratic National Convention site] was a most blatant example that what we have is not true democracy. There were two Presidential candidates picked by the machines, over which the people had nothing to say.

"It's not a question of an alternative between democracy and an autocracy. You have to restore the democratic process.

"What about this?" he said, turning to his little pile of scurrilous mail, and asking his interviewer a practical question. "Isn't there some way the Post Office should stop letters addressed to a person with things like 'Filthy Communist'?"

The visitor suggested that, apart from the contents of communications, arbitrary interception of letters on the basis of the way they were addressed might be an undue interference with citizens' rights to receive any mail directed to them.

"You mean it is my right to get letters with slanderous inscriptions on the envelope?" Dr. Marcuse asked with philosophical irony. He leaned back and reflected for a moment. "Ah, I guess that would be the case," he said.*

UNDER the conditions prevailing in this country, tolerance does not, and cannot, fulfill the civilizing function attributed to it by the liberal protagonists of democracy, namely, protection of dissent. The progressive historical force of tolerance lies in its extension to those modes and forms of dissent which are not committed to the status quo of society, and not confined to the institutional frame-

* *The New York Times*, September 29, 1968, p. 71.

work of the established society. Consequently, the idea of tolerance implies the necessity, for the dissenting group or individuals, to become illegitimate if and when the established legitimacy prevents and counteracts the development of dissent. This would be the case not only in a totalitarian society, under a dictatorship, in one-party states, but also in a democracy (representative, parliamentary, or "direct") where the majority does not result from the development of independent thought and opinion but rather from the monopolistic or oligopolistic administration of public opinion, without terror and (normally) without censorship. In such cases, the majority is self-perpetuating while perpetuating the vested interests which *made* it a majority. In its very structure this majority is "closed," petrified; it repels a priori any change other than changes within the system. But this means that the majority is no longer justified in claiming the democratic title of the best guardian of the common interest. And such a majority is all but the opposite of Rousseau's "general will": it is composed, not of individuals who, in their political functions, have made effective "abstraction" from their private interests, but, on the contrary, of individuals who have effectively identified their private interests with their political functions. And the representatives of this majority, in ascertaining and executing its will, ascertain and execute the will of the vested interests which have formed the majority. The ideology of democracy hides its lack of substance.

In the United States, this tendency goes hand in hand with the monopolistic or oligopolistic concentration of capital in the formation of public opinion, i.e., of the majority. The chance of influencing, in any effective way, this majority is at a price, in dollars, totally out of reach of the radical opposition. Here too, free competition and exchange of ideas have become a farce. The Left has no equal voice, no equal access to the mass media and their public facilities —not because a conspiracy excludes it, but because, in good old capitalist fashion, it does not have the purchasing power because it is the Left. These conditions impose upon the radical minorities a strategy which is in essence a refusal to allow the continuous functioning of allegedly indiscriminate but in fact discriminate tolerance, for example, a strategy of protesting against the alternate matching of a spokesman for the Right (or Center) with one for the Left. Not "equal" but *more* representation of the Left would be equalization of the prevailing inequality.

Within the solid framework of preestablished inequality and power, tolerance is practiced indeed. Even outrageous opinions are expressed, outrageous incidents are televised; and the critics of established policies are interrupted by the same number of commercials as the conservative advocates. Are these interludes supposed to counteract the sheer weight, magnitude, and continuity of system-publicity, indoctrination which operates playfully through the endless commercials as well as through the entertainment?

Given this situation, I suggested in "Repressive Tolerance" the practice of discriminating tolerance in an inverse direction, as a means of shifting the balance between Right and Left by restraining the liberty of the Right, thus counteracting the pervasive inequality of freedom (unequal opportunity of access to the means of democratic persuasion) and strengthening the oppressed against the oppressors. Tolerance would be restricted with respect to movements of a demonstrably aggressive or destructive character (destructive of the prospects for peace, justice, and freedom for all). Such discrimination would also be applied to movements opposing the extension of social legislation to the poor, weak, disabled. As against the virulent denunciations that such a policy would do away with the sacred liberalistic principle of equality for "the other side," I maintain that there are issues where either there is no "other side" in any more than a formalistic sense, or where "the other side" is demonstrably "regressive" and impedes possible improvement of the human condition. To tolerate propaganda for inhumanity vitiates the goals not only of liberalism but of every progressive political philosophy.

I presupposed the existence of demonstrable criteria for aggressive, regressive, destructive forces. If the final democratic criterion of the declared opinion of the majority no longer (or rather not yet) prevails, if vital ideas, values, and ends of human progress no longer (or rather not yet) enter, as competing equals, the formation of public opinion, if the people are no longer (or rather not yet) sovereign but "made" by the real sovereign powers—is there any alternative other than the dictatorship of an "elite" over the people? For the opinion of people (usually designated as The People) who are unfree in the very faculties in which liberalism saw the roots of freedom: independent thought and independent speech, can carry no overriding validity and authority—even if The People constitute the overwhelming majority.

If the choice were between genuine democracy and dictatorship, democracy would certainly be preferable. But democracy does not prevail. The radical critics of the existing political process are thus readily denounced as advocating an "elitism," a dictatorship of intellectuals as an alternative. What we have in fact is government, representative government by a non-intellectual minority of politicians, generals, and businessmen. The record of this "elite" is not very promising, and political prerogatives for the intelligentsia may not necessarily be worse for the society as a whole.

In any case, John Stuart Mill, not exactly an enemy of liberal and representative government, was not so allergic to the political leadership of the intelligentsia as the contemporary guardians of semi-democracy are. Mill believed that "individual mental superiority" justifies "reckoning one person's opinion as equivalent to more than one":

> Until there shall have been devised, and until opinion is willing to accept, some mode of plural voting which may assign to education as such the degree of superior influence due to it, and sufficient as a counterpoise to the numerical weight of the least educated class, for so long the benefits of completely universal suffrage cannot be obtained without bringing with them, as it appears to me, more than equivalent evils.*

"Distinction in favor of education, right in itself," was also supposed to preserve "the educated from the class legislation of the

* *Considerations on Representative Government* (Chicago: Gateway Edition, 1962), p. 183.

uneducated," without enabling the former to practice a class legislation of their own.*

Today, these words have understandably an antidemocratic, "elitist" sound—understandably because of their dangerously radical implications. For if "education" is more and other than training, learning, preparing for the existing society, it means not only enabling man to know and understand the facts which make up reality but also to know and understand the factors that establish the facts so that he can change their inhuman reality. And such humanistic education would involve the "hard" sciences ("hard" as in the "hardware" bought by the Pentagon?), would free them from their destructive direction. In other words, such education would indeed badly serve the Establishment, and to give political prerogatives to the men and women thus educated would indeed be anti-democratic in the terms of the Establishment. But these are not the only terms.

However, the alternative to the established semi-democratic process is *not* a dictatorship or elite, no matter how intellectual and intelligent, but the struggle for a real democracy. Part of this struggle is the fight against an ideology of tolerance which, in reality, favors and fortifies the conservation of the status quo of inequality and discrimination. For this struggle, I proposed the practice of discriminating tolerance. To be sure, this practice already presupposes the radical goal which it seeks to achieve. I committed this *petitio principii* in order to combat the pernicious ideology that tolerance is already institutionalized in this society. The tolerance which is the life element, the token of a free society, will never be the gift of the powers that be; it can, under the prevailing conditions of tyranny by the majority, only be won in the sustained effort of radical minorities, willing to break this tyranny and to work for the emergence of a free and sovereign majority—minorities intolerant, militantly intolerant and disobedient to the rules of behavior which tolerate destruction and suppression.

Ibid., p. 181.

Sidney Hook is Professor of Philosophy at New York University. He is the author of Quest for Being, Paradoxes of Freedom, and Fail-Safe Fallacy.

Although Marx was a prophet of social revolution, his predictions about when, where and how it would occur were not confirmed. Nor did he foresee the rise of Fascism and the welfare state. Actually, it was the advent of the welfare state that eroded the doctrinaire and evolutionary character of Western Marxism. For it showed that democratic political processes could affect the operation of the economic system, abolish some of its worst evils and open a perspective for profound change in the power relations of different classes.

The very success of reform brings despair to the heart of those who, like Herbert Marcuse, wish to revolutionize the entire basis of human society and abolish all injustice. The main reason for their despair is the belief that the workers, who should have been the carriers of social revolution, have become part of the Establishment in all the developed economies of the West. Corrupted by the sorry affluence of their society, striving for the same values, goods and services of the middle-classes, the workers, declares Marcuse, are now a "conservative, even counter-revolutionary force." The situation is hardly remediable, because the vested interest of the workers in the System extends to their very nerve endings, to their biological make-up.

Who, then, will be the carriers of the revolution? For not all the scientific and technical advances in the world will by themselves bring liberation. That can now be achieved, Marcuse asserts, only by "a new type of man" with "a new sensibility" whose "biological dimension" will render him forever immune to the degrading seductions of an affluent society. The new, biological type of man is not the new type of Soviet man—who seems to want the same things in life as the workers corrupted by capitalist prosperity, who misguidedly strive for the same high standard of living as their employers. The new man must be instinctually different, "A type of man with a different sensitivity as well as consciousness; men who would speak a different language, have different gestures, follow different impulses; men who have developed an instinctual barrier against cruelty, brutality, and ugliness."

Where can such a new man—really superman—be found? We obviously cannot rely on biological mutations. Marcuse is very unclear on this point. He tells us that the construction of a new society "presupposes" such a man, and that the new sensibility must "precede" the revolution. But he also asserts that the new man cannot be "envisaged" except through revolution. All this makes the prospect of human liberation very dubious.

It does, however, reveal the spirit of Marcuse's thought. Convinced that he has gone beyond Marx, he has actually returned to the Utopian, undemocratic positions Marx criticized as playing into the hands of reaction. For Marx, the emancipation of the working class depended upon its own historical struggles to improve its lot; it could not be effected by an élite party or group of supermen. And the view that genuine revolutionary social change must be preceded by "the revolution within," whether spiritual or biological, was for Marx the oldest text of social illusion. Human nature may be a historical variable, but this emphasis upon developing "a new type of man" reeks of totalitarianism. It brings to mind the horrid definition of the intellectual, attributed to Stalin, as "the engineer of the human soul."

Disappointed with the workers, Marcuse finds his last best hope for a truly free society—described as if it were a sexy heaven on earth—in active minorities, "mainly among the young middle-class intelligentsia and the ghetto population." Although a minority, they represent "the common interest" of the oppressed majority, and are therefore justified in acting in its name. Marcuse leaves it far from clear that these groups have escaped the contagion of their society; and by his own account of their behavior they seem rather a comedown from the kindly supermen of the "new sensibility."

So far, Marcuse's ideas are a rehash of discredited fantasies. But when he begins to apply them to politics, they become mischievous. Absurdities in the marketplace tend to prepare the way for atrocities. Marcuse admits that existing democracy "provides the most favorable ground for the development and organization of dissent." But he scorns it. The very reforms, concessions and freedoms that democracy makes possible lull the majority into endorsing decisions not in its best interests, as Marcuse understands those interests. What good is its freedom if the majority chooses wrongly— as it must do in a class society? Therefore, he concludes, social change must take place not through "the rules and methods of democratic legality" but through extra-parliamentary "rebellion."

Among the reasons he offers for rejecting existing democracy as spurious is that government is "factually exercised" by élites. But this is true of any representative system. The relevant questions are: To whom are élites responsible? Is their power limited by other powers, judicial and social? Can they be changed or dismissed by expressions of the majority will? Disregard these questions, as Marcuse does, and the whole distinction between dictatorship and democracy becomes meaningless, and Orwell's double-speak becomes the public idiom.

Marcuse frankly acknowledges that he is prepared to replace the present existing élite by another governing élite which does *not* have majority support. He follows Lenin and Stalin here, not Marx. One naturally asks: What guarantee is there that the regime of his undemocratic élite will not be as repressive as Stalin's or Hitler's? Marcuse's response is hardly reassuring:

"Our entire discussion was based on the proposition that the revolution would be liberating only if it were carried out by the non-repressive forces stirring in existing society. The proposition is no more, and no less, than a hope."

For this forlorn hope—since the "new man" is still in the limbo of the unborn—Marcuse is willing to incite to rebellion and insurrection despite their tragic costs.

In selecting those who are to revolt, Marcuse's élitism is at its most arrogant. He pins his hope for rebellions on some student groups, some elements among the *lumpenproletariat,* but mainly on the Negroes. In the past, when the civil-rights movement showed that black people wanted the same goods and services as whites, Marcuse sneered at their capitulation to middle-class values, and was indifferent to whether they had the right to vote. Since the ghetto riots, he has discovered their force for rebellion. "The ghetto population of the United States constitutes such a force. Confined to small areas of living and dying, it can be more easily organized and directed." (sic!)

It is not likely that the black population will permit itself to be directed by Marcuse or anyone else in behalf of a forlorn hope.

The spirit that pervades this book, and most of Marcuse's writings, is more Prussian than Marxist. He doesn't argue his positions as much as he proclaims them. Confused by Hegel, the law of contradiction has no terrors for him. Inconvenient facts are simply ignored. He writes, for example, "as the common Enemy of all capitalism, communism promoted the organization of a common interest superseding the inter-capitalist differences and conflicts." How, then, account for capitalist England and capitalist America making common cause with Communist Russia against capitalist Germany in World War II? Although he speaks of the direct democracy of the rebels, of the "new men," he has no conception of the ethics of democracy, for he unqualifiedly endorses Castro's regime and "the Chinese cultural revolution." Apparently insensate, mindless glorification of Mao as an illustration of "biological solidarity" at work; and the breaking of the fingers of musicians who play Western music in China is an expression of "instinctual creative force." This is pure Orwell.

In the interests of a libertarian society, Marcuse would ruthlessly repress all who differ with him about how to make man and society freer. He enjoys rights in this spurious democracy he is frank to admit he would deny to others. The most effective response to his dogmatic intolerance is not to subject him to the repressions he would visit upon others, nor to deprive him of the rewards, comforts and protection of the welfare state to which he clings with as great a tenacity as those whom he denounces for their spiritual corruption, but rather to expose his views most widely to the criticism and laughter they deserve.

For Marcuse's reputation as a thinker is not likely to survive a careful reading of this book.*

*Refers to Marcuse, *An Essay on Liberation*, Boston: The Beacon Press.

Robert Welch founded the John Birch Society in 1958. He is dedicated to fighting the international Communist conspiracy. He opposes the liberal Establishment's control of public opinion in the United States, and sharply distinguishes between the republican and democratic forms of government.

Now, how do we go about asking men, in the words of Santayana, to "trust the soul's invincible surmise?" How do we go about all of the immediately more urgent tasks and undertakings which I have been foreshadowing—of which this moral and ethical base is the bedrock, to be chiseled into a more recognizable foundation as we go along? We come at long last to the question of ways and means and methods—to what our bureaucratic friends would call implementation—in connection with all of these plans and aims and hopes.

In the earlier sections of this long and fragmented discourse I used the word "organization" several times in connection with suggested future plans. It was a very broad and inaccurate term, employed because no other was available to convey the thought there being expressed without too much interruption of that thought. But the "organization" of which I am thinking is of an entirely different nature from anything that word might at first bring to your minds, just as the raising of resources is of a far more drastic and more *realistic* nature than anything attempted in this fight before.

I am proposing, as the most immediately tangible outcome of this meeting, the formation of The John Birch Society. And I ask you not to give undue thought, at present, to the name. In the small packets for each of you there are copies of my little book, *The Life of John Birch.* I hope you will read it when you have the opportunity, if you have not already done so—or even if you have.

You will find that John Birch, a young fundamentalist Baptist preacher from Macon, Georgia, who did as much as any other one man, high or low, to win our war and the Chinese war against the Japanese in China, was murdered by the Chinese Communists at the first opportunity after the war because of the powerful resistance he would have been able to inspire against them. You will find, and I believe agree, that John Birch possessed in his own character *all* of those noble traits and ideals which we should like to see become symbolized by The John Birch Society. And the kind of life, of peaceful opportunity and responsibility, which John Birch wanted for his fellow Americans, and for his Chinese friends, and for all men of good will, is exactly the kind of life we should like to see possible everywhere. We could use other names than that of John Birch, of course. But I think you will gradually see, as time and meditation do their work, that the name is fitting, significant, and helpful, in many ways and for many reasons.

It is important that it should be, for I am not suggesting any ephemeral organization of loose ties and uncertain loyalties. It is my fervent hope that The John Birch Society will last for hundreds of years, and exert an increasing influence for the temporal good and the spiritual ennoblement of mankind throughout those centuries. For I am staking my whole aspiration to play my part, in forwarding man's one increasing purpose, on whatever can be accomplished through The John Birch Society. I want no other title than that of its Founder, and have no other ambition for anything resembling fame or historical remembrance.

The John Birch Society is to be a monolithic body. A republican form of government or of organization has many attractions and advantages, under certain favorable conditions. But under less happy circumstances it lends itself too readily to infiltration, distortion and disruption. And democracy, of course, in government or organization, as the Greeks and Romans both found out, and as I believe every man in this room clearly recognizes—democracy is merely a deceptive phrase, a weapon of demagoguery, and a perennial fraud.*

For withstanding the stresses and strains of internal differences and external animosities, throughout changing political climates over long periods of time; for the building of morale and loyalty and a feeling of unified purpose and closely knit strength; for effective functioning in periods of crisis and a permanence of high dedication throughout more peaceful decades; for these and many other reasons The John Birch Society will operate under completely authoritative control at all levels. The fear of tyrannical oppression of individuals, and other arguments against the authoritative structure in the form of governments, have little bearing on the case of a voluntary association, where the authoritative power can be exercised and enforced only by persuasion. And what little validity they do have is outweighed by the advantages of firm and positive direction of the Society's energies. Especially for the near future, and for the fight against Communism which is the first great task of the Society, it is imperative that all the strength we can muster be subject to smoothly functioning direction from the top. As I have said before, no collection of debating societies is ever going to stop the Communist conspiracy from taking us over, and I have no intention of adding another frustrated group to their number. We mean business every step of the way.

There are many reasons why, in the fight immediately ahead, we cannot stop for parliamentary procedures or a lot of arguments among ourselves. One is the increasing confusion, cleverly planned by the Communists, as to what persons, books, activities and organ-

*Our Liberal critics would have you believe that this statement, for an American, is practically heresy. This is because these same Liberals have been working so long and so hard to convert our republic into a democracy, and to make the American people believe that it is *supposed to be a democracy*. Nothing could be farther from the truth than that insidiously planted premise. Our founding fathers knew a great deal about history and government, and they had very nearly a clean slate on which to write the blueprint for our own. They gave us a republic because they considered it the best of all forms of government. They visibly spurned a democracy as probably the worst of all forms of government. But our past history and our present danger indicate that they were right in both particulars.

izations really are anti-Communist. In other words we are now being more and more divided and deceived, by accepting within our walls more and more Trojan horses, large and small, made out of all kinds of timbers, and with all kinds of enemy agents inside. Some of them have no more harmful purpose than merely to drain off, into innocuous wastefulness, money and effort which might otherwise find its way into really patriotic and anti-Communist activities. Others are primarily designed to offer protective coloration to Communists who can thus get themselves publicized as active in anti-Communist organizations. Others, like the very pretentious American Friends of Vietnam, in my opinion form major parts of a whole plan and drive for gradually turning some country over to the Communists, while pretending to be leading the opposition. But most of them are intended, as much as anything else, to add to and create the increasing confusion which makes even the most patriotic American feel utterly frustrated in trying to figure out who is friend and who is enemy—and hence more willing to give up the whole struggle.

Now there are ways of sizing up both individuals and organizations in this battle, which come only with experience, a knowledge of the interlocking pieces and personalities, and a feel for the way the Communists work. And while of course I can make mistakes too, I know from the way my opinion of various characters, formed entirely independently, has then proved to coincide with the opinion of J. B. Matthews, time after time when I have had a chance to check with him, that I have a fairly sensitive and accurate nose in this area. And of course I also have the benefit of J. B.'s files, almost incredible memory, and judgment built out of long experience, to lean on whenever I wish. So we do not intend to be frustrated by indecisions of this nature nor to let our members be. But the confusion and the problem will get steadily worse; and the need for somebody who can simply say "Help this guy, or let him help you, but stay away from that one" is also going to increase.

Actually, we are going to cut through the red tape and parliamentary briar patches and road blocks of confused purpose with direct authority at every turn. The men who join The John Birch Society during the next few months or few years are going to be doing so primarily because they believe in me and what I am doing and are willing to accept my leadership anyway. And we are going to use that loyalty, like every other resource, to the fullest possible advantage that we can. Whenever and wherever, either through infiltration by the enemy or honest differences of opinion, that loyalty ceases to be sufficient to keep some fragment in line, we are not going to be in the position of having the Society's work weakened by raging debates. We are not going to have factions developing on the two-sides-to-every-question theme.*

Those members who cease to feel the necessary degree of loyalty can either resign or will be put out before they build up any splintering following of their own inside the Society. As I have said, we mean business every step of the way. We can allow for differences of opinion. We shall need and welcome advice. And we expect to use the normal measure of diplomacy always called for in dealing with human beings. But whenever differences of opinion become translated into a lack of loyal support, we shall have short cuts for eliminating both without going through any congress of so-called democratic processes. *Otherwise, Communist infiltrators could bog us down in interminable disagreements, schisms, and feuds before we ever became seriously effective.†*

*The folly of the two-sides-to-every-question argument is emphasized in a brief story we have told elsewhere and often. The minister had preached a superb sermon. It had moved his whole congreagation to a determination to lead nobler and more righteous lives. Then he said: "And that, of course, is the Lord's side. Now for the *next* half hour, and to be fair, I'll present the devil's side. You can then take your choice."

†The whole theme of these several paragraphs, and the monolithic structure of the Society, have of course been seized on by the Liberals (and worse) as the basis of vicious and persistent attacks against the Society and myself. Their criticism is about as slippery and phony as everything else the Liberals turn out today under the label of argument.

Our members are told specifically and emphatically in our bulletins, about once every three months, never to carry out any of our requests or to do anything for the Society that is against their individual consciences or even contrary to their best judgement. If they find themselves too constantly and continuously in disagreement with our activities, then probably they do not belong in the Society and may wish to resign. But it is only a real troublemaker that we put out of the Society ourselves. So far, with many thousands of members and two years of experience, we have dropped less than a dozen. (We have had a total of about one hundred resignations in the two years). One of the two dropped directly by the Home Office was a

The purpose of The John Birch Society, as officially stated, will be to promote less government, more responsibility, and a better world. The purpose, as unofficially described and discussed among ourselves, will be exactly the same thing. Our short-range purpose, our long-range purpose, and our lasting purpose, is to promote less government, more responsibility, and a better world. That says it

lonesome widow who did not have the slightest interest in, or idea of, what The John Birch Society was all about. She simply wanted companionship and a place to go, and she constantly bogged down her chapter meeting with her personal affairs. The other turned out not even to be a member. But he had been going regularly to the meetings of one of our chapters, posing as an important member of our Home Chapter, and turning the meetings more and more—before we knew about it—into sessions in advanced anti-Semitism. We simply asked this man to stay away from our meetings, straightened out the chapter, and have had no further trouble from that source.

We have refused to accept just one chapter since the Society was founded, and this was because of the extreme racist views of some of its prospective members. How little we go along with such views is shown by the fact that we have two all-Negro chapters, of which we are very proud, and several chapters in northern states with good citizens of both white and colored races who meet together. We are bitterly opposed to *forced* integration, in schools or *anywhere else*, but on far sounder grounds than the "racial superiority" arguments. It is because, according to the Constitution, the Federal Government has absolutely nothing to do, legally, with public education; because every American, white or black, should have the right to select his own associates for every enterprise and occasion; and because all of the trouble over integration—which is doing inestimable damage to both the black and white races—is Communist inspired, encouraged, and implemented for Communist purposes. And while these remarks may appear to be of a rambling nature, it seems well worth while to get them down on paper at this point to avoid misunderstandings in the future.

When we were viciously attacked in one of the Midwestern papers a few months ago, on the basis of the monolithic structure of the Society, our members came to our support with a veritable flood of letters to that paper, quoting passage after passage from the Blue Book to show how unfounded were the charges advanced. Our members themselves are fully aware, from actual experience as well as from study of our materials, that the monolithic structure is purely for the sake of *efficiency, effectiveness,* and *steadfastness* of purpose within the Society itself—from which anybody can resign, with our good will and good wishes, at the drop of a hat. Our members themselves soon find that there is absolutely no reason to object to this protection of the Society internally against infiltration, splintering, and inside fights.

And yet our critics frequently and vehemently charge that we are a *fascist* organization, far more dangerous and tyrannical than the Communists themselves. We don't know how they attempt to justify any such charges, but in any event we should like to call to their attention *one* difference between the Communists and ourselves. You join the Communist Party, and you are told what to do. You refuse to do it enough times, and you are shot in some dark alley or pushed off a subway platform in front of a moving train. You join The John Birch Society, and you are asked to do certain things, *if you agree.* You refuse to do them enough times—and we give you your money back! Somehow it does seem to us that there is a difference.

all. It is, I think, simple, understandable, and all-inclusive as to the goals for which we should strive.

In seeking the first two of those broad objectives, less government and more responsibility, we shall make all the use we can of educational action on the political front. In always seeking more slowly, but with an inner unswerving resolution, to make this a better world, we shall use all means and depend on all efforts that are consistent with the faith which supplies our motivation.

In the political arena we shall try to make the word Americanism useful as a constructive opposite of Communism, and attract to our support many americanists who may not be members of our Society. But the words americanism and americanist are simply semantic weapons, and have no direct connection with The John Birch Society.

Members of The John Birch Society, not only in the United States, but anywhere in the world, not only *can* be good patriots in their respective countries, but necessarily *will* be. For internationalism, as it is conceived and promoted today, is an attempt to impose more government and a more centralized one-world government on all of us everywhere. For that reason it is automatically contrary to everything we stand for, and one of the movements we shall oppose with all the strength we can.

An honestly intended federation of nations, in some later years or decades, for the legitimate purpose of increasing the freedom of individuals, goods, and cultures to cross national boundaries, and hence for the very purpose of decreasing governmental restrictions on individuals, is something we would support with all our hearts. But until the intended Communist Internationale now called the United Nations has been wiped out or made over from the bottom up, our attitude towards so-called internationalism is made clear and uncompromising by the stated purpose of the Society. As Richard Cobden said, "peace will come to this earth when her peoples have as much as possible to do with each other; their governments the least possible." It is axiomatic that we shall strive to hasten the world's approach to those conditions in every way we can.

K. R. Valhal is a contributor to Statecraft. Statecraft supported the Presidential candidacy of George Wallace.

On March 29, in Detroit, Michigan, a fighting unit of armed black revolutionaries brutally murdered one policeman and seriously wounded another as they went about their routine rounds. After the murder, the police rounded up a number of suspects caught with weapons. Nine of the suspects were proven by paraffin tests to have recently fired a weapon. When the accused were taken into the court room of Judge George W. Crockett, Jr. (a black power judge), they were immediately released. In spite of the mass of evidence, the savage black power judge claimed that there was no "legal evidence" against the defendants. When the prosecutor ordered the police to immediately rearrest these wild savages, he himself was charged with contempt of court by the vicious black power judge. Crockett ordered the release of all but three of the defendants. Crockett has become a real hero to liberals and black power savages. The scene in Detroit brings back unpleasant memories of the post-Civil War reconstruction era when illiterate savages and their white liberal counterparts ran the governments of the Southern states.

The situation above exemplifies the death of law in the United States. All conservative talk about "constitutionality" is meaningless in the face of massive overt lawlessness created by the United States Supreme Court. We at *Statecraft* respect the concept of law, but the American Nation is now engaged in an internal crisis which has led to the total and absolute destruction of all concepts of traditional law. To combat this destructive crisis, we can not look back to the Constitutional Convention in 1787. We must, instead, look forward to the revolutionary struggle for the future of America.

We have previously discussed the nature of the personality of the American Revolutionary and of the Statist political program. The time has come to discuss the nature of the coming Revolution itself.

THE DEATH OF DEMOCRACY

The concept of democracy is an idea born of the noblest sentiments of man. The democratic idea allows man to control his own government. Democracy supposes that the people will choose a government based upon a free exchange of alternative proposals before an election. Empirical observations quickly reveal that these conditions are no longer prevalent within our land.

Democracy assumes an equal presentation of opposing ideas. Today both major political parties are under the total control of and in subservience to the liberal totalitarian enemy. This situation in and of itself would be easily remedied if the liberal enemy did not also have absolute control over the major means of communications. *It is through the communications control that the liberal is totally shaping the reality of our present environment. Modern mass media,* including television, motion pictures, radio, mass circulation magazines and newspapers *are almost all under absolute liberal control.* Any subject or person not favorable to the liberal enemy is consistently subjected to smears, lies, mass distortions, and the worst kind of mud slinging. These attacks are aimed at anybody who does not accept the totalitarian liberal collectivist ideology. Occasionally the liberal media gives a token frown to its Communist domestic allies. *The major political purpose of modern mass media is to create the mass image,* such as that of the Kennedy family—the new liberal dynasty chosen to rule America in perpetuity, as uncrowned kings of the land. When the traditional two party system, as it is presently constituted, holds an election the liberal mass media usually plays tweedle dum or tweedle dee. However, when a truly patriotic candidate enters upon the scene (either by capturing temporarily one of the existing parties or by creating a third party of his own) he is immediately and totally denounced. *Control of the mass media by the liberals has created, in effect, thought control.* Thus, we advance toward an Orwellian society. In a mass environment, *with almost total thought control there can be no possibility of any kind of democracy.* When political opponents are unable to present their ideas in an equal manner there can be no democracy. When Kennedys can spend millions of dollars to create an "image" there can be no democracy. When the people of a state are denied the right to vote on the control of their own property there certainly can be no democracy. The liberals have done even that however, and have taken away the right of the people to democratically review by popular vote such liberal tyranny as forced housing laws and school busing. *The liberals are so satanic and devious that they have in fact succeeded in destroying democracy in the very name of democracy.*

The death of democracy was also helped by *natural causes.* As America advances into the totally technical age, we are becoming more and more dependent upon scientists and technocrats to keep our society functioning and producing. More and more decisions in government are being made by people who are classified as either technocrats or scientists. Such government jobs as those of air pollution control expert and traffic engineer (for example) cannot be subject to democratic election. These jobs are supposed to be filled by competence. *As our society becomes more complex, most of the governmental decision making processes and power will reside in the hands of these scientists and technocrats who can never be subject to election. Thus as the majority of government power passes naturally into the hands of the non-electable,* the last glimpse of democracy fades.

Today democracy is almost totally dead. The advance of historical forces creates the impossibility of reviving the dying patient. Democracy is dying of a combination of natural and induced causes. The natural cause being the technical advance and the induced cause being that of the liberal march to totalitarianism. We must now abandon wasteful attempts at using the traditional democratic political methods to achieve national power. The liberals have known of democracy's death for some time and have been using it only when it served to advance the liberal cause. In other words democracy is great if it will give everyone who will vote liberal the chance to vote, but democracy is evil if the American people choose to retain their own right to control the use of their property or choose to retain control over the education of their own children. *The liberal double standard is simple—everything which promotes liberalism is moral and everything which hinders it is immoral.*

The death of democracy means that *the day of elections is over.* It is quite true that a number of local and even state elections will continue to produce victories for patriotic citizens. The national trend however, is permanently set by the above combination of natural and liberal forces. *There is absolutely no chance whatsoever at any time in the future for any patriot to win control, through elections, of the Executive Branch of the Federal Government.* It is quite certain that had Wallace won the 1968 election he would have immediately been assassinated by agents of the liberal-Communist controlled CIA. The plain fact is that the liberals will not tolerate (under any condition) the election of a patriot with a pro-American outlook. *The liberals will always resort to force when necessary to achieve their political ends*—whether it is in the case of a barber who wants to cut only white people's hair or parents who do not want their children bused miles away from their own home.

We must of course continue to support democracy where it still functions at the state and local levels. We should not be obsessed however with these regional situations. Our major concern should be the conquest of *National* power. He who controls the nation, ultimately controls all the subdivisions therein. We should no longer waste our time on a delusion of a possible National election victory. We must now be prepared to organize an army of the right to fight in the coming revolution.

THE REVOLUTION

The liberals have used the doctrine of extreme permissiveness to destroy traditional conservative opposition. One of the chief spokesmen for this permissiveness was Doctor Benjamin Spock, upon whose advice millions of parents raised their children. America is now reaping the harvest of the seeds of destruction sown by Spock and his liberal permissiveness in the outgrowth of the mass white trash-anarchist hippy movement. The SDS itself is an army of Spockites, who were trained to destroy under the doctrine of Spockish liberalism.

When the liberals used permissivism as a political tactic to gain power, they accidentally created their own Frankenstein monster. Although the doctrine of liberalism attacks the concept of authority, *the covert goal of liberalism is now and has always been total authority by the liberals over every aspect of the life of man. To gain this authority, the liberals have had to denounce the very concept they are seeking.* The liberals have always made use of anarchy to justify increasing their own political power and increases in mass giveaways of the taxpayers' hard-earned money. As stated in a previous article *the liberals are deliberately creating a situation of short-term anarchy to justify the establishment of an absolute Orwellian totalitarian liberal government.* The liberals have seriously miscalculated their ability to stop the uncontrollable advance of anarchy. Even now they themselves are suffering attacks from their own anarchistic creations—the SDS and others like them. The liberals failed to understand that nihilism and anarchy are impossible to use as a *directed* political force. It is most certainly possible to take advantage of a nihilistic or anarchistic situation. But it is totally impossible to use mobs of anarchists and nihilists for any long-term political goal. *The mobs will not take sufficient political discipline.* The liberals' lust for total power is so great that they would rather destroy everything around them than turn over power to the one group of people who would restore order and authority—the productive and patriotic citizenry.

Revolutions are not created by men or political parties alone.

Revolutions are, instead, created by a combination of historical events and the abilities of great political leaders. All of the historical forces are now in motion to create a violent revolution in America. No amount of traditional conservative wishing away or hand-wringing can stop this revolution. The only way to stop it would be for the government to display a massive show of authority and remove all the potential revolutionary leaders from the physical presence of America. Such overt forceful action by the liberals will never come about because it is diametrically opposed to their long-term goal of total power via anarchy. *The only people who would be inclined to use the force of government against the coming revolution will never be able to obtain national political power through the traditional political system. There is no effective way for patriots to prevent the coming revolution.* The patriots and producers of America have only one choice: *whether to fight or whether to lie down and die.* The revolutionary situation will be aided by massive economic fluctuations, which in turn will make more people aware of the political crisis. Many of these people can be recruited into our own patriotic action organizations. The revolution, once started, cannot be stopped. *The only solution for American patriots and producers is to organize now to fight in the revolution to defend America from the massive onslaught of jungle savagery.*

THE ARMY OF THE RIGHT

Our duty must now be to raise an army of citizens to defend our nation from internal destruction. This Army of the Right must not just be an army, but should be, instead, the total political organization *capable of operating the government once we have achieved power.* Far too many people talk about "overthrowing the government" without being competent to run a new government after they would overthrow the old government. We must, in fact, be able to create a shadow government made up of competent individuals in all governmental fields. Every action unit of our party should be a disciplined political unit. We are not interested in individual forays against unimportant liberals. *Our aim must be no less than the total overthrow of liberalism in all facets of American society.* It would be a serious mistake to concentrate solely upon the government, for liberalism is entrenched in all American social institutions: the church, the schools, the economy, the mass communication system and finally the government itself. *The overthrow of liberalism and the coming revolution cannot be accomplished by any half baked coup d'etat aimed solely at the center of government.* It is true that we might raise sufficient men to capture the city of Washington, but what good would that do when the rest of the country would be in the hands of the enemy? Our aim, therefore, must be to create a mass army of aroused citizens willing to take up arms and fight for America against the liberal enemy and the other destructive forces.

We state here that *the social contract between the citizens and government requires a mutual interest between both.* We use the word "citizens," not just residents, but active producing citizens of the nation. We do not consider nonproductive and destructive people to be worthy of American citizenship. The first duty of the citizens is to give loyalty to that government which gives them protection. Contrary to previous ideas, the state does not serve man nor does man serve the state. *The relationship of man and the state is one of mutuality. They must serve each other's interests. When the government breaks its part of the social contract by refusing to give protection to the citizens, it is not due any loyalty from the nation's citizens.* The decent and productive citizens of America should have absolutely no loyalty to a liberal government which has become their *enemy.* Every action of the liberal government has become an action against productivity and against patriotism. To-day the situation is so bad that the liberal government is brutalizing even our small children at the hands of wild savages, strictly to satisfy the liberal political lust for power. Any group of people who victimize millions of school children, through such devices as busing, should be taken out and lined up against a wall and shot.

If we hope to win the revolution we must organize now. We must not be afraid of "radical" action to save our country—the men who stood at Valley Forge had no such fear. The *Statecraft* action unit in Alexandria, Virginia constitutes the first part of the New Army of Northern Virginia. This army must be joined by others across the country. The coming revolution will not be a civil war between different sections of the country. It would be instead a war of annihilation between the forces of destruction and the forces of production.

THE NATIONAL REVOLUTION

We who consider ourselves American nationalists and patriots must recognize that *our only chance to win the coming revolution is to create a revolutionary force of our own.* Our goal is to purge liberalism from all social institutions. This purge can only be accomplished by a truly revolutionary force. Such a revolutionary force can only be built up by the mass use of propaganda. Propaganda is the most vital tool in creating a revolutionary organization. We should, first, therefore concentrate all efforts on massive propaganda. Our propaganda should have the purpose of: (1) attracting recruits, (2) attacking the enemy, (3) awakening the public, (4) arousing fear in the hearts of our enemies, and (5) creating a psychological, charismatic mission of revolution within the movement.

The next step of revolutionary activity should be in the areas of organization and military training. These subjects will not be discussed in this article for purposes of space. It should be sufficient to state that *we should never strike by force unless we have a reasonable chance of succeeding.* We should also seek to convert as many members of the armed forces and police to our cause as possible. America's armed forces and police have been the group which has suffered the most physically from liberalism. The situation is so bad that the lives of our armed forces have become pawns in the international socialist chess game between the liberals and their Communist friends overseas. Many members of the armed forces and police should readily identify with the goals of the National Revolution. The National Revolution would restore the police and our armed forces to their proper place of social respect.

During this time we must create a professional group of patriotic agitators who will constantly stir up the citizens against the liberal enemy. When we have organized a sufficient number of people, our movement should come openly out onto the streets to demonstrate its strength and to strike fear into the heart of the liberal enemy. The open demonstration of our strength will itself attract new recruits to our cause. *We should try to avoid secret political conspiracies. Our goal is quite open. It is the total overthrow of liberalism from all areas of American life.* Our openness is our protection. We can use tactics somewhat similar to those of the militant leftists. At the time we emerge as a mass movement in public, we must have sufficient strength to block any liberal attempt to destroy us.

When the mass outbreak of anarchy occurs across the nation our people must be armed and ready to fight. Their first goal must be to suppress the immediate forces of anarchy—the savage mobs and their white trash allies. When we accomplish this goal, we must then turn the force of our violence against the liberal enemy. As the situation gets out of hand in the early stage of the revolution, the liberals will probably panic and call upon all available people to fight the mobs when they realize that they themselves are in physical danger. *This time of mass anarchy will be our opportunity to strike.* Thus like Alexander Kerensky, the liberals will have used an army which will turn and destroy them.

To those who say "let's not fight, let's not be too radical," I answer: your choice is between fighting to live or cowering to die. A victory of the forces of destruction who would surely destroy what is left of the private property system. Millions of American businessmen would probably be murdered. Millions of American workers and producers would be enslaved. Hundreds of thousands of others would fall victims to savage mobs. *Only a National Revolution can save America and only the willingness to overthrow liberalism by force can create in effect a National Revolutionary Organization.* Those who love America must now be prepared to defend her. America's defense is our holy mission in life. We must live solely for America. The future survival of the Nation is totally dependent upon the success of the National Revolution against liberal totalitarianism and its red and black allies of destruction.

PART IV

Beyond Democracy

Andrei Y. Vishinsky (1883–1954) was a Russian jurist and diplomat. He was chief prosecutor of the Moscow treason trials (1936–1938) and U.N. representative for the U.S.S.R. from 1953 to 1954.

Special attention should be given to the proscribed areas of free speech and to Vishinsky's analysis of the shortcomings of free speech in democracies.

Freedom of speech, of the press, of assembly, of meetings, of street parades and of demonstrations, being natural and indispensable conditions precedent to the manifestation of freedom of thought and freedom of opinion, are among the most important political freedoms. No society can be called democratic which does not afford its citizens all of them. Only in a state which actually guarantees these most important political freedoms, and in behalf of all citizens without exception, is expanded and completely logical democracy to be found.

While constitutions of bourgeois-democratic states ordinarily make a formal grant of these freedoms to all citizens without exception, every sort of limitation thereupon and all the capitalist social order in its entirety, have turned what are, in form, rights possessed by all citizens into rights actually possessed by a narrow and privileged minority only.* Freedom of assembly, "even in the most democratic bourgeois republic, is an empty phrase, since the rich have at their disposal all the best dwellings, social and private, as

*Even in Japan, a country where thought in an undesirable direction is per se subject to legal prosecution, the Constitution contains a hypocritical declaration as to granting freedom of the press to *all* citizens.

163

well as sufficient leisure for meetings (and protection thereof by the bourgeois mechanism of power). Proletarians of city and country, and small peasants, the vast majority of the population, have none of the three."*

And all the sharpness of even the formal limitations in the bourgeois legislation as to street parades as well as open-air meetings—mass meetings of the toilers, whom this form of meeting suits better than meeting indoors because of their lack of proper premises and the great number of those taking part—are usually particularly strict, including a complicated method of obtaining a permit, while the police, present under the pretense of protecting social order, are given broad powers, under diverse specious pretexts, to close these meetings when they find it necessary. The entire hypocrisy of bourgeois legislation regarding such "freedoms" is clearly expressed in the fact that in England, for example, it was impossible to assemble upon private property without the permission of the owner or upon state property without the permission of state organs.† Under such conditions the "right" of assembly requires per se no permit; permission is required only for the temporary occupation of a parcel of earth. The result necessary for the bourgeoisie is attained, while the semblance of "freedom" is not touched. Legislators of contemporary England have decided, nevertheless, to fill the existing gap in the sphere of legislative regulation of "freedom" of assembly, and in 1936 issued a special law (the Public Order Act)** concerning meetings and demonstrations. This law officially charged the police, after the example of continental bourgeois countries, with the duty of dispersing undesirable meetings and demonstrations and arresting those taking part in them—functions hitherto unofficially exercised by the English police.

In France the law of October 23, 1935, forbade street assemblies and required, as to street processions and demonstrations, a preliminary declaration concerning them, having granted to trustworthy organs of authority the right to forbid the proposed demon-

*Lenin (Russian ed.), Vol. XXIV, p. 9.
†Ivanovsky, *Manual of Public Law* (1910), p. 265.
**Cf. Albert Crek, *The Law Relating to Public Meetings and Processions* (London, 1937).

stration or street parade if they shall find that it may violate social order. For an inaccurate declaration, or for taking part in the organization of manifestations not declared, the law provides for the imprisonment for from fifteen days to six months and a fine up to 2,000 francs.* Freedom of assembly, meetings, and demonstrations in capitalist countries is most brilliantly illustrated by the numerous police attacks upon peaceful demonstrations of workers, the dispersal of the latter and the beating or shooting of those who took part in the demonstrations.

To turn freedom of meetings from a right which is mere form into an actual right of the toiling masses, "it is necessary at the outset to take from the exploiters all the social and elegant private buildings, to give leisure to the toilers, and to have the freedom of their meeting preserved by armed workers, not by petty nobles or capitalist officers with broken-down soldiers."†

Freedom of the press stands no better in countries of bourgeois democracy, inasmuch as "this freedom is a delusion so long as capitalists commandeer the better printing establishments and the largest stores of paper, and capital retains its power over the press —a power manifested throughout the world with a cynicism brilliant and cutting in proportion to the development of democracy and the republican social order, as in America."**

Bourgeois public law ordinarily regards the absence of preliminary censorship as the most essential and fundamental indication of freedom of the press. Thus, from this viewpoint, the U.S.A. or England, where such censorship has long since been abrogated, are rated as countries where the press is absolutely and completely free. In reality, in these countries the bond between the press and capital, the enslavement of the press by capital, appears perhaps more clearly than in any others. Thus in England the most influential conservative daily, the *Times*, is the organ of banks, connected through its directors with Lloyd's Bank, with the largest railroad companies, with insurance companies and with a number of the biggest capitalist firms (Armstrong, Vickers, and others). The *Daily*

* *Journal officiel* (1935), pp. 11, 203.
† Lenin (Russian ed.), Vol. XXIV, p. 9.
** *Ibid.*, p. 10.

Telegraph, the other very powerful organ of the press, likewise conservative, is considered the organ of heavy industry. The newspaper enterprises of Lords Rothermere and Beaverbrook uniting a number of newspaper trusts, dictate to their papers the direction in which social opinion is to be molded.*

Newspapers in the U.S.A. are still larger capitalist enterprises connected with specified banks and trusts in whose stock the capital of the newspaper owners is invested. Hearst, for example, a big American capitalist connected with war industry, banks, and concerns which are exploiting the countries of Latin and South America, owns twenty-nine papers with a total circulation of ten million readers. These papers, by order of Hearst, carry on a bloodthirsty agitation against the Communist Party, the revolutionary workers' movement and the U.S.S.R. How the freedom of the press are maintained by capitalists—is brilliantly told in the recent book of the talented American journalist George Seldes.† Freedom of the press consists essentially in the possibility of freely publishing the genuine, not the falsified, opinions of the toiling masses, rather than in the absence of preliminary censorship. This was clearly shown in the experience of the press in tsarist Russia.

The Revolution of 1905 compelled the tsarist government to abrogate a number of Draconian laws against the press, including that requiring editors to make a large preliminary deposit, that granting the administration the right to impose assessments on editors without court proceedings, and likewise that providing for the preliminary censorship of periodical publications in the cities and—from and after April 26, 1906—of "other than periodical" issues also. This by no means left the press free, however. The abolition of preliminary censorship was accompanied by increased strictness of subsequent censorship threatening, on the basis of Temporary Rules Concerning the Press (November 24, 1905), editor-publishers and

*Lord Northcliffe, owner of one of the newspaper trusts in England, in his pamphlet, *Newspapers and Their Millionaires*, openly declares: "Certain provincial papers, like certain London papers, are maintained by rich persons in order to strengthen their political or social position. There is nothing strange in this. . . . *The Westminster Gazette* was always a 'kept' paper, passing—over a long period of years—from one millionaire to another."

†George Seldes, *Freedom of the Press* (1937, Russian transl. by Kalmer).

authors with imprisonment for every sort of attempt to take seriously the freedom of the press declared by the "imperial" manifesto and by the very "rules" themselves.* Preliminary censorship was abolished, but confiscation, enormous fines, and the closing up of newspapers, which took on the character of an open epidemic from 1905 on, put such a noose around the neck of the press that it appeared strangled.†

To make the press actually free "it is necessary at the outset to take away from capital the possibility of hiring writers, buying printing houses, and bribing papers, to which end it is necessary to overthrow the yoke of capital and to overthrow the exploiters and crush their resistance."**

Even before the October Revolution, Lenin, by way of preparing the masses to seize power, wrote (October, 1917):

> Only the Soviet government could have successfully struggled with such pitiful injustice as the seizure by capitalists—with the aid of millions pillaged from the people—of the biggest printing presses and most of the newspapers. It is necessary to shut down the bourgeois counterrevolutionary papers,†† to confiscate their printing establishments, to declare private advertisement in newspapers a state monopoly, and to transfer them to the administrative paper published by the Soviets, and telling the peasants the truth. Only in this way is it possible and our boundless duty to knock out of the hands of the bourgeoisie a mighty instrument for lying and defaming with impunity, for deceiving the people, for leading the peasantry into error, and for preparing counterrevolution.

The victory of the Socialist Revolution in the USSR, which transferred to the hands of the worker class, along with the basic means

---

*E. A. Vallo de Barr, in his *Freedom of the Russian Press After October 17, 1905* (published in Samara in 1906), writes bitterly that the Temporary Rules (above referred to) involuntarily recall the famous words of Figaro, replete with irony, as to establishing the freedom of the press on condition that the press should not touch the powers nor the church nor policy nor morality nor officials nor honorary classes nor anybody who has any connection with anyone.

†Cf. *Martyrology of the Russian Press*, appended to Vallo de Barr's text.

**Lenin (Russian ed.), Vol. XXIV, p. 10.

††Naming *Rech, Russkoe Slovo*, and the like.

and instruments of production, buildings for meetings, printing houses, and stores of printing paper, meant the broad realization of freedom of speech, of the press, of assembly, and of meetings. For the first time in the world, these became genuine freedoms of the masses.

> To the end of assuring in behalf of the toilers actual freedom of assembly, the RSFSR, conceding the right of its citizens freely to organize assemblies, meetings, processions, and the like, grants to the worker class and the poorest peasantry the use of all premises suitable for the organization of popular assemblies, together with their furniture, lighting, and heat (Art. 15 of the RSFSR Constitution, 1918).

Having given the toilers freedom of speech, assemblies, street parades, press, and so on, the Soviet government explicitly excluded the nonlabor classes from enjoyment of this freedom. Lenin spoke on this matter at the First Congress of the Comintern: Any class-conscious workman who has not broken with his class will understand immediately that it would be folly to promise freedom of meetings to exploiters at a time (and in a setting) when the latter are resisting their overthrow and defending their privileges. When the bourgeoisie was revolutionary it did not give "freedom of assembly" to monarchists and nobles who had summoned foreign troops and had "assembled" to organize attempts at restoration either in England in 1649 or in France in 1793. If the present bourgeoisie, long since turned reactionary, demands of the proletariat that, notwithstanding the future resistance of capitalists to their expropriation, the proletariat guarantee in advance freedom of assembly to the exploiters, the workers will merely smile at the bourgeoisie's hypocrisy.* Having assured genuine freedom of the press to the toilers, the Soviet government did not extend this freedom to nonlaboring strata. Concerning freedom of the press, the first Soviet Constitution, of 1918, said:

> To the end of assuring in behalf of the toilers actual freedom to express their opinions, the RSFSR annuls the dependence

*Lenin (Russian ed.), Vol. XXIV, p. 9.

of the press upon capital and hands over to the worker class and poorer peasantry all the technical and material resources for publishing newspapers, pamphlets, books, and all sorts of other productions of the press, and gauarantees that they may circulate freely throughout the land (Art. 14).

One of the first and most important measures of the Soviet government in assuring actual freedom of the press in behalf of the toilers was the closing—by the War-Revolutionary Committee in the very first days after the revolution in Petrograd—of numerous organs of the counterrevolutionary press. Enemies of the proletariat raised a hullabaloo on this occasion, screaming about violation of the freedom of the press. In sanctioning these actions of the War-Revolutionary Committee, the decree concerning the press, issued by the Council of People's Commissars (October 27/November 9, 1917),* made it clear to the toilers that the liberal screen of "free press" is actually a cover for the freedom for the "have" classes (after possessing themselves of the lion's share of all the press) to poison the minds of the masses and introduce confusion into their consciousness without let or hindrance. "Everyone knows," the decree said further, "that the bourgeois press is one of the bourgeoisie's most mighty weapons. Particularly was it impossible at the critical moment when the new authority, the authority of the workers and peasants, was only in the process of being stabilized to leave this weapon—at such moments no less dangerous than bombs and machine guns—entirely in the hands of the foe.

This decree evoked sharp attacks from the "Left" SR's as well as from the Trotskyists and Bukharinists who, traitors to the socialist revolution, masked themselves under the name "Bolsheviks." It is extraordinarily important to note that it was at the very session of the All-Russian Central Executive Committee, November 4/17, 1917, when this decree concerning the press was under consideration, and after the Bolshevik resolution completely approving this step of the Council of the People's Commissars had been adopted by majority vote, that the "Left" SR's, in token of their protest,

*Cy. 1917, No. 1, Art. 7.

declared that they refused to accept responsibility and recalled their representatives from the War-Revolutionary Committee and other organs. In alliance with the "Left" SR's, a group of strike-breakers—fascist hirelings in the persons of Rykov and others—came out with a vehement declaration about leaving their posts, allegedly because of the Bolshevik Party's refusal to come to terms with the tolerationist parties and also because of the supposedly "terrorist" policy of Soviet authority (an allusion to the closing of counterrevolutionary organs of the press).

The great October Socialist Revolution destroyed each and every possibility of the rich bribing the press and capitalists being free to employ their wealth to fabricate social opinion. It created in the Soviet state, for the first time in the world, a truly free press, a means of expressing the opinions of the toilers with genuine freedom. Guided by the Bolshevik All-Russian Communist Party, the press in the USSR became a mighty instrument for the true education of the masses, for their self-organization, for fostering new discipline among them, for criticism and self-criticism, and for mobilizing the masses to eliminate all shortcomings in state and social building—for the building of socialism.

Paralleling the growth of our socialist land, our press has increased and grown strong. In 1936 the number of copies of our papers struck off at each issue was 37,971,000, almost fourteen times greater than that in 1913. The total number of newspapers was 9,250, almost eleven times as many as in 1913. The total number of books struck off was 571,071,000, more than six and one-half times the number of 1913. Newspapers in the USSR appear in 69 languages, and books in 111 languages, of the USSR peoples.* Hundreds of thousands of worker correspondents and peasant correspondents take an active part in all types of periodicals.

Soviet law stands on guard for the Soviet press. The law, Concerning the Chief Administration for Literature and Publication (June 6, 1931),† provides for political-ideological control of productions of the press and obligates the Administration, a constituent

---

*Cf. *Twenty Years of Soviet Authority* (1937), pp. 103–104.
†Cy. 1931, No. 31, Art. 273.

part of the RSFSR People's Commissariat for Education, "to prohibit the issuance, publication, and circulation of productions: *(a)* containing agitation and propaganda against Soviet authority and the proletarian dictatorship; *(b)* publishing state secrets; *(c)* arousing nationalist and religious fanaticism; or *(d)* of a pornographic character."

The RSFSR Criminal Code (Arts. 182, 185) prosecutes those who violate Soviet legislation concerning the press.

A number of circulars of the USSR Public Prosecutor's Office have instructed prosecutors as to the necessity of the utmost endeavor to have the courts apply stern punitive measures to persons persecuting worker and peasant correspondents and thereby encroaching upon the freedom of the press.* The first assemblies of the organizations and societies of the toilers take place according to the plan of these organizations and societies and upon the call of the proper executive organs thereof without any permission whatsoever from the organs of authority. District, area, and regional (territorial) councils, conferences, and congresses are called with the permission of the regional (territorial) executive committees and the Council of People's Commissars of the Autonomous SSR. Republic congresses, conferences, and councils, with the participation of representatives of the localities, are summoned with the permission of the appropriate Republic Council of People's Commissars. Congresses, conferences, and councils summoned by state organs of the USSR, by All-Union cooperatives and by social organizations are summoned with the permission of the Council of People's Commissars of the USSR.*

Full initiative as to street parades and demonstrations in the USSR is given to the social organizations and societies of the toilers and, in the first instance, to the Communist Party as the directing nucleus of all these social (as well as of state) organizations. Rules of the People's Commissariat for Internal Affairs relative to the

*Cf. the circular of Dec. 3, 1933, "Concerning the Struggle with the Persecution of Worker and Peasant Correspondents" (*For Socialist Legality*, 1934, No. 1).
*Cf. directive of the USSR Council of People's Commissars (May 15, 1935, Cz. 1935, No. 26, Art. 209) and of the All-Russian Central Executive Committee and RSFSR Council of People's Commissars (June 20, 1935, Cy. 1936, No. 6, Art. 29).

organization of these parades and demonstrations contain rules of a purely technical character touching the observance of social order, supervision over which is a responsibility of the worker-peasant militia.

In our state, naturally, there is and can be no place for freedom of speech, press, and so on for the foes of socialism. Every sort of attempt on their part to utilize to the detriment of the state—that is to say, to the detriment of all the toilers—these freedoms granted to the toilers must be classified as a counterrevolutionary crime to which Article 58, Paragraph 10, or one of the corresponding articles of the Criminal Code is applicable.

Freedom of speech, of the press, of assembly, of meetings, of street parades, and of demonstrations are the property of all the citizens in the USSR, fully guaranteed by the state upon the single condition that they be utilized in accord with the interests of the toilers and to the end of strengthening the socialist social order. Their breadth and genuineness and the assuredness of their socialist character are confirmed in Article 125 of the Stalin Constitution:

> In conformity with the interests of the toilers and to the end of strengthening the socialist social order, citizens of the USSR are guaranteed by law; *(a)* freedom of speech, *(b)* freedom of the press, *(c)* freedom of assembly and meetings, and *(d)* freedom of street parades and demonstrations. These civil rights are assured by granting to the toilers and their organizations the uses of printing establishments, stocks of paper, public buildings, streets, means of communication, and other material conditions essential for their realization.

Harold C. Gardiner, S.J., is the author of The Catholic Viewpoint on Censorship, *in which the following selection appears in Chapter Three, "The Partnership of Law and Liberty."*

This selection, like the others in this section, is a clear expression of the doctrine of "higher values" (a form of infallibility), in terms of which the exercise of censorship is justified.

. . . what are the reasons for the Church's restrictions (strictly interpreted though they be) in the matter of reading? Once the reasons are grasped, the higher freedom toward which they are intrinsically directed will become clear.

The Church is the divinely appointed carrier of Christ's revelation and of Christian morals. His revelation is enshrined in the dogmas of the Church; morals are summed up in the Ten Commandments as understood by Christian tradition. The Church is to hold, pass on, and defend the faith and morals of the Catholic body. To perform this task, she has been equipped by her Founder with all that is needed to make her a "perfect" society. This technical phrase does not mean that every member of the Church is a saint; it means that the society which the Church is has in its essential constitution all that it needs to preserve, propagate, and defend itself. It follows that the Church has a threefold authority: legislative, executive, and judicial. It can establish laws (always, mind, within its mandate of preserving faith, morals, and collective survival—for no other purpose); it can carry them into execution; it can judge their observation and punish transgressions against them.

It will be noted that these are the same aspects of authority that the Church vindicates for the civil power. The state, too, on its level, is a "perfect" society. Hence, the Church, by reason of its divine mandate, has not only the right but the *duty* of safeguarding the faith and morals of its subjects. This it does through such positive legislation as demanding observance of Sundays and holy days of obligation, abstinence and fasting at certain times, and—what we are concerned with—the restriction, under certain definite circumstances, of specific books and certain types of reading matter.

The Catholic Church has never gone along with the profound-sounding but really vapid statement we hear these days in connection with the effects books have or can have on morals. In the attempt to show that censorship of any type is unneeded, the opponents of restriction of reading matter for the young often come up with the statement that "no book has ever seduced a girl." But many a book *has* seduced many a girl, and people more mature than girls as well. Minds have been swayed to truth *and* to falsehood through reading, and a mind lured into error is a mind seduced—a type of seduction that may well be more lamentable and more pernicious than physical seduction. Though it is not wise to go all the way with some who make horror, crime, and sex comic books the root of our juvenile delinquency, there can be no doubt that *some* specific horrible offenses by the young can be and have been traced even to a specific comic book. Case histories of this type can be found in the perhaps too-exaggerated indictment of the comics by Dr. Frederic Wertham in his *Seduction of the Innocent* (Rinehart, 1954). When the works of André Gide were placed on the Index in 1955, there was a great outcry in many quarters. But years before, one who apparently knew whereof he spoke, Paul Claudel, had said that every young man in France he ever met who had lost his faith had been sadly influenced by Gide. Happily, on the other hand, we need do no more than recall the experience of St. Augustine and the mysterious voice saying to him, *"Tolle, lege* [Take and read]"—an experience that started his conversion and gave the Western world one of its intellectual giants—to realize that books cannot only seduce minds but inspire them as well.

Indeed, it has always seemed to me that those who belittle the deleterious influence of books are defeating their own case. They seem to have a low opinion of the very printed word they are trying to save from destruction at the hands of censorship, for if books cannot "seduce" anyone, how can they inspire anyone—or are all books of equal insipidity? The Church at the very least pays books the compliment of thinking that they are—some of them, at any rate—of tremendous importance; it regards them as foes of Christian life worthy of a kind of respect, as one respects the strength of the caged tiger. If some books are not explosive enough to be viewed with alarm, it would seem to follow that no books are worthy to be viewed with interest.

So much by way of digression. To come back to the point: the Catholic Church does most firmly hold that some books can "seduce," that they are of grave danger to the faith and morals of the generality of the Catholic body. Holding that, she is compelled, by her own internal logic and constitution, to protect the faithful. (The state, too, as we have seen, is equally *impelled*, if and when a grave danger to the commonwealth arises.) Hence the Church may forbid a book on the grounds of danger to faith and morals, and she may do it in one of two ways. She may specify the particular book by title and author (this is done by "placing the book on the Index") or by indicating types or categories of reading under which unspecified books may fall (these categories are contained in Canon 1399).

The *Index Librorum Prohibitorum* (the latest edition appeared in 1948, with an appendix including books proscribed up to December 31, 1945) is a listing of some four thousand titles.* No one, of course, has ever figured out how many books have been printed since Gutenberg came up with his invention around 1400; over the centuries millions of titles have appeared. The point is that the number of books that have been given the dubious distinction of

*The number, as of 1952, was 4,126. An interesting breakdown according to half centuries shows the number of books condemned in each period: 1600–49:469; 1650–99:862; 1700–49:723; 1750–99:463; 1800–49:576; 1850–99:778; 1900–49:255. These figures are taken from *What Is the Index*, by Redmond A. Burke, C.S.V. (Milwaukee: Bruce, 1952), p. 52.

being placed on the Index is rather on the infinitesimal side compared to the number of titles issued through the centuries. This fact in itself is indicative of the restraint with which Rome works in the matter of restricting the freedom of members of the Church in the field of reading.

Further, of these four thousand books, probably two thirds are technical, professional works, many of which are unknown even to workers in the same professional fields and which probably could not be found outside an extremely antiquarian library. A surprising feature of the titles on the Index—surprising to those who are not familiar with the nature of the Index—is the fact that most of the proscribed works in theology and philosophy were written by priests. In the whole field of literature, in which Catholic readers might probably feel that their freedom was being most restricted, there are not more than several hundred titles on the Index. The national literature that leads the field is the French—Zola, Balzac, Hugo, to name a few, have some or all of their works on the I ndex. There is one English novel on the list—Richardson's *Pamela* (Sterne's *Sentimental Journey* is named, too, if one would call it a novel)—and not a single American novel has been listed; in fact, there are but few American-authored books of any type in the roster.

The charge, then, so frequently heard, that the existence of the Index is a paralyzing restraint on the intellectual freedom of Catholics, is surely a much-too-sweeping indictment. The average Catholic would be inclined or tempted to read but very few titles on the Index even if all its restrictions were lifted tomorrow. Further, as we shall see later, the restrictions of the Index are not absolute. If one objects *in principle* to the Index, then, of course, the restrictions it imposes are unjustifiable; but if one approves the general principles that some restrictions are possible and even necessary, and that the Church has the authority so to limit the freedom of its members for a greater good, then the wonder grows that the Index is so temperate in tone and minimum in extension. Certainly its scope lends no color to the suspicion of tyranny over intellectual freedom. Incidentally, the Index is not a deep, dark secret; it is an actual book which can be purchased in most Catholic bookstores and consulted in public libraries. Don't expect, however, that it will make very exciting reading; you will hardly be impelled to rush out to try to get permission to read Michael Amatus' (1725) *De Piscium atque Avium Esus Consuetudine apud quosdam Christi Fidelium in Antepaschali Jejunio* ("On the Customs of Some Christians of Eating Fish and Birds in the Pre-Easter Fast") or Gideon Harvey's (1701) *The Art of Curing Diseases by Expectation*. I am far from suggesting that the books on the Index are all quaint museum pieces; many of them, to be sure, are of little importance today, but in their times they posed a real threat to the faith and/or morals of the Catholic public to whom they were addressed. Several centuries from now many may wonder why Alberto Moravia was ever considered important enough to be placed on the Index, but Rome had a good reason for warning all, and especially the Catholics of Italy, of the distressing effects his books were having, with their despairing commentary on modern life.

The second mode of controlling books and reading is contained in two sections of Canon Law. In Canon 1385 there is a question of *censura praevia* (prior censorship). This applies to authors; Catholics, whether clerics or lay, may not publish books that explicitly deal with matters of faith or morals without permission from ecclesiastical authority. This permission is commonly sought from the bishop of the diocese in which the author resides (it can also be petitioned from the bishop of the diocese in which the book is either printed or published). Such treatments of faith and morals include, for instance, the Holy Scriptures or notes and commentaries on them; books on theology, philosophy (especially ethics), ecclesiastical history, books of prayer and devotion, and, in general, books in which "there is something of particular relevance to religion and public morals."

The procedure is as follows. The author submits his manuscript for pre-publication inspection by the "censors" of the diocese. As we shall see later, these are competent and carefully selected specialists. If, after careful consideration, they find nothing in the book that is opposed to faith or morals, they issue (they must do so, indeed) a *nihil obstat.* This Latin phrase means merely "there is nothing against" publication. Acting on this decision of the experts, the bishop of the diocese in almost routine fashion appends his *imprimatur*, which means "let it be published." This official approval, let it be understood, does *not* mean that the bishop has necessarily read the book (he has his officials for the purpose), nor does it necessarily signify that the bishop is according the book his hearty approval. Indeed, there may well be, let us say, some overtones in the book that indicate that the author is of the Democratic party persuasion; a bishop who happens to be a devout Republican cannot for that reason refuse to give the book his *imprimatur*, though he may heartily disagree with every bray of the donkey that echoes in its pages. The *imprimatur* is, we may say, a negative approval; it simply means that the freedom of the author to publish is stated after a decision that nothing in the book is contrary to traditional Catholic teaching on faith and morals.

In Canon 1399 the restriction is shifted from *pre* to *post:* restrictions on reading books that are already published (and these normally, as is clear, will be by non-Catholic authors, save in the category of literature, when such books are forbidden by the Code).

There are twelve categories of books mentioned in Canon 1399 (the last category deals with printed pictures of Our Lord, the Blessed Virgin, the angels and saints and "other servants of God," when and if such representations are contrary to the "mind of the Church"). The other eleven categories are: editions or translations of the Holy Scriptures made by non-Catholics; books which propound heresy or schism or in any way attempt to subvert the very foundations of religion; books which have for their principle or one of their notable purposes to attack religion or right morals; books by non-Catholics which professedly treat of religion, unless there is nothing in them that is contrary to the Catholic faith; books of Holy Scriptures and commentaries concerning them and books of revelations, miracles, prophecies, and new devotions published without proper ecclesiastic permission; books which attack or ridicule any Catholic dogmas; books which approve superstition, magic, spiritism, and other such practices; books which favor divorce, suicide, and so on; books which purposely treat of or teach lascivious or obscene matters; liturgical books that have been so changed as not to agree with approved editions; books containing apocryphal indulgences.

As is obvious, the books forbidden here which touch most on the freedom of the average Catholic reader are the books on religion by non-Catholics and those which are *ex professo* (as the Canon puts it) obscene. Catholics do not generally have to be warned, nor are they actually interested in, books that attack their faith. Further, it should be noted that the rule for the "strict interpretation" of Canon Law still holds. When it is stated, for instance, that books that *propound* heresy are forbidden, the word must be taken to mean "to promote or defend by argument"; it would be an unlawful extension of the meaning to widen it to include an incidental reference to heresy, even though the reference were favorable. Similar operative words in the Canon are to be interpreted in their minimum sense. It would carry us far afield in the present work to comment on all such words in the law; one who is interested in pursuing the matter further has but to consult any commentary on Canon Law or specifically any book on the portions of Canon Law that deal with this matter of the censorship and prohibition of books.* The meaning of the word "obscene" will occupy our attention at some length later.

Who has the power so to restrict the freedom of the Catholic to read? Not every official in the Church. The Holy See can, of course, declare books forbidden for the universal Church; this is commonly done by a decree of the Holy Office, one of the Roman congregations. A bishop may forbid a book to the reading of members of his diocese, wherein, for instance, a particular book is causing danger to souls because of peculiar circumstances. No parish priest or pastor, however, has this power; he may, and sometimes must, counsel against the reading of a particular book, but it is not within his power to forbid it unless it clearly falls within the provisions of Canon Law, or would probably be a serious temptation to a particu-

*Such, for example, as Bouscaren and Ellis, *Canon Law: A Text and Commentary* (Milwaukee: Bruce, 1946), or Redmond A. Burke, *op. cit.*

lar individual. If we may recall the famous case of Betty Smith's *A Tree Grows in Brooklyn*, no Catholic priest had the power to *forbid* (in the sense of establishing a law) the reading of the book, however much he may have found it distasteful, vulgar, or "common"; it clearly did not fall in the category of an "obscene" book, as Canon Law understands that word; the priest might have dissuaded its reading, but beyond that he could not, in justice, have gone.

The obligation laid on Catholics to abide by the restrictions of Canon Law in the matter of reading is a serious obligation, for the simple reason that the purpose of the law is serious—namely, to safeguard Catholic dogma and Christian morals. To clarify this obligation, it is perhaps necessary to say a few words on the nature and binding-power of "positive" legislation. This is legislation which defines and specifies obligations that already exist through the natural moral law. This natural law—man's recognition of God's eternal law—demands, for example, good social relations if one is going to live in a society. The state will step in and say, "Well and good, but in order to be a good citizen, you will have to obey some traffic regulations," and accordingly makes some positive laws about speed and so on. Canon Law is likewise positive law; it defines and specifies the general law that Catholics should be good Catholics, holding fast to faith and living according to sound morals. To abide by the disciplinary regulations of Canon Law is a *means* to achieve the end.

Now, positive law, whether ecclesiastical or civil, binds *all* members of its own society—Church or state—precisely because it is legislation for the common good. It may be that a particular individual *knows* that the law is not necessary for him; a man may know that he is the world's safest driver and that therefore he can drive at eighty miles an hour with positively no danger to the life or limb of anyone. Well, he still *may* not drive that fast where the law says fifty miles is the limit; if he does, he breaks the law and is subject to fine, protest as he may that he is above the law. The reason, obviously, is that the law has to be based on the objective common good and not on one's subjective interpretation of what the law ought to be to fit his particular case. It is far better to restrict the freedom of an individual than to permit every individual to be a law unto himself, for that way lies social chaos.

The same character of positive law obtains when that positive law is ecclesiastical. It may be that an individual knows with sincere and complete conviction that if he reads a book that is a most blatant attack on the Catholic dogmas he holds with all his heart he would not for an instant find his faith being insidiously undermined. It could be—though self-deception is an easy state of mind to slide into. But, granted the truth of the supposition, it does not matter; the law still binds, for it was made for the common good and cannot take into consideration the peculiar gifts or strength of character of the individual. The only way anyone, whether in ecclesiastical or civil life, can get a relaxation from the positive law is to go to the lawmaker and get a statement that the particular law does not bind him. If you can flash a certificate signed by mayor, police department, traffic-control bureau, and whatever other agency is necessary, then you may drive at eighty miles; otherwise you will be smitten with a fine every time you are caught. So it is with the obligation of Catholics with respect to restrictions on reading, and this leads us to the point mentioned above; namely, that the limitation of reading, whether expressed in the Index or in the twelve categories of books, is not *absolute.*

This is a part of the picture that is rarely adverted to when our non-Catholic friends refer to the supposed intellectual shackles that fetter Catholic intellectual freedom. The statement always runs, "But there are *so many* books you Catholics *can't* read," whereas it ought to be something like, "There are, aren't there, some books you have to get permission to read?" For the possibility of obtaining permission is written right into the Code.* In ordinary cases, permission to read forbidden books is obtained through one's bishop, and permission will not be granted unless there is a good and sufficient reason for the book to be read. One engaged in professional literary work, for instance, might really find it necessary to read all the works of Zola, let us say. Again, if one were teaching the history of religions, it would probably be of prime importance

*Cf., for example, Bouscaren and Ellis, *op. cit.,* pp. 724–25.

to him to know many of the classic works that propound (i.e., "promote and defend by argument") heretical doctrines. But if there is good reason for the book to be read, and if (obviously a necessary condition, else the permission would defeat the very end and purpose of the law) the danger to the prospective reader's faith and morals is not discernible, permission is as a rule fairly easy to get. It must be added, however, that *no one*—not even the Pope of Rome—can give *anyone* permission to read a book whose reading would be a sin, would place the reader in proximate spiritual danger. If one has permission to read a book and still finds that he cannot "take" the book, his conscience obliges him to stop reading it, and he will sin if he violates the mandate of his conscience. Exemptions from the positive law do not ever carry with them license to violate the natural moral law. So our friend who has all the legal permissions in the world to drive eighty miles an hour has to stop it when he finds that his reflexes are slowing up and he is endangering his own and others' necks; otherwise, despite what his permission grants, he will be in his own conscience (if an accident happens) guilty of manslaughter and/or suicide.

Let us return for some consideration of the *censura praevia*. This is, as we have seen, the only real censorship in the strict sense of the word. In most of the discussion in this country on the problems of censorship, the question really hinges, not on prior censorship of books, but on the possibility and advisability of their control *after* publication. But since prior censorship is apparently so repellant to many, it may be worth while to examine the spirit in which the Church exercises it. If we keep in mind the points that have already been established about the presumption in favor of freedom, about the higher freedom that is always envisioned in any restrictions of freedom, and so on, it will not come as a surprise to anyone that the Church, while demanding prior examination of some books before permission is granted to publish, is reasonable in the provisions it sets up.

The rules for censors which are laid down in the Code, and which apply both to censors of the Roman Congregation of the Holy Office and to censors in the various dioceses as well, may be summarized as follows. Censors are to be well versed in the subject with which the book under examination treats, as well as with the language in which it is written. In the performance of their office they must "put aside all undue influence that might arise from a consideration of persons and attend only to the dogmas of the Church and to common Catholic doctrine. It is clear from this that censors are not to judge according to their private opinions or the tenets of a favorite school, but according to *common* Catholic doctrine. . . ." If they judge that a book is sound in doctrine but that its publication may, for some reason or other, be inopportune, they may give their opinion as to the inopportuneness, but must, at the same time, clearly approve publication as regards soundness of doctrine. Wherever possible, leniency must be shown, and if a book is refused clearance under the phrase *donec corrigatur* (until corrections be made), the author must be heard in his own defense and the fact that the book was so refused clearance must not be publicized if the author agrees to correct the passages that violate the common teaching of the Church. Finally, any strictures that may have been leveled against the book are to be secret between the author and the examiners and not revealed even to the author's representatives, unless the author agrees. In this way, the legislation, while preserving the purity of Catholic teaching, endeavors with all its power to preserve the author's good name and to give him every possible benefit of the doubt. This is, to be sure, censorship in the strict sense, which the Church must, from its very nature, exercise; but -,but it would be captious to deny that it is censorship exercised with prudence, consideration, and charity. . . .

The first selection that follows is written by an undergraduate and deals with the question of career recruitment on campus. Until the Vietnam war, no one thought of challenging the practice. However, it is now argued by some that if we disapprove of the activities of an organization, institution, or corporation on moral grounds, we are justified not only in refusing to patronize it but in preventing others from doing likewise. The same argument has been used in the past to prevent the use of campus facilities by Communists and others.

The second selection also deals with recruitment. In it we find an overt and explicit disregard of democratic procedures justified on "moral" grounds.

The third selection is an unsigned pamphlet wherein certain demands are specified as *non-negotiable* (another form of infallibility). It also contains an interesting critique of negotiation as a tool for repression on the part of the Establishment.

Corporations Make Profit from Murder and Suppression;
Labeling Recruitment a "Free Speech" Issue Is Irrelevant

Last week, Students for a Democratic Society led College students in expelling General Electric recruiters from the campus. During the occupation of the Placement Office, several objections were raised by students who were waiting to be interviewed by recruiters. They argued that SDS was preventing individual students from making a free choice whether or not to get jobs with General Electric and violating "free speech."

There are many people at the College who agree that the Army,

Marines, Dow Chemical, etc. are doing bad things. For the past several years thousands of students have participated in many demonstrations against the war in Vietnam and against the draft. We were saying to the people in power: "Stop the War!" To Dow Chemical recruiters, we said: "Stop napalming women and children in an unjust war!" Others added that Dow Chemical and any other corporation should not be allowed to make profits on this war in which thousands of Americans and Vietnamese died, and are dying. For years we talked, and talked, and demonstrated and then talked some more. Little has resulted from our efforts. However, we have come to realize that the relatively few people who have power not only do not listen to the masses of working people and students in this country, but also exploit and oppress them. They continue to increase their profits while more of us are sent to die for them, and our living cost continues to go up (largely because of inflationary war spending and war taxes).

on Tuesday, March 11, [1969,] SDS led about 150 students and faculty to the Placement Office to protest the recruitment by General Electric. The students entered the office and asked the GE recruiter to leave the campus. After 15 minutes of political discussions interspersed by chants of "Racist GE must go," the recruiter left.

In several well-documented leaflets, SDS has shown that GE is actively using and encouraging racism to further its profits and to oppress workers, especially blacks. Also, we have shown (and this is further backed up by a story in Tuesday's *Wall Street Journal*) that GE is engaging in labor practices which are unfair even by the standards of the Federal government. We have pointed out that GE makes huge profits from weapon systems which are designed to indiscriminately napalm and kill men, women, and children. In a very real sense, GE (i.e., GE's owners) grow rich on the blood and suffering of people both in the US and abroad.

We oppose this.

Many students ask: "Don't these corporations and the military have a right to recruit at the College because they have the right of free speech?" and "Don't students have the right to go to GE if they want to?"

Certainly, these are important questions, not to be taken lightly by SDS or by anyone else. We hope that you will consider the following answer (however briefly stated) to the questions as seriously as we consider the questions.

General Electric, as well as their supporters on campus, try to hide the real meaning of their operations behind high-sounding statements about "free speech" and "rational discourse." While they want us to *passively* sit around and play verbal games, the corporations are *actively engaged* in making profits from murder and oppression. If they came here to talk and consult us about the development of new projects, then we would talk with them. For example, if the Army were to come to the campus and ask us whether or not this country should be fighting in Vietnam (and abide by our decision) then we would participate and tell them, no! They do not come here for that purpose (we think that they never would, nor can they). They come to recruit students to participate in their existing projects and to support their *active* undertakings of making profits on the blood and sweat of people around the world. Since they are not just *talking* about their oppressive policies but are *actively* involved in them, the question is not truly one of free speech. We think that we should not only *verbally* expose and denounce them; we must *actively* stop them from furthering their activities. At the College this means we must stop them from recruiting.

By the same token we do not think that a student has an abstract, individual right to help GE, or any other such corporation, exploit and oppress. We feel that no man has a right to do these things and therefore does not have a right to serve any company which uses these practices (as we have shown with GE).

Morality and Majority Vote

C.C.N.Y. Students Demand Recruiting

Engineering students at City College demanded yesterday that the administration again allow companies to recruit them on campus and threatened to take "militant" action against student radicals seeking to block campus recruitment.

Tuesday afternoon a scuffle between students from the School of Engineering and some of the student radicals ended in bloody noses and other minor injuries for several of the youths and the indefinite suspension of two of the dissidents. In the evening the college announced the suspension of on-campus interviews.

Yesterday, small clusters of angry engineering students argued again with radicals outside Steinman Hall.

"How dare you take away my right to be interviewed for a job? How dare you close down my placement office?" one engineering student shouted.

"Damn it, next time we're going to send you people out of here in ambulances," he yelled at a slim youth with shoulder-length blond hair.

The college re-affirmed yesterday that it would indefinitely bar recruiting on campus. Officials said tensions between the two groups were running so high that they feared another, possibly more violent, confrontation.

A petition signed by 795 engineering students was presented to Dr. Buell Gallagher, president of the college. It demanded that he reopen the placement office and that "anyone who interferes with our right to be interviewed be prosecuted to the full extent of the law."

Some of the engineering students have pointed to a college-wide referendum on recruitment held last year, in which students voted by a large majority to open the campus to all recruiters.

Student radicals, on the other hand, have maintained that the issue is a moral one, not capable of resolution by a majority vote.

Referring to Hughes Aircraft and Northern Aeronautics—two concerns that recruited on Tuesday and that produce war material —a student radical said, "We don't think the university is a place that should allow recruitment by companies that make money out of killing people."

The two students who were suspended are Ron McGuire and Jeff Steinberg. They entered the locked fourth-floor room where a Hughes Aircraft interview was in progress by climbing down from the roof of the Finley Student Center and into an open window.

Mr. Steinberg said later that a member of the college's Young Republican Club, stationed in the room as a guard, had tried to shove him out of the window as he was entering. He said that only the ledge outside had prevented his falling.

Non-Negotiable Demands

Strike on Monday—If Seven Demands Aren't Met

The Ad Hoc Committee to End Political Suppression invites all students to join in a mass strike against the administration, beginning Monday, April 21, [1969,] if our demands are not met.

The strike has been called as a result of weeks of demonstrations, confrontations, intense intellectual and emotional involvement. It has been provoked by the administration's stubborn refusal to halt its present policies of political suppression. A strike is the one tactic around which enough support can be mobilized to force the administration to grant these demands, which concern every person on this campus. A strike enables each individual student to choose in an active way whether to support the struggle. We of the Ad Hoc Committee will peacefully picket and, as in the past, use no coercion, threat or force against students. Rather, we seek to discuss the issues and join with thousands of students who have not yet supported us, as well as with those who have previously attended our rallies or joined our occupation of the S.S. Building.

At the end of March, our newly formed committee brought four demands against the administration. Later, three additional demands were added. Large numbers of students and faculty, as well as SA, SGS, and the *Phoenix*, have supported these seven demands:

(1) Reinstatement of three SDS members who were suspended for "contempt of court" through a "trial" ultimately controlled by the administration; and (2) dropping of charges against them, resulting from their participation in a demonstration against corporate recruitment. These are the only demands that have been met —the first through the action of the Student Court and the second in response to the actions we have taken. If the administration had been willing to grant these demands a month ago, our protest would

have appeared unnecessary. Instead, students were aided in recognizing other examples of political suppression on campus and in formulating new demands, which are still unanswered by the administration.

We demand the rehiring of Sheila Delaney, who was not rehired as an assistant professor because of political reasons. This is our third demand. Our fourth demand is that use of the Max-Kahn Report, a policy of the Board of Higher Education which enforces secrecy in firing, rehiring and tenure procedures, be discontinued at QC. This report clearly serves as a smokescreen for political firings.

On April 1, Pres. McMurray summoned 700 members of the specially-trained Tactical Police Force onto campus to arrest 39 peaceful demonstrators. These 39 were subsequently charged with criminal trespassing in the second degree, a misdemeanor carrying a possible sentence of 90 days. (5) We demand that administrative and civil charges against the 38 arrested students be dropped. (6) We demand that all civil and administrative charges against Henry Lesnick, a faculty member arrested in the sit-in, be dropped. (7) We demand that the administration guarantee in writing that no police will ever be called on campus, except in case of direct danger to life. Student and faculty rights are directly threatened when the administration is free to bring in police to suppress political dissent.

The administration has responded to these demands in two ways. First, through use of force. This is seen in its use of police and its collusion with Queens District Attorney Mackell's Grand Jury investigation of "campus disruptions" at QC. The Grand Jury is attempting to intimidate students by claiming our movement is manipulated by a small gang of "ringleaders" and by raising the threat of indictment and prosecution. We consider this an insult to the integrity of our movement and an extension of the same policies of political suppression we are fighting on campus. There is the possibility of further arrests and even expulsion of those who have been most active in the movement. Political suppression continues to exist at QC.

Second, the administration has attempted to evade the issues raised by the struggle. It has done so through a student convocation, a faculty convocation, a four-day moratorium and various committee meetings, as well as in discussions with individuals, negotiations with faculty members, and public statements. The administration's position has remained firm: it has refused to implement our demands. Its proposals, as in the current Governance Committee report, have not even addressed these issues. It is clear that the administration's wish for "dialogue" is a stalling tactic and a means of obscuring the clarity of our position.

Our demands are very simple, although we believe them to have profound importance as a means of exposing and combatting political suppression at QC. We have demanded that the administration halt a number of repressive actions. The administration has refused. Moreover, it has hardened its position. By calling for "negotiations," it hopes to force us to accept major concessions, which we have refused to do. We will not compromise our opposition to political suppression. That is what we mean when we say that our demands are non-negotiable.

For weeks, students have waited for the administration to act. It has become clear that students must themselves act in order to ensure that these demands are met. That is why we are calling for a strike: as the most effective way to involve the entire campus in the struggle. If the administration does not meet our demands, we call upon all students who are in sympathy with our demands *to not attend classes during the strike.* There will be students leafleting at every gate and picket lines in front of classroom buildings. There will be rallies and discussions throughout the day.

Thousands of students and faculty have already become involved in the movement. Our strength lies in our numbers. The administration cannot ignore the voices of thousands of students and teachers. We can succeed if we work together. Don't cross the picket lines —join them!

 PART V

Academic Freedom

This article is self-explanatory. It discusses an instance of pressure applied to the academic community from without (churches, courts, and so forth) is order to restrict academic freedom. The authors were all members of the philosophy department at the City College of New York during 1940, the year of the case under discussion.

The authors of the essay are Daniel J. Bronstein, Abraham Edel, Lewis Feuer, Yervant H. Krikorian, Joseph Ratner, Philip P. Wiener, which group includes all the members of the Department during 1940, the year of Professor Russell's appointment.

I

In recommending the appointment of Professor Bertrand Russell and throughout the controversy that arose thereafter, the Department of Philosophy of the City College was guided by certain principles concerning the nature of teaching and the place of the college in a democratic community. The City College is a tax-supported institution in New York City. The taxpayers, in the widest and fairest sense of the term, are the people of New York. The college serves the needs of the community by providing higher education for those young people who are able and willing to acquire it. This education is free and open to all, irrespective of race, religion, political belief, economic status, and country of origin. In its long history, the college has served this purpose well. Its general influence in the community has been a progressive one.

Not all groups in the community have favored the work of the

194 CLEAR AND PRESENT DANGER

college. There have been some who have resented the fact that it was educating the children of workers and of the lower middle class, that it was giving opportunities to immigrant groups and thus helping them toward full equality in American society. For some elements, the college has always been an undesirable extension of democracy and social equality. As a consequence it has not been expanded as rapidly as the community's needs required. The various groups opposing the college have shown themselves ready to attack it on the slightest pretext and have waged constant warfare against its good name. The Russell case is a dramatic and portentious episode in the history of the college.

Our conception of the obligations and responsibilities of the teacher at the City College is guided by our view of the reciprocal relations between higher education and the life of the community: the college has to meet the educational needs of the community, it has to transmit the enduring values of culture, and it has to clarify the purposes and increase the scope of the democratic ideal toward which enlightened mankind has been painfully striving. Only by keeping firmly and clearly in mind the various functions of a liberal college can there be developed satisfactory criteria for deciding, then, to what degree and in what respects it is desirable for the college to be responsive to the majority opinion of the community. History provides ample evidence that progress and the general welfare of mankind are best served by freedom of inquiry. Academic freedom is not freedom from communal responsibility but an instrument for fulfilling that responsibility.

Unless the college enjoys the right to explore possibilities, higher education cannot contribute to progress but will be a definite hindrance and obstacle. The gap between what is taught in college and what is going on in the community will be widened. The students on graduation will not be prepared for adult participation in the life of the community. To restrict college education to the inculcating of ideas and attitudes that will support the *status quo* at all costs is in fact to constrain the college to supporting the past.

There is another consideration which is almost always completely neglected in popular movements that have as their objective making the college "safe." Most people, not excluding educators, tend to be conformists. No elaborate precautions are needed, nor special pressures and inducements, to make the overwhelming majority of educators, in private as well as in public institutions, feel and think in terms of the dominant social pattern. They will do that anyway. What is sorely needed is adequate support and encouragement for the few who exhibit intellectual courage and originality. The practice of rewarding the inventor and the discoverer in the technical, scientific and technological fields has contributed greatly to the enrichment of American material culture. American spiritual culture will be as greatly benefited by rewarding creative minds in social fields. It is our firm belief that it is essential for democracy that such minds enjoy the right to work and teach in publicly supported educational institutions.

The common purpose of enlightened teaching in all fields is to stimulate reflection, to develop independent thought on the part of the student. This is especially true of the function of philosophy. To help the student understand the ideas of others and to clarify his own, to help him systematize his thoughts and achieve some consistency of belief, is the essential educational objective of philosophy, both within the college and without. In the educative process the principal function of the teacher of philosophy is to act as a catalytic agent. It is not his function to impose a set of ideas upon the student, but to present alternative points of view and to discuss them fairly. This process, when successfully carried out, develops in the student both intellectual self-reliance and the dissociation of ideas from personalities. Thus the teacher is enabled to preserve his individuality and present his unique contribution without running the danger of indoctrinating his students.

The essential qualities for a teacher are fair-mindedness, intellectual honesty, the ability to understand and formulate views contrary to his own, imaginativeness, analytic power. These qualities are neither dependent upon nor necessarily correlated with any specific dogmas, whether of religion, politics, economics, or morals. The removal of religious and political tests for educators is a cornerstone of the free democratic education in America, and remains fundamental to the preservation of social freedom and progress.

These general principles are the foundations of the democratic faith. The Board of Higher Education in 1938 gave them fuller realization through the reorganization of the college's administrative structure. This reorganization gave the teaching staff a new and enhanced role in all functions of the college—in the formulation of educational policy, in reaching decisions concerning educational standards, and in selecting the teaching personnel. The effect on the individual teacher has been to widen his scope and deepen his sense of responsibility. The teacher has become an increasingly effective part of the college, co-operating with his fellow-teachers and administrators in working out the purposes of the institution in and for the community.

II

The Russell case is significant because it involves these basic principles. When Professor Morris Raphael Cohen and Professor Harry Allen Overstreet retired from City College, it was agreed both by the Philosophy Department and by the administrative authorities of the college that the addition of an outstanding philosopher to the staff would be highly desirable. Mindful of the statement made on one occasion by the Chairman of the Board of Higher Education—"Nothing is too good for City College"—the department, after carefully considering the available professors of philosophy throughout the learned world, recommended that an invitation be extended to Professor Bertrand Russell, one of the most eminent of living philosophers. The college authorities and the Board of Higher Education unanimously and enthusiastically accepted the recommendation. In the words of one member of the Board, it was the "educational scoop" of the year. Professor Russell was eagerly sought by many American universities of high standing. He had taught at the University of Chicago, was teaching at the University of California at Los Angeles, and was scheduled for the William James Lectures at Harvard. Our chief concern had been that he might not find an offer from City College sufficiently attractive. Following the Board meeting of February 26, 1940, Acting President Nelson P. Mead issued a statement to the press to the effect that the college was singularly fortunate in being able to secure the services of a man of such international reputation and distinction as Bertrand Russell.

The department and the administration were surprised and shocked at the character and vehemence of the attacks which certain groups immediately launched against Professor Russell's appointment. From Bishop Manning's first pronouncement to Justice McGeehan's decision, the attacks seemed to us to be based on a conception of the educational process in colleges and universities that is contrary to the fundamental principles of education in a democracy.

The main charge directed against Professor Russell by Bishop Manning was that Russell was morally incompetent to be a teacher of youth. The Bishop asked: ". . . What is to be said of colleges and universities which hold up before our youth as a responsible teacher of philosophy and as an example of light and leading a man who is a recognized propagandist against both religion and morality, and who specifically defends adultery . . . ?" In support of his public query, he cited disconnected passages from a few of Russell's books dealing with sex and religion. And in Justice McGeehan's decision the consideration of Russell's moral fitness played a decisive part.

The Justice was on firm ground when he stated that ". . . the personality of the teacher has *more* to do with forming a student's opinion than many syllogisms,"* and also when he stated that the more eminent the teacher, the greater his influence is likely to be on impressionable and developing minds. "It is contended that Bertrand Russell is extraordinary. That makes him the more dangerous."

However, the Justice's evaluation of Professor Russell's character is, in our opinion, wholly erroneous. The influence of Russell's character would be beneficial not only to the students but also to the whole college and through the college to the community. For

*Italics ours.

we cannot conceive how it could be detrimental to anyone to be exposed to Russell's qualities of intellectual and moral courage, to his integrity, his uncompromising devotion to truth, his profound concern for the advancement of human welfare, his tolerance in all provinces of human thought and action, his love of freedom, his disinterestedness and unselfish maintenance of principles. It is our belief that these qualities make Professor Russell eminently desirable as a teacher, not merely of logic and the philosophy of mathematics but also of ethics.

It is evident that, in the attacks of Bishop Manning and Justice McGeehan, the objection to Professor Russell on moral grounds has its source in a basic opposition to freedom of thought in general and to academic freedom in particular. Any thinker who stimulates people to reflect critically over fundamental human questions is "dangerous." In this sense Professor Russell is truly a "dangerous" man. As Mrs. Russell pointed out felicitously in a letter to the editor of the *Journal of Social Studies*, a student publication at City College, "To them [groups opposing Professor Russell] argument itself is impious. It is not so much my husband's actual opinions they object to as his belief that ethics is a subject for argument, that it is for human beings to discover by thought and experiment what rules of conduct and what social institutions will do most to promote human welfare in any given age, and that morality is made for man and not man for morality."

III

The opponents of Professor Russell were consciously and unconsciously advocating that a publicly supported educational institution should teach one specific ethical-religious doctrine. This, in essence, is sectarianism in education and would inevitably lead to the introduction of religious tests for appointment to public colleges. We need hardly point out that such a development would subvert the basic law of the land. The separation of church and state, and its consequence, the elimination of religious tests for public or civil service offices, are among the great historical achievements of the Constitution of the United States. It is essential to the continuance of American culture that students be given not only the opportunity but the intellectual training necessary for examining different conceptions about man and society. Only in this way can independent self-reliant minds be developed. Only in this way can the rising generation grow into ethical maturity.

The strength of the movement to override the traditional American separation of church and state is evidenced in the recent legislation in New York State permitting time off from school for sectarian religious instruction. It is also evidenced in the widespread attempt in the domain of general social theory to base political democracy on an exclusively religious foundation. It is true that the religious emphasis on the dignity of man has historically been an important factor in developing the democratic outlook. However, it is important for an understanding and preservation of our traditional liberalism to recognize that the democratic idea can be firmly and effectively established on a non-religious basis. This is implicit in the practical separation of church and state established by the Constitution. And in the realm of philosophic theory there are several different systems which furnish a non-religious basis for the whole of liberal thought and action.

IV

The McGeehan decision not only crystallized the views and attitudes of those who opposed Professor Russell's appointment, but in some respects went much further. The decision is particularly dangerous to academic freedom and to public higher education.

The central and novel contention of the McGeehan decision would, if carried out literally, make a criminal of every critical-minded person. In a statement to the Bertrand Russell-Academic Freedom Committee which was read before the Board of Higher Education, Professor Arthur O. Lovejoy, former President of the American Association of University Professors, and of the American Philosophical Association, wrote:

The gravest feature of Justice McGeehan's decision consists in the assumption which he makes in order thus to bring the case within the scope of the criminal law. That assumption is that *the expression of an opinion that an existing legal prohibition is ill-advised and socially undesirable is to be judicially construed as an incitement to other persons to violate the law, and therefore as itself unlawful.* Thus Justice McGeehan declares Mr. Russell "not fit to teach in any of the schools of this land" on the ground that "he encourages the violation of the Penal Law of the State of New York"; and in his second opinion Justice McGeehan states, as the final and most decisive of the "ultimate facts" justifying the original decision, that Mr. Russell "does not deny that he has expressed opinions in conflict with existing penal laws which he characterizes in his proposed answer as 'antiquated' and 'in need of revision.' " No evidence is cited that Mr. Russell has in fact ever incited anyone to break any law of the State of New York or of the United States; it is simply assumed that criticism of the ethical premises underlying certain laws is *eo ipso* an incitement to break them. This principle, generally applied, would be destructive of liberty of speech and of the press; for it implies that any advocacy of alterations in, e.g., the criminal law is an encouragement to crime, and consequently criminal.

There is in fact no limit to which such "logic" may be carried. If criticism of present standards of sexual morality is incitement to adultery, then criticism of present property arrangements is incitement to theft, criticism of a cigarette tax incitement to smuggling, criticism of an existent poll-tax incitement to insurrection, and criticism of any matter on which the criminal law directly or indirectly touches can be turned into incitement to illegality. Such a "legal doctrine" is potentially a weapon against academic freedom. It can be used by any elements of a community that regard a mere whisper of change, or the least criticism of existing arrangements, as a threat to "law and order."

A second issue of major importance which the McGeehan decision raised is the relation of the courts to administrative bodies established by legislative act. In effect, the justice assumed the right of the court to nullify the law which expressly gave to the Board of Higher Education the power of appointment. On this phase the *Herald Tribune* wrote an incisive editorial which said in part: "If it were sustained the net of the decision would seem to be that any Supreme Court justice could cancel any City College appointment (and could he not, on these same grounds, cancel any appointment to any private institution, for that matter?) if he happened to find anything in the candidate's past record which led the justice to think that his teachings might tend to encourage his students to any violation of any penal law." The *New York Post* said editorially: "The issue becomes one of whether the Board of Higher Education controls City College, or whether any one of the several dozen justices of the Supreme Court can set himself up as a super-Board of Higher Education and veto the acts of duly constituted authorities in the field."

Such assumption of right on the part of the court in relation to an administrative agency having the powers of appointment and policy-formation is particularly inimical to the democratic process. With the creation of federal administrative bodies, which is an increasing phase of the development of American life, this issue has become one of far-reaching national importance.

There are a number of other special issues raised by the McGeehan decision; for example, at a time when America was becoming host to an increasing number of refugee scholars, the Justice's ruling would deprive the City College of the opportunity to make appointments of aliens. It also jeopardized the very positions and tenure rights of the college staffs.

v

The triumph of those who opposed Professor Russell's appointment was an encroachment of the demagogic process on the democratic process. The demagogic process depends for its success upon making mass appeals to blind prejudice and on combining divergent and contradictory issues in one cohesive confusion. The democratic process, on the other hand, seeks its objectives by enlightenment and by clarification of issues.

The twofold technique of the demagogic process is clearly exhibited in the activities of Professor Russell's attackers. They began by charging Professor Russell with immorality and atheism—accusations which are most potent in arousing unthinking passions. Then the anti-alien element was introduced, then the charge of communism, then pacificism, then political comments which Professor Russell allegedly had made during the first World War. The charge of immorality and atheism remained throughout the controversy the center of attack; it functioned as the basic social glue which gave a semblance of coherence to the additional arguments advanced for annulling Professor Russell's appointment. One of the most frequently used epithets was "barnyard morality." Justice McGeehan's judicial decision followed the popular standards of expression and mode of analysis. He denounced the appointment as "an insult to the people of the City of New York"; he reached the threshold of fame with his dictum that the appointment was equivalent to creating a "chair of indecency."

The treatment accorded Bertrand Russell is not an isolated or accidental case. It is important for the defenders of academic freedom and the advancement of American life to recognize this. The opponents do. They were quick to use the Russell case as a breach through which to press forward toward their more comprehensive objectives. Very rapidly the attack was broadened to include the Board of Higher Education, which had established a reputation for progressive reforms. From that point on, nothing of liberal or progressive practices and ideas in college education has been immune from assault. A resolution was introduced into the State Legislature calling for a sweeping investigation of the educational system; the outcome of this legislative interest was the Coudert subcommittee of the Rapp-Coudert Committee.

In its widest significance, the Russell case—like the condemnation of Socrates, the inquisition of Galileo, the Scopes trial, and many other comparable cases—is a symbol of the everlasting struggle for the freedom of the human mind. Professor Russell pointed this out in his reply to the editorial suggestion of the *New York Times* that he should have resigned his post as soon as the opposition acquired momentum. As he wrote in part:

> But however wise such action might have been from a personal point of view, it would also, in my judgment, have been cowardly and selfish. A great many people who realized that their own interests and the principles of toleration and free speech were at stake were anxious from the first to continue the controversy. If I had retired I should have robbed them of their *casus belli* and tacitly assented to the proposition that substantial groups shall be allowed to drive out of public office individuals whose opinions, race, or nationality they find repugnant. This to me would appear immoral.

> It was my grandfather who brought about the repeal of the English Test and Corporation Acts, which barred from public office anyone not a member of the Church of England, of which he himself was a member, and one of my earliest and most important memories is of a deputation of Methodists and Wesleyans coming to cheer outside his window on the fiftieth anniversary of this repeal, although the largest single group affected was Catholic.

> I do not believe that the controversy is harmful on general grounds. It is not controversy and open differences that endanger democracy. On the contrary, these are its greatest safeguards. It is an essential part of democracy that substantial groups, even majorities, should extend toleration to dissentient groups, however small and however much their sentiments may be outraged.

> In a democracy it is necessary that people should learn to endure having their sentiments outraged.

All through the public controversy City College was never alone in its defense of academic freedom. The vigor and spontaneity with which liberals all over the nation rallied to the cause of intellectual freedom was a heartening demonstration of the vitality of democratic ideals in the United States.

We cannot name all the individuals and organizations who took part in this defense. Among them were college and university presidents and deans, leading educators, faculty members of our own as well as of other colleges, scientists and liberal theologians, publishers, columnists, newspapers, labor unions, parents' organizations, teachers' organizations. The student bodies, in particular at City College and the University of California at Los Angeles, added their invaluable support. It is especially gratifying that a large number of the members of the American Philosophical Association and its Western Division, which was meeting at the time, came to the support of our common professional ideals.

To all individuals and organizations who joined us in defending democratic ideals in education we take this opportunity of expressing our deep appreciation.

Gary Shapiro is an instructor in the philosophy department at Columbia University and a member of the radical New University Conference.

This article is an instance of the justification of pressure from within the academic community itself to restrict academic freedom. It raises the question of the purpose of academic freedom. Are academics free to tell only the "truth"? Whose truth? It also raises the question of whether the personal failures and shortcomings of individuals are in any way relevant to academic freedom. Or is this whole argument ad hominem? Analogously, are the decisions of former Justice Fortas invalidated because of his questionable personal ethics?

To most teachers and intellectuals "academic freedom" designates the precious value of free inquiry and the thorough investigation of all questions. Professional academics and the liberal intellectual community usually maintain that this freedom is a universal and timeless value; it is important to remember that it came to be historically important in the Enlightenment when intellectuals began to see their responsibility in terms of providing critiques of existing social institutions as a means of promoting human freedom. Great champions of intellectual freedom like the philosophes and Kant are obviously in this tradition. How then is it possible for radicals—and especially radical intellectuals—who claim to be concerned with the basic problems of oppression and liberation to repudiate their own cause by denouncing academic freedom or attempting to limit its value? One radical answer is that "academic freedom" as it is often used no longer has the libertarian content that it once did; we must expose the distortion of the concept and restore its fuller meaning with attention to the present prospects for intellectuals in this society. (The liberal finds it too easy to denounce the apparent paradox involved in a libertarian "attack" on "academic freedom"; as with Marcuse's notion of repressive tolerance the failure lies in refusing to see that the contradiction is within himself and his institutions, not in the writer's words).

I am not speaking of the question which is often raised as to whether other values take precedence over academic freedom. Certainly there are immediate and pressing human needs—survival and minimum welfare—which must exclude study when it is necessary to make a choice. The case has often been made that the problems outside the university are so pressing that they cannot be ignored merely for the sake of preserving academic freedom for a few. Rather than entering into that controversy I question the basic terms in which it is discussed, namely, the assumption that the university is today a sanctuary of academic freedom in the traditional sense of the phrase.

Today "academic freedom" plays a basic ideological role in justifying the university's participation in a corporate and militaristic society. It does so only because those who frequently employ this concept have largely perverted its meaning. This becomes especially clear when we examine some of the uses which presently are being made of the idea of academic freedom. An example at hand is the statement called "The University as a Sanctuary of Academic Freedom" which was circulated at Columbia by part of the liberal establishment.

The statement begins innocuously enough, even if it is, perhaps, a bit self-righteous: "The tradition of the university as a sanctuary of academic freedom and center of informed discussion is an honored one, to be guarded vigilantly." The statement then goes on to say what freedom is: "the rights of professors to teach, of scholars to engage in the advancement of knowledge, of students to learn and to express their views, free from external pressures or interference." I have emphasized the last phrase because it is crucial to understanding the present liberal-conservative interpretation of academic freedom. Apparently it is believed that the SDS disruption of classes was an "external pressure" on the academic community which endangered its freedom. In reality, "external pressure" can hardly come from the university's own students who, as a matter of fact, were protesting the institution's growing complicity in American imperialism and racism. The "academic community" is not a relatively closed group sharing common objectives of advancing knowledge, but contains within it whole schools, institutes, and groups of academics whose obvious function is to aid imperialism (School of International Affairs, S.E. Asia Institute, Jason project, etc.). I for one resent being called part of the academic community if it implies that I share the goals of those who do such work. Finally, what kind of freedom is endangered by disruptions of classes and other protests directed at the way in which the university is becoming an integral part of the ruling apparatus? It is the freedom for teachers now in the university to be listened to and for their students to listen to them and "express their views" (in the way which the teacher deems appropriate). This is the "freedom" of the authoritarian classroom. One might have supposed that academic freedom was an ideal for the university community as a whole, and that it meant freedom within this community: freedom to challenge prevailing views and substantive evils, freedom for all perspectives (especially those critical of the society) to be elaborated and explained. This is closer to the academic and intellectual freedom sought by the Enlightenment.

It is instructive to see why this broader intellectual freedom and sanctuary is not mentioned in the statement. If we turn away from the traditional rhetoric of the statement to some more serious observations and proposals of some of its signers we begin to see that the academic freedom they praise is freedom for the corporate university to perform its functions in the economic-military system without interference (I hope that not all signers of the statement endorse the following quotations; if they do not, they should begin to reflect on what they do mean by academic freedom.) Daniel Bell envisions the future society as being led by "the research corporations, the industrial laboratories, the experimental stations, and the universities."* The individual leaders will be "the scientists, the mathematicians, the economists, the engineers of the new corporate technology ... not only the best talents, but eventually the whole complex of social prestige and social status will be rooted in the intellectual and scientific communities." As technology becomes continually more complex, the corporations and military find the university an indispensable supplier of trained manpower and researchers. Perhaps we are on the verge of a new stage of capitalism in which the universities will take a major role—if so then the university need not be concerned with external interference except as a challenge to its authority—not as an impediment to its academic freedom. As for that, Professor Brzinski of the School of International Affairs gives us a fairly clear vision of what will happen in the neo-capitalist university: "The largely humanist-oriented, occasionally ideologically-minded intellectual dissenter, who sees his role largely in terms of proffering social critiques, is rapidly being displaced either by experts and specialists, who become involved in special government undertakings, or by the generalist-integrators, who become in effect house-ideologues for those in power, providing overall intellectual integration for disparate actions." Professor Brzinski is tireless in defending the freedom of "house-ideologues" to teach their classes how to intellectually integrate "disparate actions" (Vietnam, racism, the growing dependence of the economy on weaponry and waste); as for those who proffer "social critiques" of the system, nobody will interfere with their academic freedom—they will simply be "displaced." (Columbia has a long tradition of firing social dissenters, dating from the time of Daniel de Leon and Charles Beard; it has been revived since last spring.)

This new concept of academic freedom is very much like the relatively new concept of free enterprise. The latter is an amalgamation of two ideas—free market and private enterprise—which seemed to the laissez-faire economists to describe freedom within

*This and subsequent quotations from Bell and Brzinski are from Noam Chomsky, "The Menace of Liberal Scholarship," *The New York Review of Books*, January 2, 1969.

the economic system. The production and exchange of goods was thought to take place by free contracts among independent individuals. In corporate capitalism there is no "free" market and no "private" enterprise—there is free enterprise, meaning capitalism unchecked by any "external pressures" such as concern for human life or welfare. In the university there is no real "freedom" of these sections of the apparatus of domination. It would be an interesting and somewhat grotesque intellectual exercise to attempt to fathom why the official reasons given for denying credit to ROTC are not equally applicable to the divisions which serve the CIA, the State Department and the corporations. Having traditional academic freedom as an ideal might lead us to question a School of International Affairs whose function is to turn out CIA men and other agents of U.S. imperialism rather than to analyze the nature of third world rebellions and other large social movements without "external pressure or interference." It might lead us to wonder why the Business School does not make the slightest pretense of evaluating the U.S. economy from many competing points of view, but simply trains people to administer it smoothly.

In fact NROTC is only the tip of the iceberg of military-corporate influence at Columbia. Only a few departments have been left relatively untouched by its demands, and even they often manifest a bureaucratization of form in teaching, standards of academic excellence, and even the intellectual conception of the area of study, all of these developments having occurred at the same time as the growing intrusion of the military-industrial state onto the campus. The "value-free" social sciences, even in such reputedly liberated parts of Columbia as the College and Graduate Faculties, show the growing cohesion of the requirements of the warfare economy and the substance of the curriculum. People must be taught to accept the system and trained to administer and rationalize it. Consciousness must keep up with social change—thus the need for "generalist-integrators." Accordingly, the prevailing view in the social sciences is one which studies the way in which various systems function and maintain their stability; since the R.S. is one of the main systems studied, the results obtained comprise a knowledge of how to keep things going with the least possible adjustment and admiration for the way in which a society which performs so many "disparate actions" can be given an "overall intellectual integration." The social scientists, of course, reject the notion that they place any premium on the stability of the system—this is just their "objective" way of studying things. This one-sided emphasis on functionalism and system-stability masks an allegiance to the status quo and an anxiety about the disruption of its orderly processes. Disruptive students are like third-world guerrillas; the ringing announcement at the end of the statement mentioned would not be out of place in a Johnson/Nixon speech on Vietnam: "It is our intention not to surrender the safeguards of freedom that men have erected at great sacrifice over several centuries." The implication that freedom has already been realized (in the U.S. or at the university) is of course inconsistent with the classical liberal and democratic tradition which always saw freedom as something to be extended to more people and to new areas of life. There is a need to discuss just who and what is free within the university, rather than to repeatedly invoke a phrase that has lost most of its original content.

In the Government department, political theory is fast disappearing to be replaced by comparative government—the study of how different systems function. Political theory, after all, raises those sticky questions about freedom and human values made fashionable by such "humanist-oriented ... intellectual dissenters" as Locke, Rousseau, and Marx. (Political theorists are not being denied their freedom, simply "displaced.") In introductory economics students learn how the capitalist system functions; if they have questions about the course or the orientation they must go to the section-men, one of whom recently admitted that he knew nothing about other economic systems. If one challenges such narrowness of vision or attempts to point out that the ideology of the classroom is related to that of the government he is an enemy of "academic freedom."

The ideal of academic freedom is a powerful and moving one for most intellectuals. When we attempt to envision the world which we desire to create, we hope that inquiry in all areas of thought and action will be free, that all points of view will be heard, and that the place of criticism will be respected. We believe this because we consider ourselves, at least potentially, members of a rational community—one which is genuinely democratic in its communication, inquiry, and action.

It is an illusion to suppose that outside of a few humanistic fields Columbia or any other major American university approaches that ideal. This is hardly surprising; Columbia gets about half of its money from the government and is run by trustees who represent Lockheed Aircraft, the District Attorney's office and other freedom-loving interests. It might be excusable that many liberals do not see the connection; it is grotesque that they can protest against a few disruptions of classes in the name of an ideal which is daily dishonored at Columbia in large areas of the university.

The ideology of "academic freedom" is now being heard from strange sources; when Nixon jumps on the band-wagon perhaps a few more liberals will be disquieted. As we move towards the Bell-Brzinski vision of the corporate university within the corporate society let us hope that more students and intellectuals will realize the irony contained in the defense of the university as "sanctuary": "Academic freedom and the sanctuary of the campus . . . cannot be invoked by those who would subordinate intellectual freedom to political ends."

Professors Bell and Brzinski have a more accurate perception of the reality: the "sanctuary" is already being used for political ends. In the words of the New University Conference statement on the student rebellion:

> . . . if the university were a democratic institution, if it stood against racism, if it refused to serve imperialist and militarist ends, if it were genuinely diverse in the interests it served and in its internal composition, then there would be no special need for challenging it—and community might be possible on the campus. But then, too, it would have a difficult time surviving in a society such as ours.

Professor Sidney Hook (see page 124) is a well known philosopher and a controversial figure in political discussions both within and outside of the academic world. It should be noted that he also contributed to the defense of academic freedom in the case of Bertrand Russell. Most recently, he has founded a national organization of academicians called University Centers for Rational Alternatives.

I began my college career in the fall of 1919, almost a half century ago. My academic lifetime spans half a dozen revolutions in American education. But have no fear, I am not going to reminisce. I want to stay young, at least in spirit, and I learned from my teacher, John Dewey, whom I observed closely for the last twenty-five years of his life, what the secret of staying young is, and that is *not* to reminisce about the past. Actually, I never heard John Dewey reminisce until he was in his nineties, and that was as a reluctant response to my deliberate prodding in order to extract biographical data from him.

However, there is a way of talking about the past that is not merely reminiscence or idle reverie. It occurs when we make comparisons of the past and present for the sake of a present purpose or for the sake of finding a new way out of present difficulties.

Fifty years ago when I began my college studies, it would be no exaggeration to say that the belief in academic freedom was regarded as faintly subversive even in many academic circles. The AAUP [American Association of University Professors], organized by two philosophers, Arthur Lovejoy and John Dewey, was in its infancy without influence or authority. Today, except in some of the cultural and political backwaters of the U.S., academic freedom, although not free from threats, is firmly established. In some regions it has the support of law.

Fifty years ago, the power of the chief university administrator was almost as unlimited as that of an absolute monarch. Today the administrator is a much harried man with much less power and authority among faculty, and especially students, than his forebears. Today, there may be temperamentally happy administrators but their present life is an unhappy one. There seems to be an open season on them, and to such a degree that for the first time in history there is an acute shortage of candidates for the almost three hundred vacant administrative posts in institutions of higher learning. When I did my graduate work at Columbia, Nicholas Murray Butler was both the reigning and ruling monarch. I don't believe that in his wildest dreams he could have conceived of the Columbia scene today. The strongest argument I know against the resurrection of the body is that if it were within the realm of possibility, Nicholas Murray Butler would have risen from his grave and would now be storming Morningside Heights.

Having been an administrator in a small way myself, I have learned what an ungrateful job it is, and at the same time how necessary. Without administrative leadership, every institution (especially universities, whose faculties are notoriously reluctant to introduce curricular changes) runs downhill. The greatness of a university consists predominantly in the greatness of its faculty. But faculties, because of reasons too complex to enter into here, do not themselves build great faculties. To build great faculties, administrative leadership is essential. In the affairs of the mind and in the realm of scholarship, the principles of simple majority rule or of "one man, one vote" do not apply. The most "democratically" run institutions of learning are usually the most mediocre. It takes a big man to live comfortably with a still bigger man under him, no less to invite him to cast his shadow over the less gifted.

TARGETS OF ABUSE

The paradox today is that as administrative power decreases and becomes more limited, the greater the dissatisfaction with it seems to grow. The memory of favors or requests denied remains much stronger than the memories of requests granted. Faculties are fickle in their allegiance. Overnight the most beloved of administrators can become the target of abuse, a figure of obloquy in the eyes of the very faculty, or a large section of it, which he himself has helped to build. In the very year that Clark Kerr received the Meikeljohn medal for academic freedom, the faculty at the University of California campus at Berkeley panicked in consequence of the events resulting from the *fourth* student sit-in.

In effect it repudiated him by adopting a set of resolutions that made him the scapegoat for the student lawlessness that it conspicuously refused to condemn. The faculty even voted down a motion that would have given the students complete freedom of speech except to urge the commission of *immediate acts* of force and violence. Another example: Vice President Truman of Columbia University was vigorously applauded at Columbia's commencement last June for, among other things, opening new avenues of communication with students. Only a few days ago he was roundly booed by a section of the Columbia faculty.

Why any scholar (and administrators are largely recruited from the ranks of scholars) should want to become a *full-time* administrator has always puzzled me. The duties, sacrifices and risks seem altogether disproportionate to the rewards. In speaking of administrators, one is tempted to characterize them with the words Lecky used in his great history of European morals about the fallen women of Europe: "The eternal priestesses of humanity blasted for the sins of their people." Well, university administrators are no longer priests, but whenever a crisis arises they are sure to be damned if they do and damned if they don't.

SYNTHETIC STORMS

One thing seems clear. In the crisis situations shaping up throughout the country, administrators are not going to enjoy a peaceful life. Their prospect of weathering the storms that will be synthetically contrived for them depends upon their ability and willingness to win the faculty for whatever plans and proposals they advance in the name of the university. For if they permit students or any other group to drive a wedge between them and the faculty, they will discover the sad fact of academic life that in such rifts the faculty will either play a neutral role or even assume a hostile one.

Not only on good educational grounds, therefore, but on prudential ones as well, the administration must draw the faculty into the formulation of institutional educational policy. I say this with reluctance because it means the proliferation of committee meetings, the dilution of scholarly interest, and even less time for students. But this is a small price to pay for academic freedom and peace.

In talking about academic freedom, nothing signifies the distance we have come in the space of my lifetime so much as the fact that we now are concerned with the academic freedom of *students*. For historical reasons I cannot now explore, academic freedom in the United States meant *Lehrnfreiheit*, freedom to teach. *Lernfreiheit*, freedom to learn, has only recently been stressed. It does not mean the same as it meant under the German university system that presupposed the all-prescribed curriculum of studies of the *Gymnasium*. If academic freedom for students means freedom to learn, then two things should be obvious. There is no academic freedom to learn without *Lehrnfreiheit* or academic freedom to teach. Where teachers have no freedom to teach, students have obviously no freedom to learn, although the converse is not true.

Second, students' freedom to learn was never so widely recognized, was never so pervasive in the United States as it is today—whether it be construed as the freedom to attend college or not, or the freedom to select the *kind* of college the student wishes to attend or his freedom of curricular choice *within* the kind of college he selects. Above all, if academic freedom for students means the freedom to doubt, challenge, contest and debate within the context of inquiry, American students are the freest in the world, and far freer than they were when I attended college.

I recall an incident when I was a student in a government class at CCNY. The teacher conducted the class by letting the students give reports on the themes of the course. All he contributed was to say "next" as each student concluded. But when in reporting on the Calhoun-Webster debates, I declared that it seemed to me that Calhoun had the better of the argument, that his logic was better than Webster's although his *cause* was worse, the instructor exploded and stopped me. After emotionally recounting his father's services in the Civil War, he turned wrathfully on me and shouted: "Young man! When you're not preaching sedition, you are preaching secession!" Whereupon he drove me from the class. (The "sedition" was a reference to an earlier report on Beard's economic interpretation of the Constitution that he had heard with grim disapproval.) And this was at CCNY in 1920! The incident wasn't typical, but that it could happen at all marks the profundity of the changes in attitudes toward students since then. John Dewey's influence has made itself felt even in the colleges today.

Moral Premise

Of course, there is still a large group of potential college students who are deprived of freedom to learn because of poverty or prejudice or the absence of adequate educational facilities. And as citizens of a democratic society whose moral premise is that each individual has a right to that education that will permit him to achieve his maximum growth as a person, our duty is to work for, or support, whatever measures of reconstruction we deem necessary to remove the social obstacles to freedom of learning. It is perfectly legitimate to expect the university to study these problems and propose solutions to them. All universities worthy of the name already do. This is one thing. But to therefore conclude that these problems must become items not only on the agenda of study but for an agenda of action is quite another.

For it therewith transforms the university into a political action organization and diverts it from its essential task of discovery, teaching, dialogue and criticism. Since there are profound differences about the social means necessary to achieve a society in which there will be a maximum freedom to learn, the university would become as partisan and biased as other political action groups urging their programs on the community. Its primary educational purpose or mission would be lost. It would be compelled to silence or misrepresent the position of those of its faculty who disagreed with its proposals and campaigns of action. Class and group conflicts would rend the fabric of the community of scholars in an unceasing struggle for power completely unrelated to the quest for truth.

OBJECTIVITY IMPERILED

If the university is conceived as an agency of action to transform society in behalf of a cause, no matter how exalted, it loses its *relative* autonomy, imperils both its independence and objectivity, and subjects itself to retaliatory curbs and controls on the part of society on whose support and largesse it ultimately depends.

This is precisely the conception of a university that is basic to the whole strategy and tactics of the so-called Students for a Democratic Society. I say "so-called" because their actions show that they are no more believers in democracy than the leaders of the so-called Student Non-Violent Co-ordinating Committee are believers in non-violence. And indeed the leaders of the SDS make no bones about that fact. In manifesto after manifesto they have declared that they want to use the university as an instrument of revolution. To do so, they must destroy the university as it exists today.

I wish I had time to list some of the clever strategems they have devised to focus their opposition. On every campus there are always some grievances. Instead of seeking peacefully to resolve them through existing channels of consultation and deliberation, the SDS seeks to inflame them. Where grievances don't exist, they can be created. In one piece of advice to chapter members, they were urged to sign up for certain courses in large numbers, and then denounce the university for its large classes!

Freedom of dissent, speech, protest is never the real issue. They are, of course, always legitimate. But the tactic of the SDS is to give dissent the immediate form of violent action. The measures necessarily adopted to counteract this lawless action then become the main issue, as if the original provocation hadn't occurred. Mario Savio admitted after the Berkeley affair that the issue of "free speech" was a "pretext"—the word was his—to arouse the students against the existing role of the university in society.

SEEK TO DESTROY

One of the leaders of the SDS at Columbia is reported to have said: "As much as we would like to, we are not strong enough as yet to destroy the United States. But we are strong enough to destroy Columbia!" He is wrong about this, too—the only action that would destroy Columbia would be faculty support of the students!—but his intent is clear.

Actually, the only thing these groups, loosely associated with the New Left, are clear about is what they want to destroy, not what they would put in its stead. In a debate with Gore Vidal, Tom Hayden, one of the New Left leaders, was pointedly asked what his revolutionary program was. He replied: "We haven't any. First we will make the revolution, and *then* we will find out what for." This is truly the politics of absurdity.

The usual response present-day academic rebels make to this criticism is that the university today is nothing but an instrument to preserve the status quo, and therefore faithless to the ideals of a community of scholars. Even if this charge were true, even if the universities today were bulwarks of the status quo, this would warrant criticism and protest, not violent and lawless action in behalf of a contrary role, just as foreign to their true function. But it is decidedly *not* true!

There is no institution in the country in which dissent and criticism of official views, of tradition, of the conventional wisdom in all fields, is freer and more prevalent than in the university. The very freedom of dissent that students today enjoy in our universities is in large measure a consequence of the spirit of experiment, openness to new ideas, absence of conformity and readiness to undertake new initiatives found among them.

ARROGANT CLAIM

The first casualty of the strategy of the campus rebels is academic freedom. It is manifest in their bold and arrogant claim that the university drop its research in whatever fields these students deem unfit for academic inquiry and investigation. This note was already sounded in Berkeley. It is focal at Columbia. It is a shameless attempt to usurp powers of decision that the faculty alone should have. After all, it is preposterous for callow and immature adolescents who presumably have come to the university to get an education to set themselves up as authorities on what research by their teachers is educationally permissible.

Unless checked, it will not be long before these students will be presuming to dictate the conclusions their teachers should reach, especially on controversial subjects. This is standard procedure in totalitarian countries in which official student organizations are the political arm of the ruling party. Already there are disquieting signs of this. At Cornell a few weeks ago—*before* the martyrdom of Dr. King—a group of Black Nationalist students invaded the offices of the chairman of the economics department and held him captive in order to get an apology from a teacher whose views on African affairs they disagreed with. Only yesterday, another group at Northwestern demanded that courses in "black literature" and "black art" be taught by teachers approved by the Negro students.

And there are spineless administrators and cowardly members of the faculty who are prepared to yield to this blackmail. Under the slogans of "student rights" and "participatory democracy" the most militant groups of students are moving to weaken and ultimately destroy the academic freedom of those who disagree with them.

Let us not delude ourselves. Even when these militant students fail to achieve their ultimate purpose, they succeed in demoralizing the university by deliberately forcing a confrontation upon the academic community that it is not prepared to face and the costs of which it is fearful of accepting. In forcing the hand of the academic community to meet force with force, the citadel of reason becomes a battlefield. The students glory in it, but the faint of heart among their teachers turn on their own administrative leaders. These militants succeed in sowing distrust among students who do not see through their strategy. They also succeed in dividing the faculties.

EMBITTER RELATIONS

There is always a small group—a strange mixture of purists and opportunists desirous of ingratiating themselves with students—who will *never* condemn the violence of students but only the violence required to stop it. These students succeed, even when they fail, in embittering relations between the administration and some sections of the faculty. They succeed, even when they fail, in antagonizing the larger community of which the university is a part, and in arousing a vigilante spirit that demands wholesale measures of repression and punishment that educators cannot properly accept.

How is it possible, one asks, for events of this character to happen? There have always been extremist and paranoidal tendencies in academic life, but they have been peripheral—individuals and small groups moving in eccentric intellectual orbits. But not until the last four or five years has the norm of social protest taken the form of direct action, have positions been expressed in such ultimatistic and intransigent terms, have extremist elements been strong enough to shut down great universities even for a limited time.

There are many and complex causes for this. But as I see it, the situation in the university is part of a larger phenomenon, viz., the climate of intellectual life in the country. I do not recall any other period in the last fifty years when intellectuals themselves have been so intolerant of each other, when differences over complex issues have been the occasion for denunciation rather than debate and analysis, when the use of violence—in the right cause, of course!—is taken for granted, when dissent is not distinguished from civil disobedience, and civil disobedience makes common cause with resistance, and readiness for insurrection. A few short years ago, anti-intellectualism was an epithet of derogation. Today it is an expression of revolutionary virility.

FANATICISM RAMPANT

In the fifties I wrote an essay on "The Ethics of Controversy," trying to suggest guidelines for controversy among principled democrats no matter how widely they differed on substantive issues. Today I would be talking into the wind for all the attention it would get. Fanaticism seems to be in the saddle. That it is a fanaticism of conscience, of self-proclaimed virtue, doesn't make it less dangerous. This past year has presented the spectacle of militant minorities in our colleges from one end of the country to another, preventing or trying to prevent representatives of positions they disapprove of from speaking to their fellow-students wishing to listen to them.

The spectacle shows that we have failed to make our students understand the very rudiments of democracy, that to tolerate active intolerance is to compound it. If we judge commitment by action, the simple truth is that the great body of our students is not firmly committed to democracy or to the liberal spirit without which democracy may become the rule of the mob.

I do not know any sure way or even a new way of combatting the dominant mood of irrationalism, especially among students and even among younger members of the faculty whose political naivete is often cynically exploited by their younger, yet politically more sophisticated, allies. What is of the first importance is to preserve, of course, the absolute intellectual integrity of our classrooms and laboratories, of our teaching and research against any attempt to curb it. We must defend it not only against the traditional enemies, who still exist even when they are dormant but also against those who think they have the infallible remedies for the world's complex problems, and that all they need is sincerity as patent of authority. Fanatics don't lack sincerity. It is their long suit. They drip with sincerity—and when they have power, with blood—other people's blood.

We need more, however, than a defensive strategy, safeguarding the intellectual integrity of our vocation against those who threaten it. We need—and I know this sounds paradoxical—to counterpose to the revolt of the emotionally committed the revolt of the rationally committed. I do not want to identify this with the revolt of the moderates. There are some things one should not be moderate about. In the long run, the preservation of democracy depends upon a passion for freedom, for the logic and ethics of free discussion and inquiry, upon refusal to countenance the measures of violence that cut short the processes of intelligence upon which the possibility of shared values depends.

These are old truths but they bear repeating whenever they are denied. Even tautologies become important when counterposed to absurdities.

We as teachers must make our students more keenly aware of the centrality of the democratic process to a free society and of the centrality of intelligence to the democratic process. Democracy has our allegiance because of its cumulative fruits, but at any particular time the process is more important than any specific program or product. He who destroys the process because it does not guarantee some particular outcome is as foolish as someone who discards scientific method in medicine or engineering or any other discipline because of its failure to solve altogether or immediately a stubborn problem.

COURAGE NEEDED

There is one thing we cannot deny to the intransigent and fanatical enemies of democracy. That is courage. Intelligence is necessary to overcome foolishness. But it is not sufficient to tame fanaticism. Only courage can do that. A handful of men who are prepared to fight, to bleed, to suffer and, if need be, to die, will always triumph in a community where those whose freedom they threaten are afraid to use their *intelligence* to resist and to fight, and ultimately to take the same risks in action as those determined to destroy them.

Yes, there is always the danger that courage *alone* may lead us to actions that will make us similar to those who threaten us. But that is what we have intelligence for—to prevent that from happening! It is this union of courage and intelligence upon which the hope of democratic survival depends.

PART VI

Academic Political Activism: Pro and Con

The University of California at Berkeley was until recently one of the largest, fastest growing, and most progressive of American universities. It was the first state-supported university to achieve an international reputation for excellence, primarily in the sciences and technology. In September of 1964 the administration, headed by Clark Kerr, issued an order banning the solicitation of funds for political and social movements originating off-campus. That ban was opposed by the Free Speech Movement (FSM) headed by Mario Savio, and was finally rescinded. The original members of the FSM argued, and rightly so, that the ban was an infringement on the right of free speech. Since then Kerr and Savio have departed, and the movement has progressed first to removing the anonymity of the University and more recently to political reform within the State of California.

In view of the incidents reported in the following editorial, it is ironic that the FSM originally insisted that the University should restrict itself to maintaining normal running of the school and protecting the right of teachers to hold classes.

Campus Totalitarians

The alarming concept that extremism in the hands of allegedly idealistic young radicals is no vice is beginning to undermine the very foundations of academic freedom.

The extent of the erosion of principles without which free society cannot survive has been underscored by reports of a deliberate campaign of harassment conducted by militant New Left students against Dr. Arthur Jensen, an educational psychologist at Berkeley. Dr. Jensen has come under attack for a research paper, published in the Harvard Educational Review, which suggests that hereditary factors, in addition to environmental ones, may account for lower averages in I.Q. scores shown by Negroes and other disadvantaged groups.

The question is not whether the Jensen research is valid. There is much evidence that it is being abused by some who want to bolster their racist prejudices, although this was clearly not Dr. Jensen's intention. As Dr. Joshua Lederberg, the Nobel Prize geneticist at Stanford University, has pointed out, the study serves as a reminder that diseases, malnutrition or dietary imbalances, either during prenatal or early childhood stages or as a consequence of conditions of past history, may have to be investigated further for their influence on the heredity of various ethnic groups. While Dr. Lederberg disagrees with some aspects of the Jensen hypothesis —particularly the doubts it throws on compensatory education programs, which at best are still in their experimental infancy—he also leaves no doubt that its publication was a scientific contribution and should be treated as such.

This is the heart of the matter. The young totalitarians who have harassed Dr. Jensen and whose tactics of pressure and smear have led to the resignation of one of the scholar's staff members pose a threat to the future of free inquiry that can no longer be ignored. A campus on which classes must be shifted to secret meeting places in order to avoid disruption may soon cease to be a campus at all.

There is special irony that these outrages against free speech are being perpetrated at Berkeley, where the student rebellion originated under the banner of the Free Speech Movement. The subjugation of science—including theories of heredity—to the orthodoxies of political revolutions has been the mark of Fascist, Nazi and Stalinist totalitarianism. Surrender to such tactics cannot be tolerated on the American campus.

In late April and early May of 1968 the first serious disturbances at a highly reputable university occurred at Columbia. They started ostensibly with a protest against, among other things, the building of a gymnasium and the University's connection with the Institute of Defense Analysis. The protest led to the seizing of buildings, police confrontations, and a "strike." Full-scale analyses are still rather controversial.

For our purposes, it is important to note that the research papers of Professor Orest Ranum of the history department were mysteriously burned after he had opposed the strike by continuing to hold his classes. Moreover, Columbia has become, along with Berkeley, a striking instance of a "politicized" university. The following selections present diverse views and consequences of the situation.

The New York Times

Rebels at Columbia Are Called "Issueless"

"I think they are desperate and issueless. Ugliness and meanness is all they have left."

That was the reaction of James S. Young, associate professor of government, who was struck with a club by Columbia University students yesterday as they charged into Fayerweather Hall.

Professor Young and a colleague, Professor Harvey Mansfield, who was also roughed up by the students, discussed the experience in an interview shortly afterward. They both promised to return to the classroom today.

"I was swirled around and shoved and saved from falling by Jim," Professor Mansfield recalled. "It was frightening."

The two professors said that Dr. Andrew W. Cordier, Columbia's acting president, had told them that the university would press charges if the attackers could be identified.

But neither of the two, who were still badly shaken hours after the incident, was able to recognize their attackers, although they both have wide acquaintances among the students.

Both are well-known, well-liked and generally sympathetic to moderate reform efforts on the troubled Columbia campus. They have served in the past as mediators between the students and the administration.

But yesterday both men were indignant.

"It has gone beyond issues—it is naked force against the democratic process," said Professor Mansfield, a slender, sixty-four-year-old scholar who spent nine years as managing editor of *The American Political Science Review* and is a professor of government at Columbia.

Professor Young, a Princeton graduate who is forty years old, said that his assailants had seized him from behind as he clung to a doorknob for support.

While one young man held him, another hit him in the face with a club, inflicting an ugly bruise under the left eye.

Then they threw him to the ground, he said, where a student threatened him with the nozzle of a fire hose.

The two men had just come down stairs in the building with Peter B. Kenon, chairman of the economics department, and they were standing in the doorway about to go to lunch.

Professor Kenen, who was not available for comment later, was also pushed and shoved in the student charge.

After the scuffle, Professor Mansfield and Professor Young hurried back up to their department offices on the fifth floor, as the students barricaded the building.

Two and a half hours later, they were permitted to leave with their secretaries, Miss Edith Black and Mrs. Sophie Berson, and they crawled out through a ground-floor window. Asked why he was so determined to come back to the campus today, Professor Mansfield explained:

"The faculty must stand as a symbol of reason and sanity."

Columbia Daily Spectator

Faculty Troubled by SDS Action

Members of Students for a Democratic Society took their cause to the classrooms yesterday and many faculty members whose courses were interrupted by the students last night expressed indignation at the incidents.

Robert A. Laudicina, assistant dean for student affairs, yesterday stated that about ten professors complained to the Dean's office about the interruptions and said that many faculty members offered the administration names of suspected disrupters.

According to Dean Laudicina, several professors have also asked the University to provide special security for classroom buildings today.

Nearly forty classes in six campus buildings were interrupted yesterday when SDS members, seeking support for a planned demonstration today, entered classrooms to make announcements and distribute leaflets calling for an end to NROTC, military research, and armed forces recruiting.

In an interview last night William Martin, a lecturer in sociology whose class was briefly interrupted yesterday, stated that he may ask the College administration to issue a public statement declaring that similar class interruptions "will not be tolerated" in the future. He said he might also press disciplinary complaints against the students involved in the action.

"I will take some kind of action," Mr. Martin said. "I believe this has to be stopped."

"These actions strike right at the heart of the University," he said. "If a student doesn't believe in consecutive rational discourse, he has no place at all here."

Roland E. Wulbert, an instructor in sociology whose class was also interrupted, yesterday differed with his colleague's view of the matter.

"It would be quite another matter if it would go on over a long period of time repeatedly," Mr. Wulbert said. "But I'm not particularly upset."

The sociology instructor remarked that he could not be particularly troubled by yesterday's action in part because "some of the best students I've had all year" participated in the interruptions.

Associate Professor of Music Gordon F. Crain, who walked out of his music humanities class and alerted his departmental office yesterday when three SDS members entered his room, last night scored the student interruptions.

"I don't really know what they were doing," he commented. "But you just don't walk into anybody's class and—without explanation or permission—take over. It was just simply bad manners."

"If it happens again, I will make a scene," he said. "I'll throw them out if necessary."

Professor of German Ludwig W. Kahn, however, had a different view of the SDS action. "I thought it was funny," he said. "It was nothing to get excited about."

Radicals Interrupt Nearly Forty Classes in NROTC Drive

SIT-INS PLANNED TODAY AFTER NOON SDS RALLY

Members of Students for a Democratic Society yesterday interrupted nearly forty classes in six University buildings in an attempt to attract support for a planned sit-in demonstration today against the Naval Reserve Officers Training Corps, on-campus war research, and Columbia's expansion policies.

Approximately two dozen SDS members met at the sundial at 10:30 A.M., divided into teams of three, and fanned out to cover all major undergraduate classroom buildings and Barnard Hall. They attempted to pass out petitions in classes calling for the abolition of the campus NROTC unit, the end of on-campus military recruiting and the cessation of research for the government.

According to an SDS spokesman, the organization plans to hold "several non-violent, non-destructive sit-ins" in campus buildings today following a noon sundial rally. The sit-ins will end in a few hours, the spokesman said, and SDS will then hold an open meeting in Havemeyer Hall to discuss them.

Several conservative student groups are expected to hold counter-demonstrations today. John Meyer, Graduate Faculties, chairman of Students for a Free Campus, said yesterday that his organization would employ "militant non-violent" tactics to prevent the radicals from entering buildings.

The group has received permission from Proctor William E. Kahn to use the sundial at noon today, in accordance with the Interim Rules. This year SDS has ignored the directive and it is possible that a dispute over the use of the sundial may develop.

According to Robert A. Laudicina, assistant dean for student affairs, the University administration has not taken any security measures to prevent possible violence between students.

Student and faculty reaction to the class interruptions was vocal and, in most cases, hostile. Several faculty members shoved the protesters out of their classrooms, and others walked out or called off their classes. In most of the classes where votes were taken, students voted to have the disrupters leave immediately. There was no violence, but a number of instances of pushing and shoving occurred.

In Associate Professor of English Edward Said's class, three SDS members entered and began to speak while Professor Said was still lecturing. He demanded that they leave, announcing that he would leave if they stayed.

Most of the seventy-five students in the class shouted for the disrupters to get out, but before a vote was taken, Dr. Said stalked out. The radicals also left, and several students retrieved him from his office, where he had called campus security to report the disruption.

Professor of English Quentin Anderson refused to allow the demonstrators into his seminar, bodily shoving them out the door. "You're interfering with my class, young man—out," he said, planting both palms on a student's chest, and pushing him out the door.

In a calculus class in Mathematics Hall, students booed the disrupters when they announced they were members of SDS. When one demonstrator attempted to write an announcement on the blackboard, students in the class got up and erased it.

In another mathematics class, however, the SDS team was permitted to speak. "Excuse me, we have to talk to this class for about two minutes," an SDS member said, adding that "usually most people don't see the classroom as a political forum."

After listing the SDS demands, the students left. One explained somewhat apologetically, "For those of you who don't agree with us—and I'm sure there are many—we'll be meeting tomorrow night to explain what we did tomorrow afternoon."

A lecturer in a biology class reportedly gave the revolutionary salute—waving his clenched fist—when an SDS team entered his class, and was cheered by his students.

Several Barnard professors led walkouts after their classes were interrupted. In one history class, the professor said, "If you had asked before class you could have spoken, but we're in the middle of a discussion." The demonstrators went on talking, and were in turn interrupted by the professor who shouted, "This is enough, get the hell out of here." They left.

Students in a chemistry lecture in Havemeyer Hall tossed paper airplanes and epithets at the radicals who attempted to speak, and voted overwhelmingly for them to leave. One stood up and shouted, "Get out, we don't want you here!"

Roland Wulbert, a sociology instructor, defended the SDS group which entered his class, although his students demanded that they leave so the lecture could continue. Several students walked out angrily; the debate over whether to listen to the radicals took up the rest of the period.

"The day went well in that we started to break down the division between classrooms and the outside world," an SDS spokesman said yesterday. "That is not to say we are going to come in every day and impose anything," he continued. "We just want to present our program."

During the interruptions, however, many students asserted that they had paid for their classes and wanted to be instructed in what they had signed up for. "I can find out what you have to say anytime," one enraged student shouted when his sociology class was disrupted, "but I can't hear about Piaget anywhere else."

Beyond Honesty

Journalists in this country have contended that a responsible newspaper must report the news in an "objective" impartial manner. Newspapers, the traditionalists have said, must provide a chronicle of events and the reader—not the reporter—must be left to interpret and analyze the news. Opinion was to be strictly confined to the editorial page and the news columns were to be somehow free of all judgment and interpretation.

During the past century, a similar and parallel tradition developed within the University. The campus, it was said, was an apolitical sanctuary for "free inquiry and rational discourse." And the University—like the newspaper—was to remain neutral and aloof from partisan causes.

As we take editorial control of *Spectator* today, we must question whether a newspaper or a university can or should be objective and value-free.

In the most recent issue of *Columbia College Today*, George Keller, recounting the events of last spring, contends that by the fourth day of the protest, "*Spectator* had dropped all pretense of objective reporting." We do not believe this newspaper tried to maintain a pretense of objectivity last spring. But if it ever did, we intend to drop that pretense now.

Objectivity is an illusory goal: it presumes that the news occurs in only one way and that the good reporter will relate the news "as it happens to be." But news does not just "happen to be." The reporter, the editor and the reader each bring their own perspective to events: To pretend that any newspaper can report the news devoid of perspective and interpretation is absurd. To seek such a detached view would be sterile. We can only hope to report events as we see them and to report them as accurately and with as much insight as we can.

In the past few months, critics have accused *Spectator* of blowing certain events out of proportion. Our only answer is that we must have a sense of proportion to put out a newspaper. And if our proportions appear unjustified to the critics, it is not because we are biased and they are objective, but because our sense of proportion does not conform to theirs.

This newspaper contains a variety of opinions, but our heterogeneity is not a source of neutrality. Each of us brings his values to the decisions we make, and the outcome is a collective judgment, not an impartial one.

The editors of this paper must decide each day what news will be covered and how prominently that news will be played. And in so doing, we bring our own priorities to events.

We recognize that this journal must remain independent and we will not allow the newspaper to serve the interests of any organization or faction on campus. But neither will we pretend to report the news with complete disinterest ourselves.

However, while we are prepared to shed the pretense of objectivity, there are those within the University who are clearly not prepared to do the same. In the past, administrators and prominent faculty members have contended that Columbia is a "value-free" institution devoted to open inquiry and free discussion. But the University has demonstrated time and time again—by its actions and inactions—that Columbia is a partisan, political corporation.

When Columbia permits the United States Navy to use facilities on this campus to train men for military service the University makes a judgment. When Columbia signs a contract with the Department of Defense to do research for the armed forces the University makes a judgment. When Columbia expands its facilities in a manner which may be detrimental to the surrounding community the University makes a judgment. And when Columbia prosecutes hundreds of students in criminal court for protesting its judgments, the University also makes a judgment.

We recognize that our paper does not merely reflect events; it also affects them. We know that it is not enough to be honest about what we see—though we pledge to maintain honesty. We know that we are not merely a passive instrument of events and we are therefore prepared to go beyond honesty and accept responsibility for trying to change this University and its role in society.

Campus Disruptions Scored by One Hundred Senior Faculty

On March 10, one hundred Columbia faculty members issued a statement condemning force and disruptive activities which "deny students their right to an education and scholars their right to be heard."

In the belief that "the life of the free university is at stake," the sponsors of the statement invited the rest of the more than four thousand Columbia teachers to add their names to the one hundred. They called on faculty members at other universities to "take steps to clarify the nature and the value of the universities for themselves, their students and people in the community at large, and to define the measures that should be adopted to defend academic freedom."

"We are convinced," the initial sponsors wrote to their colleagues, "that most students have the same devotion as their teachers to free inquiry within the university, and we will welcome the opportunity to discuss the principles in this statement with individual students or interested groups at our own university."

Acting President Andrew W. Cordier said that he "noted with deep satisfaction the statement of a large group of faculty members regarding the University as a sanctuary of academic freedom. The substance of this statement deserves the support of the entire University community, the faculty, the student body and the administration."

Dr. Cordier said that the statement was "a demonstration of deep concern for the welfare and best interests of the University—interests that must be preserved by our collective will and action."

The text of the statement with the one hundred signers' names follows:

THE UNIVERSITY AS A SANCTUARY OF ACADEMIC FREEDOM

The tradition of the university as a sanctuary of academic freedom and center of informed discussion is an honored one, to be guarded vigilantly. The basic significance of that sanctuary lies in the protection of intellectual freedoms: the rights of professors to teach, of scholars to engage in the advancement of knowledge, of students to learn and express their views, free from external pressures or interference. These freedoms can flourish only in an atmosphere of mutual respect, civility and trust among teachers and students, only when members of the university community are willing to accept self-restraint and reciprocity as the condition upon which they share in its intellectual autonomy.

Academic freedom and the sanctuary of the university campus extend to all who share these aims and responsibilities. They cannot be invoked by those who would subordinate intellectual freedom to political ends, or who violate the norms of conduct established to protect that freedom. Against such offenders the university has the right, and indeed the obligation, to defend itself. Nor does the sanctuary of the university protect acts violating civil or criminal law, which are illegal whether committed on or off the campus.

Current attempts to disrupt or prevent the holding of classes are a matter of urgent concern to us. These tactics are fundamentally inimical to university life. No genuine education can take place if teachers and students are cast in an adversary role. Disruptions deny students their right to an education and scholars their right to be heard.

The claim is false that only by disruptive tactics can criticism be made effective and university policies changed. In the past important policy and curriculum changes have been made through faculty and student action, in which rational discussion has been used to find constructive solutions to our problems. We recognize the need for further reforms and hope that all members of the university community will join in the process of orderly discussion leading to such changes, but we cannot accept force as a substitute for reasoned argument in deciding matters affecting the curriculum, instruction, and administration of the university.

In September of 1968 the faculty of this University adopted interim rules in order to insure the right to demonstrate peaceably and at the same time guarantee that the normal functioning of the university would not be impeded. It is desirable that university discipline be administered through bodies representative of the academic community, but this can be effective only if their members accept their responsibility to protect each other's rights and demonstrate the will to act. The argument that "justice delayed is justice denied" applies to the university community as well as to persons charged with violations of campus rules. Justice is denied the community if disciplinary cases go unresolved and all proceedings are subsequently abandoned.

We hope that present juridical bodies and any university-wide senate to be established will not shirk their responsibility in these matters. Teachers and students are entitled to meet their classes without interference, and the university is obliged to secure that freedom. We call upon all members of this and other universities to defend by example and by action the fundamental principles of a free university. It is our intention not to surrender the safeguards of freedom that men have erected at great sacrifice over several centuries.

(signed)

Rejoinder

Classroom disruptions are certainly not to be defended for their own sake. But the issue is not as clear-cut as our senior faculty members would have us believe. Such disruptions are not a matter of life and death for this University as the faculty statement indicates. As Acting President Andrew Cordier pointed out Monday —albeit for different reasons—only 25 of 110,000 classes this year have been disrupted. Although classroom disruptions seem to be a counter-productive tactic, alienating large numbers of faculty members and students, the fear that the intrusion of politics into our

educational lives may destroy the University is unjustifiable. Too
many professors are so possessive of their fifty minutes of class time
that they are unable to recognize or accommodate themselves to
the fact that in the past year Columbia has become a highly politicized institution.

Letter to the Editor

To the Editor:
 Since the statement on "The University as a Sanctuary of Academic Freedom" has been circulated publicly, may I use your column for my response? I will not add my name to that statement
because I find three attitudes, among others, implicit or explicit in
the document: that the spirit of free inquiry and the sanctity of the
classroom needs defense only against students; that its defense is
the province of the faculty and administration alone; that discipline
is a main, if not the main, weapon by which to preserve the sanctuary of academic freedom.
 The rights "of scholars to engage in the advancement of knowledge . . . free from external pressures and interference" have long
been undermined by classified research which has imposed external
restraints upon the publication of its findings. If it is true, as I am
told, that some faculty members use university premises, equip-
ment and time meant for learning and teaching for unpublishable
research intended for the eyes of private industrial or other clients,
then that too undermines the spirit of free inquiry and uninhibited
freedom of discussion.
 The sanctity of the classroom has long been profaned by NROTC
instruction carried on by men whose allegiance is not to intellectual
freedom but to its irreconcilable, if not blatant, foe—the military.
Assertions by NROTC "faculty" have always the external interference of their Navy fealty. Their promotions are passed upon by the
Navy, not the University. And the spirit they implant of mindless
and unquestioning obedience to a superior clashes with the spirit
of untrammeled inquiry essential in a university.
 Extricating the University from its entanglements with industry

and the military seems to be a necessary condition for restoring the university as "a sanctuary of academic freedom."

The second and third attitudes require much more and better debate and discussion than I can provide. Any issue of *The New York Times* offers evidence that students today, in high school as well as college, are quite different from the student radicals of the Thirties. Of these numerous differences, I select only that we considered ourselves then auxiliaries of an adult movement. The radical movement today is a youth, primarily student, movement. They want more to say about all the institutions run by people of my generation which direct and even threaten our lives. It seems to me that just as the Senate proposal calls for students to be engaged in the governance of the University, so the protection of the University must also engage the students. Indeed, it was the students who first, and irresistibly, drew our notice to NROTC and classified research.

Students also cherish the traditions (refurbished) of untrammeled inquiry, what Veblen termed the pursuit of idle curiosity. With few exceptions, they enjoy teaching and learning as a process in which we all take part, whether in the classroom, laboratory, seminar, dormitory or West End. We all teach and we all learn; it is a mutual enterprise. Therefore, students must share in its conduct where it is formalized in class. The authority of the teacher runs only so far as he is an authority on the subject matter, and perhaps on some other matter, and perhaps on some other matters because he has lived longer. His authority on matters of the arrangement and rearrangement of the traditional format of the classroom ought to be shared with the students to an extent far greater than it is today. Such participation by students will help assure that the purposes for which teachers and students meet in the classroom will be fulfilled. And if they are, we will all of us see to it that the process of learning and teaching is not violated or subverted. And those few who may seek to violate or subvert it will be rebuffed.

I will mention briefly the failure of the document to define classroom disruption: Is it disruption if the class votes to hear the intruding student discuss or announce some event? if the class votes to hear him for two minutes and he takes three? if the class votes not to hear what the student has to say, and he leaves quietly, although he interrupted the class? or if he (or they) insist on shouting it anyway? Does the teacher who is unprepared, or prepared for classes of ten years ago, disrupt the process of learning and teaching? Or the pride of students who come loping in ten minutes after the start of the fifty-minute hour because that's when the Hamilton elevator got to the seventh floor? What of the teacher who shifts or cancels classes because he's consulting in Washington or Detroit?

Only when students are fully engaged as subjects, not objects, in the arrangements of learning and teaching will "these freedoms flourish in an atmosphere of mutual respect, civility and trust among teachers and students." I am truly sorry that I cannot join the scholars, so many of whom I hold in esteem as well as affection, who have signed the statement: it seems to me to have eloquently designed solutions for some other university in some other age.

Samuel Coleman

Department of Philosophy

Dwight Macdonald

I'm grateful to Ivan Morris for an opportunity to explain why I concluded, after visiting the campus to see for myself, that the Columbia student strike was a beneficial disturbance. My fund-raising letter for the New York chapter of SDS which stimulated his Open Letter to me was undertaken mostly because I admired the Columbia SDS for the spirit and the courage with which they gave the initial stimulus to the strike. (The amount needed has now been raised, I'm glad to report, and the new SDS headquarters are a reality.)

But first let me deal with Professor Morris's specific accusations —or, more accurately, assumptions. He accuses "the leaders of the demonstrations" of a "resort to violence," including arson, and me of justifying "violence of this kind." But so far as I saw in my five visits over six weeks to the campus, or read in the not overly sympathetic (to the strikers) New York Times, there was remarkably little violence: scuffles between "jocks" and strike sympathizers around Low Memorial (black eyes, bloody noses total damages, and the jocks weren't exactly pacifists), vulgar taunting of the police and some throwing of pop bottles at them when they invaded the campus those two frightening nights—I deplore the taunts and the missiles but much more so the invasion—and minimum resistance when the police cleared the occupied buildings, unless Professor Morris considers, as the cops do, that going limp and refusing to move when ordered by a policeman are categories of "violence." No, that commodity was monopolized by New York's Finest, as they used to be called, and they used it freely, sending a Dean and a University Chaplain to the hospital along with many students and some faculty members. Or perhaps by "violence," he means the immobilization of Dean Coleman in his office? I don't justify that —I'm even against restricting the freedom of movement of Dow recruiters, or, indeed, anybody, but it seems not a crucial charge: the Dean could have freed himself by a phone call to the campus cops; that he didn't was a tactical decision; he and his three fellow immobilizers were not threatened, were well fed and treated by their own account, and they emerged from their ordeal unruffled, unstruck, and unindignant; anticlimax.

Or by "violence" does Professor Morris mean the occupation of the buildings (which I do justify)? If so, he confuses illegality with violence. I oppose the latter, on tactical as well as principled grounds, and I've criticized in my *Esquire* column the romantic exhortations of certain New Left and Black Power leaders for a scorched-earth violentist policy aimed at bringing on a "revolutionary" catastrophe. I can see a catastrophe resulting from such tactics, but it will be a counter-revolutionary one. In the last year, however, as a founder of Resist and a Vietnam tax refuser, I've lost some of my bourgeois inhibitions about illegality. In certain circumstances—as when an Administration, of a nation or a university, chronically ignores lawful protests against its destructive policies— it seems to me more moral to break a law with Dr. Spock than to obey it with President Johnson, or President Kirk. (This is also, by the way, a bourgeois reaction.)

As for the burning of Professor Ranum's manuscripts, must I explain to my old friendly acquaintance Ivan Morris that I think it base and disgusting, and that far from "justifying" it, I should have had nothing to do with a group that used or tolerated such acts. But how does he link that act with my letter, which was written a week before it happened, or, more important, with the demonstrators he assumes were responsible for it? Is he not aware that the fire broke out after all the demonstrators had been removed by the cops from Hamilton Hall and were safely on their way to jail? I don't know who set it—hope he is arrested and given the maximum—or the four or five other small, so to speak symbolic, quickly extinguished fires that broke out in other buildings around the same time that night. Perhaps some nut fanatics among the students, perhaps ditto from outside the campus, perhaps police provocateurs. The *Times* reported at least one police spy—disguised as a hippy—who was up to no good on the campus. There is also testimony from eyewitnesses who saw the police, at the time of the first "bust," breaking up furniture and otherwise vandalizing the occupied buildings during or after the removal of the demonstrators—destructive acts which are often blamed on the students.

Whoever the arsonists, to assume, as Professor Morris does—also some others who have troubled to write me, usually *molto vivace* if not *agitando*, explaining just why they wouldn't be caught dead giving a nickel to SDS, really unusual to hear from people who *won't* contribute—as I was saying, whoever the arsonists, it seems to me absurd, logically, to assume they were encouraged by the strike leaders, SDS, or others (for there were others, one shouldn't forget). To believe this one must also believe they lacked all tactical sense, indeed all common sense. For one would not have to be a genius of maneuver to foresee that arson—and arson escalated to such vindictive meanness as burning the papers of a faculty member who had prominently opposed the strike, thus adding an instant solution to one detective problem: motive—that this was admirably calculated to alienate all the sympathizers so hardly won and patiently wooed. Fortunately, not many of us jumped to the soggy conclusion Ivan Morris has bogged down in. In my case, leaving aside the fact that no evidence has yet been produced as to who did it, I cannot believe that the student leaders who for six weeks out-maneuvered President Kirk—perhaps no great feat—and, more impressive, accumulated increasing support on the campus until the original "tiny minority" had won the sympathy of the majority of Columbia undergraduates for its six demands, I cannot believe that such leaders could have calculated that burning Professor Ranum's papers would help their cause. And if it is argued that the atmosphere of "violence" and illegality, no quotes, created by the strike leaders may have stimulated some of their less stable followers to set the fires, I would have to agree, adding that such are the risks of any rebellious effort to shatter an undesirable *status quo,* and the question is are the probable gains greater than the probable risks? (Note that I have refrained, with some difficulty, from saying you can't make omelets without breaking eggs. To think I should come to this in my sunset years!)

I've written so much that I haven't space for much detail on my own reasons for backing the strike. When I first read about it in the press, I was against it on general principles: I don't approve of "direct action" that interferes with the freedom of others, nor could I see the justification for a minority occupying college buildings and closing down a great university—or even a small, mediocre university. That was in general. But, as has often happened in my life, the general yielded to the pressure of the particular. On Friday I went up to Columbia to see for myself. I was egged on by my wife, who was sympathetic to the strike, on *her* general principles, and stimulated by Fred Dupee who, when I phoned him to ask what in the world was going on, said: "You must come up right away, Dwight. It's a revolution! You may never get another chance to see one." I came up and he was right. I've never been in or even near a revolution before; I guess I like them. There was an atmosphere of exhilaration, excitement—pleasant, friendly, almost joyous excitement. Neither then nor on any of my four later trips to the campus did I have any sense of that violence that Ivan Morris sees as a leading characteristic of the six weeks. Everybody was talking to everybody those days, one sign of a revolution; Hyde Parks suddenly materialized and as abruptly dispersed, all over the place; even the jocks were arguing. It was as if a Victorian heavy father had been removed from his family's bosom (or neck)—later I got a load of President Kirk on TV and I realized my simile was accurate—and the children were exulting in their freedom to figure out things for themselves. A fervid rationality was the note, a spirit of daring and experiment, the kind of expansive mood of liberation from an oppressive and, worse, boring tyranny that Stendhal describes in the Milanese populace after Napoleon's revolutionary army had driven out the Austrians. The SDS putsch became a revolution overnight: like the Milanese, the Columbians had realized with a start how dull and mediocre their existence had been under the Kirk Administration.

But what really changed my mind about the sit-ins was my own observation of two of the "communes" as the occupied buildings were ringingly called: Mathematics Hall, which I was let into—after a vote, everything was put to a vote in the communes—on Friday and Fayerweather Hall, into which I was allowed to climb —all access was by window—on the Monday afternoon before the Tuesday morning police raid. Mathematics was the Smolny Institute of the revolution, the ultra-Left SDS stronghold (said to have been liberated by a task force led by Tom Hayden in person) while Fayerweather was the Menshevik center—the "Fayerweather Formula" was an attempt on Monday to reach a compromise with the Administration, but Dr. Kirk was as firmly opposed to it, doubtless on principle, as was Mark Rudd of the SDS. The two communes, nevertheless, seemed to me very much alike in their temper and their domestic arrangements. Rather to my surprise (as a reader of *The New York Times*), the atmosphere in both was calm, resolute, serious, and orderly; I saw no signs of vandalism, many efforts to keep the place clean and the communal life disciplined. I sat in on a meeting at Mathematics—the communes were forever having meetings, must have become as deadly as a non-stop political caucus, but at least it was, or seemed to be, participatory democracy —which discussed the tactics to be used if the jocks tried to put them out as against those suitable for resisting the police. Everybody had his say as far as I could tell—had same impression at the Hamilton Hall sit-in before the second police raid—and the conclusion arrived at was sensible: resist the jocks because their armament was muscular only, hence the fighting would be on equal terms; don't resist the police because they had superior force—clubs, guns, tear gas—and also were trained in violence (this proved a true prophecy). One communard added that fighting was not the only possible strategy with the jocks; they could also be talked to, perhaps even persuaded because, unlike the cops, "they're like us"; I thought this a shrewd point. In general, what struck me about the two communes I visited was the resourcefulness and energy with which the students were meeting problems they had never had to think about before, such as getting in and distributing food supplies, arranging for medical first aid, drawing up rules for living together in an isolated society (for, as it turned out, six days) with some decorum and harmony, electing leaders, working out a line in democratic discussion that had to keep changing to meet the latest development in the complicated interaction between the white communards, the blacks in Hamilton Hall, the sympathizers and the opponents of the strike on the campus, the Administration, the Trustees, and the various faculty groups, plus the "community" in Harlem and in the immediate neighborhood. My impression is that the communards met these problems rather well, showing that intellectuals can be practical when they have to be. Also that they got a lot of education, not paid for by their parents, out of those six days, and that so did the thousands of students who milled around on the campus arguing tirelessly the questions raised in the first place by the SDS zealots. I'm told that one of the jocks admitted, under pressure of debate, that while he still didn't think a Tiny Minority had any Right etc., he had learned more in those six weeks than in four years of classes.

Harvard erupted in mid-April of 1969. This time the issue was the abolition of ROTC at Harvard. It began with demonstrations and moved on to the eviction of deans, the occupation of a building, a police "bust," and a "strike."

Harvard's Rule of Unreason

Several hundred lawless students at Harvard have accomplished what the virulently illiberal forces of the late Senator Joseph McCarthy failed to achieve. They have disrupted and suspended the historic rule of reason and academic freedom without which Harvard could never have become the symbol of the nation's quest for intellectual integrity and excellence.

It would be dangerous self-deception to pretend that the damage done can soon be repaired by any agreement among warring factions. After the forcible expulsion of the university's dean and the occupation of the administration building by a band of self-appointed revolutionaries, an invisible wall of distrust will remain, perhaps for generations.

The overreaction of the local police when they were summoned to restore order will provide fodder for the rebels—a certainty already reflected in the three-day strike planned by some moderates in the student body. There was no excuse for the savage club-swinging that marred the police activity. But the insurgents set a precedent in rule by terror in their own manhandling of the Harvard deans. The only effective way to prevent abuse of police power on the campus is through renunciation of the use of force by members of the academic community.

The records of Harvard's readiness to listen to—and act on—demands for change is persuasive evidence that the student confrontation was wilfully sought, not to reform but to destroy. In every area from the institution of a pioneering major in Afro-American studies to termination of academic credit for membership in the Reserve Officers Training Corps, Harvard showed not only an awareness of the need for change but did change.

The fundamental sickness transcends Harvard. There is a tragic relationship between the recent endorsement of "positive violence" by a group of clergymen protesting welfare cuts and the illusions of righteous coercion on the part of Harvard's Students for a Democratic Society. The former have forgotten that the Inquisitors thought their violence positive; the latter probably consider it historically irrelevant that the righteous fervor of Hitler Youth and Komsomol paved the way for "reforms" that made non-negotiable all demands by the revolutionary establishment.

The time has clearly come to stop pretending that the disruptions are adolescent pranks or justifiable excesses of young idealists. What is at stake now is nothing less than the perpetuation of universities as centers of reason in a free society. To permit them to be paralyzed or subverted by any lawless, coercive force of whatever political ideology or objective is to give up on the survival of free society itself.

On April 19, 1969, black militant students seized the Cornell student union in order to protest the reprimanding of three students who had demonstrated for a separate black college. The militants carried firearms. After the dean of faculty agreed to ask the faculty to nullify the reprimand (originally issued by a new student-faculty board), the students left the building. The faculty as a whole, however, voted to uphold the original reprimand. Mass demonstrations of students (black and white) and some faculty followed, and Cornell was warned that it had "three hours to live." The faculty then capitulated.

Later it was argued that the militants had responded to a cross burning on campus and/or had armed themselves for self-defense in the face of threats.

Cornell Defended

To the Editor:

I write in defense of the recent action recommended by the administration of Cornell University and supported (on the second attempt) by the university faculty. The issues and their causes are so complex that only their bare bones can be presented here.

A militant student needs no gun to derpive a middle-aged professor of his academic freedom; bare hands are sufficient. The momentary display of rifles in the single incident at Willard Straight, deplorable as it may be, has no substantial bearing on the freedom of a professor to state his views in the classroom or elsewhere.

Bloodshed and wholesale destruction of property were avoided by President Perkins's actions. I see no virtue in the Kirk-Rusk syndrome; the inflexibility of such persons on matters of "principle" is in large measure responsible for campus unrest today.

The majority of students realize that a faculty is necessary for a university; not all faculties have understood that the reverse is equally true.

Remember the evolution of past editorials in *The Times?* Remember the Cox report? The handful of hooligans at Columbia turned out to be nearly eighty per cent of the undergraduate body. The 250 blacks at Cornell, at the very moment they were being referred to as "250 students," were backed by 5,000 or more students in Barton Hall.

In my opinion, peace will not return to American campuses until there is peace in Vietnam and meaningful progress on racial matters in the American community. It is unfortunate that those with the power to remedy both of these ills are unwilling to do so; the university—a frail institution with no political power of its own— must suffer as a consequence.

Bruce Wallace
Professor of Genetics
Cornell University

Ithaca, N. Y., April 28, 1969

Counter-Protesters

To the Editor:

Campus insurgents now demand that the law be invoked against counter-protesters. That law is obviously the new one created by radical coercion and administrative acquiescence, for no other law provides amnesty for the insurgents and prosecution for their opponents.

The radical students have established a dangerous precedent. Why shouldn't other coercive student groups broaden the scope of amnesty to encompass all forms of protest? By the time the cross-burners at Cornell are apprehended, they will probably be able to get complete amnesty on the grounds that they had merely engaged in punishment-free, nonviolent political activity.

So much for the principle of amnesty—and so little for the cause of justice.

Paul Elliott

New York, April 27, 1969

Teaching at Cornell

To the Editor:

Many young people on our campuses are demonstrating that they will decide the causes for which they will fight. They have remained unpersuaded by the arguments of their elders that it is necessary to "liberate" the Vietnamese people, but they have not been entirely unreceptive to the influence of the Establishment.

The students have learned that, in the cause of freedom, it is acceptable to attack relatively helpless targets and to injure innocent people in the process; that the technique of overkill is respectable; that it is a sign of strength to adopt rigid positions which are largely nonnegotiable. In fact, by acting on the principle that it is necessary to destroy the universities in order to save them, the students are only showing how faithfully they follow a morality which has the endorsement of those who occupy positions of highest authority in our society.

Nell Miller

Brooklyn, May 9, 1969

A.C.L.U. Warns Student Rebels
Their Violence Is Self-Defeating

Student protest leaders and their followers were warned yesterday by the American Civil Liberties Union that continued lawlessness and violence were leading to threats of "backlash" and "counterviolence" that could destroy the college student movement and render its aims unattainable.

In a statement sent to 350 college and university campuses, the union, a defender of the legal rights of student protesters, also called on college administrators to cease "stoking the fires of discontent by refusing to consider student demands or involve students in the decision-making process."

The statement on "Campus Disorders," dated April 3, was accompanied by a letter that said:

"We feel that issues raised by student demonstrations are of such importance that we are taking the unusual step of writing directly to the presidents of colleges and universities, heads of faculty councils and student governing bodies and to editors of college newspapers."

The signers of the statement—Ernest Angell, chairman of the board of directors of the A.C.L.U., Samuel Hendel, chairman of the union's Academic Freedom Committee, and John de J. Pemberton Jr.—said that they hoped "our warning will receive the widest possible consideration with the campus community and that our views make a helpful contribution to the resolution of the issues at stake."

The statement, made public yesterday at a news conference in the A.C.L.U. headquarters, 156 Fifth Avenue, at Twentieth Street, told the student protesters that the union was "committed to the protection of all peaceful, nonobstructive forms of protest, including mass demonstrations, picketing, rallies and other dramatic forms."

Nevertheless, it continued, "we are deeply disturbed about some methods that some student activists have used in the attempt to achieve their ends—methods which violate and subvert the basic principles of freedom of expression and academic freedom."

The union said that "protests that deprive others of the opportunity to speak or be heard, or that require physical takeover of buildings to disrupt the educational process, or the incarceration of administrators and others, are anti-civil-libertarian and incompatible with the nature and high purpose of an educational institution."

In view of such activities, the statement went on, the danger is growing "that violence and threat of violence will breed a counter-violence and backlash that will defeat or set back the very objections student activists seek to serve and lead to repressive countermeasures."

Federal laws that would drop students convicted of crimes or serious violations of college regulations from scholarship eligibility are already in the books, and, the A.C.L.U. said, "no less than eighty bills" to curb campus violence are before the California and New York Legislatures.

At the news conference Professor Hendel, who was recently elected College Ombudsman by his fellow faculty members at City College, said there was "considerable evidence" that the anticipated backlash "is in progress."

The A.C.L.U. said it was opposed to repressive measures that would not likely "quiet down, but rather inflame, further the unrest."

The statement reminded the students that violence had been used in the past to further "bad causes as well as good."

"To abandon the democratic process in the interests of good causes is to risk the destruction of freedom not just for the present but for the future; not just for our social order but for any future social order as well," it said. "Freedom, the world has learned to its sorrow, is a fragile plant that must be protected and cultivated."

Faculties' Failures

To the Editor:

Abject capitulation to student violence at Cornell climaxes a series of surrenders which may destroy the university in America as a place of free inquiry and respect for morality and law. Unbridled attacks on faculties, destruction of property and wanton breaking into private files would be crimes punishable under law in any other context. [Editorial April 26.]

Yet, mature members of the university condone these criminal acts and avoid disciplinary action. Is an attack on a dean less an assault and battery when committed by students? Are destruction of property and defamation of character less criminal when perpetrated by undergraduates? Breaking into confidential files is common thievery, but such action is excused by members of the faculty.

Culpability for this campus turmoil rests squarely with the faculties. The irony is that scholars who urge free inquiry and pride themselves as pragmatists have failed in this time of crisis. Torn between academic loyalty and empathy for student rebellion, they offer no viable alternative to violence, preferring to vacillate in a morass of indecision while democratic institutions are destroyed, attitudes polarized, and violence, feeding upon violence, spreads from campus to campus.

The faculties have failed themselves, their students—who sense weakness and exploit it—and society. Because the dissidents number relatively few, the present chaos might have been avoided had the faculty galvanized the majority of middle-ground students into a positive program, recognizing the right of dissent, but not the right to destroy.

Common cause among faculty and students would have prevented deterioration into either2or alternatives—either capitulate or call in the police. Confronted by a united faculty and students, the militants would have had to desist or face rejection by their peers. That scholars chose to vacillate may well mean the tragic demise of the university as the one place in society where sanity and reason might have prevailed.

CHARLES S. Steinberg
Chairman, Committee
on Higher Education
Public Education Association

April 28, 1969

Staughton Lynd is a former member of the history department at Yale University. He made a well-publicized trip to North Vietnam despite a State Department ban on such travel. More recently he has been in the news because of a teaching offer that was later withdrawn. He is the author of Intellectual Origins of American Radicalism.

As one who has much reason to be grateful to the American Civil Liberties Union, I nevertheless believe the A.C.L.U. wrong in its position on student demonstrations, and *The* [*New York*] *Times* wrong in endorsing the A.C.L.U. position.

The crux of the A.C.L.U. position is that nonviolent disruption as well as violence is inappropriate on a college campus. The two forms of protest are lumped together because both involve action which interferes with the rights of others. In the A.C.L.U. view, only protest which does not so interfere—speech, and nondisruptive action—is consistent with a belief in the democratic process.

I believe in the legitimacy of nonviolent disruptive actions such as strikes and sit-ins. These tactics have been accepted for a generation in labor-management relations. Why is it they are rejected when practiced on a campus?

RULE OF REASON

The answer is that universities are assumed to be institutions governed by reason, not by power. Inspection of the rhetoric employed by Father Hesburgh, President Nixon and other recent critics of campus disruption makes plain how important is this assumption. Only if one can join in the assumption that the normal decision-making process in universities is non-coercive does it make sense to condemn all coercion, even if nonviolent, as inconsistent with the university's character.

The assumption is false. Universities are not governed by Socratic dialogue. Ultimate power lodges with conservative businessmen on boards of trustees whom students and faculty have no voice in choosing. The same hierarchical, rather than democratic, power structure reproduces itself in the power of senior faculty over junior faculty, and the power of all faculty over students.

Perhaps one's picture of the university depends on one's position in the hierarchy. The University of Chicago does not seem Socratic to the forty-two students recently expelled by disciplinary committees with no student voting members. The American academic world must lose its non-coercive mystique for faculty radicals (like myself) over and over again denied teaching positions by unfriendly administrations, despite the recommendations of their colleagues.

For those thus situated—the expelled student, the dismissed teacher—nonviolent disruption seems the only effective recourse. In exactly the same way, when a union organizer is fired from a factory bench, his associates walk off the job until the grievance is settled.

The Times would have it that advocacy of student strikes and sit-ins makes us "sunshine libertarians." My counter-accusation is that *The Times* is interested only in a libertarianism which does not seriously challenge the existing structure of power, on and off the campus.

The following series of selections is meant to bring out some of the ominous parallels between some current student unrest and the tactics of the Nazis during the 1920's and 1930's. Of special interest are (a) the parallel between the Nazi position and the SDS position, (b) the sociological "rationalization" of the Nazis made by eminent American faculty and journalists (including George Schuster) during the 1930's, and (c) a letter describing the same arguments employed to justify appeasement of the Nazis and black militants.

No doubt there are differences, and the reader must judge for himself if the parallels are both relevant and important. Several other facts should be kept in mind. First, the Nazi party had a branch ordered along paramilitary lines; second, during the 1920's the Nazis were not in power but were a small, militant organization engaged in confrontations and rebellions against the police and military of the democratic Weimar Republic; third, Hitler was jailed for leading an attempted putsch; fourth, while in jail he wrote an important book; fifth, the Nazi movement always had an element of anti-Semitism which grew progressively worse.

The SDS selection is taken from *Hard Core* published by SDS students at Columbia University.

Whatever Happened to SDS?

In September it seemed that Columbia might not open this year. A radical movement had shaken the university to its core in the spring and the summer had seen little response to student demands.

Columbia remained a part of the Institute for Defense Analysis, refused to finally abandon its blueprints for a racist gym, and on top of all this pushed the prosecution of a thousand students and Morningside Heights residents for their participation in the Spring protests. A new confrontation appeared imminent.

It didn't happen partly because of the attempts of the new Cordier administration to mollify campus opinion, but a much more fundamental cause of the lack of activity on campus this fall was the events of last summer off-campus. The Columbia revolt was primarily a struggle against the racist and imperialist nature of the university, and *not* a revolt for university reform, student power, or restructuring. The rebellion on Morningside Heights indicated the power of the student movement, but the summer revealed its weaknesses. The collapse of the McCarthy movement, the repression of students on the streets of Chicago, and the resulting Presidential campaign clarified the inability of the student movement to destroy imperialism or institutional racism. A new revolt at Columbia in the fall seemed wqefully inadequate to most of those invoved in the fall. The enemy's power had been revealed as never before.

As a result there has been much confusion at Columbia this year both within and ouside of Students for a Democratic Society about the role and purposes of the organization during the revolt and especially now. Many questions have been raised and many misconceptions have become widespread. What is SDS after? What are its beliefs and what is its program? What are its strengths and weaknesses? All these questions deserve answers, and while we cannot claim a complete understanding of all the complicated factors of America and the movement, we can at least begin to reply.

Over the past three years SDS has emerged as the primary student political group in the United States. A loose federation of hundreds of campus chapters, SDS views contemporary America as a profoundly unjust and oppressive society. Although there is no all-encompassing or monolithic SDS ideology, most of the membership shares the viewpoint that all of the major domestic and international problems of the United States stem from the fundamental nature of a capitalist system. SDS believes that the institutions of American society that manifest the ideology of the system can be analyzed and understood, and that their inhumane, coercive and violent nature necessitates a radical movement to replace them.

We cannot accept as natural a world wherein 10,000 people die daily of starvation, or a New York City (supposedly in the midst of a war on poverty) where 50,000 new units of slum housing appear every year. We cannot accept as God-given a society where a working man earning $7,000 a year and already in debt due to mortgage and installment payments finds himself burdened by increasing taxes to be used to suppress the Vietnamese. We cannot accept as sufficient governmental programs offering new but inadequate housing and meaningless employment to a Black America so long excluded from the economic and social benefits of our highly advanced technology, and we view as inadequate the promise that maybe future black generations will be able to share the overtaxed despair of the white working man. And we are outraged that in this very same society corporations like General Motors worry about increasing their profits from $3 to $3.5 billion and whether Fiat is challenging its Latin American car supremacy.

SDS believes that the major crises of American society can be traced to the two root causes of institutional racism and American manipulation and control of the internal political and economic affairs of many of the world's nations. SDS has grown to understand that these two basic problems are inherent in the continuing development of the American economic system of monopoly capitalism.

We are fighting to destroy capitalism as an economic system opposed to the social needs and aspirations of the majority of the world's peoples. We are socialists—not Chinese or Russian—but American socialists. We believe that this country has the technological capacity to feed all the starving peoples of the world, to eliminate inadequate housing, to fight disease—in short to meet the basic human needs of food, clothing, shelter and freedom.

But these needs cannot and will not be met so long as our technology is controlled by its current owners—families and corporate interests more concerned with vast profits than with human needs. SDS believes that there is a ruling class in this country, and notes

been elitist in character, refusing to see the connections between its struggle and the concerns of wildcat strikers, working-class high school students, G.I.'s, and black people. At this point in American history with real wages declining, inflation rising, youth dying in Vietnam, taxes mounting, and rebellion growing, SDS must begin to transmit its analysis to these groups. Only then can our movement begin to take power, and until then it will be the injustices of American capitalism that will keep us going and our revolutionary optimism that will sustain us.

Nazi Students Hit Older Generation

BERLIN, Oct. 8, 1936—The National Socialist Student League, a source of constant political agitation in the universities, has answered the recent warnings from both Minister of Education Bernhard Rust, and the noted German surgeon, Professor Ferdinand Sauerbruch, with a fiery attack on the older generation and the suggestion that it mind its own business.

Care, of course, has been taken to make no reference to the Minister of Education so that the student counter-attack, appearing as an article in the league's official organ, *Die Bewegung*, can be construed as referring solely to the suggestions made by Professor Sauerbruch before the German Medical Congress at Dresden.

Referring directly to Professor Sauerbruch, who bears the honorary title of government councillor or "Geheimrat," the article states:

"The Geheimrats can raise a hue and cry and prominent citizens groan and moan, and with a goodly portion of insolence call for the restoration of pre-war conditions. Well, whistle them in tune. We say: Do not interfere in our business. The future of Germany is our affair. The Fuehrer gave us our flag. You shall not get it back into your hands. Dress yourselves in all the insolence of the era of Kaiser Wilhelm. We, Germany's youth, we despise you."

MADE APPEAL TO YOUTH

It will be recalled that Professor Sauerbruch made the following appeal to German youth in his Dresden address:

"Full and complete understanding of the world is the result of long labor and hard experience. This experience must repeatedly be tested by the intellect. An ideology is something that only matured and tried men and women can earn for themselves. Ideology is no affair of youth, which has instead strength and faith and hope. These characteristics of youth degenerate, however, if it does not seek knowledge and understanding."

More significant politically probably is the failure to make exception to Dr. Rust's recent warning to politically agitated students in an article which certainly had all the outward appearance of a reply to just that warning. Dr. Rust warned the students to keep exercising censorship and control over their professors. The Student League declared:

Represent Left Wing

"We will be students who will keep a fanatical watch that the paralyzing spirit of reaction never again enter the classrooms and laboratories. We have risked our heads that these centers of the German mind and spirit should be free of that. We will keep them free in the face of all the narrow-minded people of yesterday who cry out: 'Away with politics; only accomplishment matters.'

"We intend to accomplish something, but not egotistically and senselessly as before the war, but for political purposes."

It is, in fact, no secret in the universities that the Nazi students represent the extreme left wing of party power. Their idols are Dr. Alfred Rosenberg, Dr. Joseph Goebbels, Walter Darre and, to some extent, Julius Streicher. They are constantly protesting, and none too tactfully, against the "bourgeois" Ministers and civil servants who still do much of the government's work.

Not swerving in their passionate adoration of Chancellor Adolph Hitler, they are nevertheless one of the most striking symbols of the violent differences of opinion and purpose that exist behind the calm façade of the Third Reich.

Unrest Held Due to Shaken Culture

May 8, 1936. Present world unrest is not entirely the result of economic and political changes but is caused primarily by an "unsettlement of culture," in the opinion of George Nauman Shuster, managing editor of *The Commonweal*.

Mr. Shuster was one of the speakers yesterday at the women's session of the Williamstown Institute in Miniature held under the auspices of the National Conference of Jews and Christians in the Hotel Commodore.

"Nazism absorbed the sense of injustice and the resolve for vengeance," Mr. Shuster said, "but itself remains what it always has been—an educational program many doctrines of which were formulated before the eighteenth century closed and the final nature of which was accurately foreseen by German thinkers of the mid-nineteenth century.

Marxism Born in Universities

"I should say that the truest thing one can say about Marxism is that it came out of the universities. Of course, the rise of industrialism created masses to whom the gospel according to Marx could be preached. But the same rise of industrialism also established a university that was the expression of the bourgeois-capitalist spirit.

"There had never previously been an academic life circumscribed by so many limitations of vision, including class-consciousness. It was not by chance that the emphasis was so firmly laid on the immediately practical, whereas previously since the days of Greece a university had been an arrangement for encouraging the speculative intelligence."

Mr. Shuster asserted that the liberal "usually misses everything but his own point of view." Escape from the present world turmoil, he said, rested either on "a cultural outlook based upon a reasoned theistic position or it is nowhere."

Dr. Frank Kingdon, president of the University of Newark, observed that "when Germany moves into the Rhineland, France builds fortresses on her border, Russia has 1,500,000 men under arms, Japan moves into Manchuria and China, Great Britain has a powerful fleet and the United States has the largest military appropriation in peacetime history, who is going to say that Italy is suffering from a madness strange to any of us?"

EVEN GREEKS CALLED INTOLERANT

Dr. Edward Sapir, Sterling Professor of Anthropology and Linguistics at Yale University, gave an anthropological view of tolerance. He noted that the Greeks were intolerant when they called every one barbarians except themselves. Mrs. Edward C. Bailly, a member of the national council, presided.

At an "interrogation luncheon" following the morning conference, speakers denounced the system of determining college entrance quotas on a religious basis.

Dean Georgianna P. McEntee of Hunter College said that bigotry often came from students least trained in their own particular religion. In answer to a question whether parents who tell children not to salute a flag because of some religious belief, or authorities who seek to require the salute were right, Dr. Robert W. Searle of the New York Federation of Churches said neither was right because they were "making a fetish out of a symbol."

Dr. Robert A. Ashworth, educational secretary of the National Conference of Jews and Christians, felt there was no escape from differences of religious opinion but that such differences could be civilized without sacrificing convictions. Mrs. Edgerton Parsons, presided.

An Open Letter to a College Faculty

There are only three possible responses to "non-negotiable" demands: resistance, capitulation, or flight. You can resist with Socrates, capitulate with Galileo, or, as the story is told, flee with Aristotle "lest philosophy be sinned against twice."

"Negotiating" with students who have seized a campus of this college is wrong on three counts. First, it tacitly accepts the use of force as legitimate. Second, it allows rhetoric to build up a head of steam which turns the situation into a pressure cooker. Third, it sets a precedent which encourages future appeals to force as a tactic.

The analogy with Chamberlain's response to Hitler's "non-negotiable" demands is illuminating. The "Cliveden set" had agreed with Keynes that the Germans had been treated unjustly by the Versailles Treaty. German rearmament was no doubt deplorable but understandable in the light of their treatment at Versailles. Moreover, Germany threatened an unthinkable holocaust if not given its due. So, guilt-ridden, fear-ridden, they temporized only to find that concessions bought, not "peace in our time," but contempt and further demands. There was no "last territorial demand."

Now we are offered, *mutatis mutandi*, the same arguments couched in sociological jargon. Thus: the blacks have been treated with gross injustice; their tactics are deplorable but excusable in view of their history; the surrounding black community will destroy the college if not given its due, etc. But this is literally irrelevant, a species of the genetic fallacy. For it appeals to historical origins as a rationalization for a highly questionable course of action. By negotiating the "non-negotiable" in the effort to do justice to Negroes in the spirit of expiation, the President of the college is falling into that fallacy. And it is highly questionable because by temporizing he is recognizing aggressive force as a legitimate mode of academic procedure. For whatever "negotiated" settlement may be agreed to, the result will be disastrous. When two thousand, not two hundred, militant students present their "non-negotiable" demands, he (or his successor) will face a far more massive and intransigent confrontation than the present one. And the motto of this college will become, all too soon, *Sauve qui peut.*

Willard Hutcheon
[City College of the
City University of New York]
April 1969

Eric Hoffer is a retired longshoreman. His political philosophy is the product of self-education. His description of mass movements in his book The True Believer is now a classic. For our purposes, we may view his message as a warning that misguided intellectuals pose a threat to a healthy society. The importance of his message for those who accept it is that what happens in the academic world has profound implications for the remainder of society.

It seems to be generally assumed that the maintenance of freedom within a society requires the presence of sturdy individuals ready and able to stand up for their rights. We are told that "Eternal vigilance is the price of liberty," and that "He alone merits liberty who conquers it afresh from day to day." How relevant are these assertions to everyday experience in a more or less free society? Does individual freedom owe its existence to individual militancy? Can a man really feel free who has to be eternally vigilant and must win his freedom anew each day?

Pascal maintained that we are made virtuous not by our love of virtue but "by the counterpoise of two opposite vices." It takes a vice to check a vice, and virtue is the by-product of a stalemate between opposite vices. The same probably holds true of individual freedom: we are free not by our own power but by the counterpoise of two opposite powers. Individual freedom is the automatic by-product of a drawn-out contest between more or less equal parties, factions, bodies, and so on. The quality of the contestants seems immaterial. A contest between two reactionary bodies can be as

268

productive of individual freedom as a contest between a reactionary and a liberal party. If Poland is at present the country with the most individual freedom in the Communist world it is due mainly to the fact that a powerful Communist party and a powerful Catholic Church—neither of which has any concern for individual freedom —are there pitted against each other in a more or less equal contest. The present situation in Poland echoes to some extent the situation which prevailed in the Occident toward the end of the Middle Ages when Church and State, each reaching out for total dominion, were engaged in a prolonged tug of war, thus unintentionally preparing the ground for the birth of civil liberty.

The growth of freedom in the Occident has been marked by a diversification and distribution of power. Starting out with a division between sacerdotal and secular power, there evolved in Western societies additional categories of power (political, economic, intellectual), subdivisions within each category (a multiplicity of churches, parties, and corporations, independent legislatures and courts, an antagonism between labor and management, and between intellectuals and men of action); and safeguards against the perpetuation of power (periodic elections, and periodic confiscations through income and inheritance taxes). The rise of totalitarianism in the twentieth century constitutes a sharp reversal of this characteristic Occidental tendency. Totalitarianism spells simplification: an enormous reduction in the variety of aims, motives, interests, human types, and, above all, in the categories and units of power. In a totalitarian state power is of one kind, and the defeated individual, no matter how outstanding, can find no redress.

It is clear, therefore, that the presence of an effective, organized opposition is a prerequisite of individual freedom. A society that in normal times cannot function adequately without unanimity is unfit for freedom. It is equally clear that the activities of an effective opposition and of free individuals subject the body social to considerable strain. A society must be in good working order and firmly anchored in a tradition of unity if it is to stand up under the ceaseless tug of parties and the willfulness of free individuals. Its government, economy, and the whole apparatus of everyday life must function smoothly and with a considerable degree of automatism. This means that a free society is also a skilled society. A wide diffusion of skills—technical, political, and social—not only makes it possible for a society to function adequately under strain, but also enables it to dispense with fervor and enthusiasm, which unavoidably blur individual autonomy, and to avoid the curtailment of freedom involved in excessive tutelage and supervision. In a genuinely free society even extraordinary tasks can be accomplished by ordinary people in an ordinary way, and the social process can run at room temperature rather than at white heat. Finally, a society needs a large measure of affluence before it can allow its members the full play of their initiative and bents. It must be able to afford the waste inherent in a riot of trial and error. There can be no real freedom without the freedom to fail.

There is no doubt that individual freedom is an unequaled factor in the release of social energies, and particularly in the activation of ordinary people. "It infuses," says de Tocqueville, "throughout the body social an activity, a force and an energy which never exist without it and which bring forth wonders." But this source of energy can be tapped only under special conditions: a society must be strong enough to support, and affluent enough to afford, individual freedom. It would thus be wholly unreasonable to expect a backward country to modernize itself in a hurry in an atmosphere of freedom. Its poverty, lack of skill, and its need for fervor and unity militate against it. In exceptional cases, like Puerto Rico and Israel, where capital and skills are available, rapid modernization is not incompatible with a considerable measure of individual freedom.

To some extent, the present dominant role of the intellectual in the modernization of backward countries also militates against the prevalence of individual freedom. Not only does the intellectual's penchant for tutoring, directing, and regulating promote a regimented social pattern, but his craving for the momentous is bound to foster an austere seriousness inhospitable to the full play of freedom. The intellectual "transforms the prosaic achievements of society into Promethean tasks, glorious defeats, tragic epics."* The strained atmosphere of an eternal drama working up toward a climax and a crisis is optimal for heroes and saints but not for the autonomous individual shaping his life to the best of his ability. The chances are that should an advanced country come into the keeping of the intellectual it would begin to show many of the hectic traits which seem to us characteristic of a backward country in the throes of awakening.

To the intellectual the struggle for freedom is more vital than the actuality of a free society. He would rather "work, fight, talk, for liberty than have it."† The fact is that up to now the free society has not been good for the intellectual. It has neither accorded him a superior status to sustain his confidence nor made it easy for him to acquire an unquestioned sense of social usefulness. For he derives his sense of usefulness mainly from directing, instructing, and planning—from minding other people's business—and is bound to feel superfluous and neglected where people believe themselves competent to manage individual and communal affairs, and are impatient of supervision and regulation. A free society is as much a threat to the intellectual's sense of worth as an automated economy is to the workingman's sense of worth. Any social order that can function with a minimum of leadership will be anathema to the intellectual.

The intellectual craves a social order in which uncommon people perform uncommon tasks every day. He wants a society throbbing with dedication, reverence, and worship. He sees it as scandalous that the discoveries of science and the feats of heroes should have as their dénouement the comfort and affluence of common folk. A social order run by and for the people is to him a mindless organism motivated by sheer physiologism.

*Raymond Aron, *The Opium of the Intellectuals* (Garden City, N.Y.: Doubleday, 1957), p. xiv.
†Lincoln Steffens, *The Autobiography of Lincoln Steffens* (New York: Harcourt Brace, 1931), p. 635.

George Wallace, then Governor of Alabama, stands (in this 1963 photograph) with his back to the "schoolhouse door" and holds up his hand to signify to Nicholas de B. Katzenback (back to camera), at that time a Deputy United States Attorney, that he is forbidding entrance to two Negroes who had planned to enroll in the all-white University of Alabama.

Queens Nassau Pix, Inc.

A student at Queens College, New York barring the entrance to a classroom.

Among the works committed to the flames by Nazi students at the University of Berlin during May of 1933 were those of Marx, Kautsky, Heinrich Mann, Erich Kästner, Friedrich Wilhelm Förster, Freud, and Erich Maria Remarque.